◆ ◆ ◆

"I have high regard for Isaac Horst's ability to explain the Old Order Mennonite customs and traditions. This book provides answers to many questions asked during conducted tours through our Old Order Mennonite communities and during presentations for Elderhostel programs. I highly recommend this book to the inquiring public."
—*Lorna L. Bergey, Secretary, Mennonite Historical Society of Ontario*

"In this book, Isaac has truly presented a real insider's view of the church community that he has called his own for eight decades. Because it is in fact the story of his life, this book is more accurate than any other I have ever read on this subject. Not only has Horst presented our ideals, he has also included unfortunate human aspects of our culture of which we cannot be proud, but which are an important part of the complete story. The true inside story!"
—*Levi M. Frey, Old Order Mennonite, Mt. Forest, Ontario*

"This is an amazingly frank and truly authentic narration of family, church, and community life among the Old Order Mennonites in the Waterloo Region of Ontario, Canada. Much of the book is in the form of dialogues with members of a visiting busload of Leamington (Ont.) Mennonites. The tour leader through the Mennonite community is none other than Isaac Horst, the elderly and most authoritative informant of the Old Order members.

"Readers will be fascinated not only with the intimate questions asked, but also with the detailed answers given by the tour leader. As far as I know, it is the most reliable source explaining the public and private beliefs and practices of Old Order Mennonites."
—*J. Winfield Fretz, Author,* Waterloo Mennonites: A Community in Paradox

"This is a useful volume that every appreciative Mennonite should read. It is an interpretive book defending the Old Order Mennonite faith and lifestyle and if need be could even be used in court to defend that cause. I regret that this book did not exist fifty years ago when the OOMs of Ontario first caught my attention."
—*Amos B. Hoover, OOM Historian, Muddy Creek Farm Library, Denver, Pennsylvania*

"This loquacious book by an elderly horse-and buggy Mennonite of Ontario welcomes the curiosity of anyone from nosy tourists to liberal cousins. Horst's method, knowing what people are likely to ask, is to pose both questions and answers. His chatty dialogue takes readers vividly into meetinghouse, schoolhouse, and farmhouse, where he cheerfully points out the colorful, nonstandard features of his people's behavior.

"Where it suits, he'll quote Tertullian or an Anabaptist author to show how traditional Mennonites see themselves trying to live by pristine Christian standards. When no other rationale for a practice seems evident, he'll simply concede that it's 'tradition.' The folkways of his spiritual family witness to the ideals of the Mennonites of eastern North America before the majority of them made large concessions to modernity."
—*John L. Ruth, Mennonite Church Historian, Harleysville, Pennsylvania*

# A Separate People

*An Insider's View
of Old Order Mennonite
Customs and Traditions*

## Isaac R. Horst

Herald
Press

Waterloo, Ontario
Scottdale, Pennsylvania

Canadian Cataloguing-in-Publication Data
Horst, Isaac R., 1918-
  A separate people : an insider's view of Old Order Mennonite
  customs and traditions
ISBN 0-8361-9122-6
1. Old Order Mennonites—Ontario—Social life and customs. I. Title.
BX8129.O43H677 2000         305.6'870713         C00-930232-8

™

The paper used in this publication is recycled and meets the minimum requirements of American National Standard for Information Sciences—Permanence
of Paper for Printed Library Materials, ANSI Z39.48-1984.

Scripture is from the *King James Version of the Holy Bible*, adapted somewhat
to current English. Selections marked RSV are from the *Revised Standard Version Bible*, copyright 1946, 1952, 1971 by the Division of Christian Education
of the National Council of the Churches of Christ in the USA, and are used by
permission.

Much of this material originally appeared as monthly columns in the *Mennonite Reporter* and is used here by permission.

The cover art "Washline" is from an original painting by Peter Etril Snyder,
a Canadian artist who has painted Mennonite country life as well as scenes
in Canada and Europe for the past thirty years. You can see more of his work
on the Internet (www.snyder-gallery.com).

A SEPARATE PEOPLE
Copyright © 2000 by Herald Press, Waterloo, Ont. N2L 6H7
  Published simultaneously in the United States by
  Herald Press, Scottdale, Pa. 15683. All rights reserved
Canadiana Entry Number: C00-930232-8
Library of Congress Catalog Card Number: 99-076119
International Standard Book Number: 0-8361-9122-6
Inside illustrations and map by Edwin B. Wallace
Cover art by Peter Etril Snyder
Book and cover design by Gwen M. Stamm
09 08 07 06 05 04 03 02 01 00 10 9 8 7 6 5 4 3 2 1

To order or request information, please call
1-800-759-4447 (individuals); 1-800-245-7894 (trade).
Website: www.mph.org

# Contents

# *Foreword*

IN August 1988, *Mennonite Reporter* sent an exploratory letter to Isaac Horst, asking if he would be interested in writing a monthly column for the paper. We knew he had written several books on the life and history of Old Order Mennonites in Ontario. We were also aware that this keen writer and communicator was not a typical member of the Old Order Mennonite Church.

My letter outlined the thinking behind our request:

> We have never reported much on our Old Order brothers and sisters, partly for fear of invading their privacy and partly for fear of misrepresenting them. Our readers, however, need to know more about the Old Order members of our Mennonite tradition, and we think a folksy, anecdotal column by an insider would give us a glimpse of the day-to-day life of your people. As outsiders, we usually tend either to idealize the Old Orders or ignore them as utterly weird. It would help us all to see a more human side.

A few weeks later, I received a simple, handwritten note from Horst: "Enclosed find two sample columns for the *Mennonite Reporter*, as you suggested." The column was launched on January 9, 1989, under the name "Old Order voice." Horst's voice was heard in the *Mennonite Reporter* until September 1, 1997, the last issue before the *Reporter* was transformed into *Canadian Mennonite*.

Horst's typewritten manuscripts kept pouring in, many more than we could use. In one letter, he said: "I hope you will not feel swamped if I send in so many articles ahead of time. I'm afraid I would panic if I had no inspiration and your barrel were empty!" After nine years, the barrel was still full and the writer still brimming with ideas.

Over the years, the letters gave way to telephone calls and even the occasional visit to our office. When *Mennonite Reporter* celebrated its twentieth anniversary, Horst was on the program, even though some lighter moments that evening "overwhelmed" him, as he puts it in "One Small Voice."

This book captures the flavor of a unique voice from within the Old Order Mennonite community. Horst's is not a simple or predictable voice; it keeps surprising us with unexpected turns and shifts in tone, giving us, in essence, a "nonconformist" defense of conservative conformity! This man of modest understatement is constantly vying with the feisty apologist within.

The "Apology" that opens this book illustrates the different levels of consciousness at work in Horst's writing. Even while begging pardon for sounding "preachy and self-righteous" (good Old Order humility), he staunchly defends his version of Old Order faith: "Why should I apologize for such Scripture texts, which are so simple to understand?" Both impulses are tempered with wry observations on the whole enterprise. "Columns are usually based on one person's opinion, and are not to be taken too seriously," he concludes.

Horst concludes a 1996 column on differences between Old Order and modern Mennonites in similar fashion: "What does all this prove? Nothing, except that many practices run in cycles. It does not mean that Mennonite churches are improving or deteriorating."

Beneath the mantle of educator is a delightful folklorist and chronicler of human foibles. In this collection, presentations of church doctrine stand next to descriptions of "dinner at Mary's" and Old Order shopping. His critique of modern life is cloaked in musings on women's roles ("Caveman Treatment?") and homespun analysis of church life ("An Old Order Frankenstein").

Horst claims he doesn't subscribe to any newspapers. But that doesn't stop him from wading into politics or other issues of the day, such as "Ontario's Legal Gambling Gambol."

His curiosity leads him in many directions. In one conversation, he suggested that someone should erect an observation tower at Martin's Meetinghouse and charge admission: "Where else can you see 200 horses at one time?" This led him to stories about a horse-loving Chicago woman who joined the Old Order, then to "hat snatchers," and to thoughts about why art begins with the outline of the human body: "It's like writing; . . . you learn the basics first and dress them up later."

The common thread weaving its way through the disparate topics and approaches in this book is the personal voice of the writer, at once tour guide and preacher and central character in the narrative. How fortunate that the voice of this rare columnist is now preserved in one volume.

—*Margaret Loewen Reimer*
*Associate Editor,* Canadian Mennonite
*January 2000*

# *Preface*

PERSONALLY, I'm not particularly fond of prefaces. I'd rather begin reading where the action starts. However, because of the unconventional arrangement of this book, a preface is as necessary as a pocket in a shirt. Without a preface, this book would be virtually unreadable.

The basic contents of this book first appeared in the *Mennonite Reporter* as monthly columns. To make it more readable and provide continuity, I have introduced conversation at some places. Yet, since all who enter into the dialogue are unidentified persons, they are merely voices in the wilderness. As lecturer, I may be no better. I, me, and myself would soon become boring to my readers.

While I was a columnist, I could voice my opinion, whether or not it made sense. As tour guide, I am expected to state facts. Rather than take the consequences of accidentally making false statements in this book, I, too, will play the role of remaining anonymous, a voice in the wilderness.

In my book, I did not wish to ramble on in Dickensian digressions. I found the solution by using this preface to set up the dialogue. I won't even use quotation marks for what the tour guide says. I leave all the "he said, she asked, and the tour guide replied" out of the conversation. As long as the important things are said, and the right questions asked, I would just as soon be the listener as the lecturer any day. It might even let me off the hook for making a stupid remark!

Seriously, I honestly believe that we, as Old Order Mennonites, do have some customs, beliefs, and points of doctrine which should not be hid under a bushel. It is easier to set much of it down in a book than to present it in personal conversation, because here the reader can't interrupt me and argue with me.

We believe the whole message of the Bible, which is the foundation of our doctrine. So if anyone disagrees with me, I would rather have him throw this book into the fire and keep the Bible.

The Swiss Brethren, called Anabaptists (Rebaptizers) and later called Mennonites, apparently originated in Switzerland in about 1525. Against the state church, they held to believers baptism, nonresistance, and separation of church and state. However, research shows that they had practically the same beliefs as the early Christians of the second and third centuries. This is the same doctrine that the Old Order Mennonites believe to this day, and which we try to follow, while admitting our human weaknesses.

Through persecution, these Swiss Brethren fled to the Palatinate in southwest Germany. Later, the generosity of William Penn, a Quaker, opened the way for their migration to America. From there, our ancestors traveled to the wilds of Upper Canada between 1800 and 1830.

By 1889, cultural change had progressed among the Mennonites to the point where the more remote and rural Mennonites could no longer identify with those living in urban areas, more aggressive in their forms of religion, and more sophisticated in dress and actions. The conservative ones withdrew from the main body. They found common ground among like-minded brothers and sisters in Pennsylvania, Indiana, and Virginia. People generally refer to these as Old Order Mennonites (OOM) or Wisler Mennonites (named after Jacob Wisler, 1808-89).

The Amish, who parted ways with other Anabaptists three hundred years ago (in 1693), are now living side by side with Old Order Mennonites. There are a few obvious differences: the Amish hold church in their homes, grow beards, and use hooks and eyes on suit coats and vests instead of buttons. Yet the Amish dress much like the OOMs, in plain and simple clothing, and also drive horses and buggies. They outnumber the OOMs about five to one.

Although I have given a few names of actual persons to add spice, most of the situations are fictitious, though like actual circumstances. I have no intention of belittling or ridiculing anyone. My natural love for people forbids this.

This work would never have appeared in print if Margaret Reimer and Ron Rempel had not encouraged me to write a monthly column for the *Mennonite Reporter*. For this, I tender my sincere thanks to them.

I also owe thanks—

• to Joe Miller, Joel Alderfer, and the Mennonite Library and Archives of Eastern Pennsylvania (now the Mennonite Historians of Eastern Pennsylvania) for permission to use excerpts from the Jacob Mensch letter collection.

• to Theron Schlabach for permission to use one paragraph, as well as some information gleaned from his book, *Gospel Versus Gospel*.

• to D. K. Cassel's descendants for quotes from the book *History of the Mennonites*.

• to A. B. Hodgetts and Thomas Nelson & Sons (Canada) Limited for two paragraphs from the book, *Decisive Decades*.

• to David W. Bercot for information gained from his book *Will the Real Heretics Please Stand Up?*

• to Reg Good, Sam Steiner, Lorna Bergey, and John F. Peters for the privilege of working with them and learning from them.

• to friends far and near, who unwittingly gave moral support and information, and who would be embarrassed to be named here.

• to my wife, finally, for faithfully bearing with me and putting up with inconveniences without complaining.

To all these, I express my sincere gratitude.

—*Isaac R. Horst*
*Mt. Forest, Ontario,*
*Canada*

# An Apology

THE observations and explanations found in this book regarding the Old Order Mennonites (OOMs) are the direct result of my monthly columns in the *Mennonite Reporter*. These columns appeared in the *Reporter* during a nine-year period, 1989 to 1997. Sometimes the following chapters bear little resemblance to the original columns. They may not have been literally tried by fire; but they have been revised to speak to a diverse audience.

Early in my literary "career," I wrote the book *Separate and Peculiar*. My purpose was to describe our customs and traditions, especially to tourists, who come to the area to see this OOM phenomenon. I soon discovered several weaknesses in the book. Since some of our customs or habits are second nature to us, it did not occur to me that they needed to be mentioned. Other responses suggested a situation like "The Parable of the Blind Men and the Elephant." Even after people had read my book, they had different and contradictory views.

Though each was partly in the right,
They all were in the wrong. (John Godfrey Saxe)

Perhaps the most important weakness was that *Separate and Peculiar* described the customs without giving the reasons behind them. As a result, some readers might have assumed that the customs were based on nothing more than ignorance, superstition, or a mixture of both.

The same applied to my *Mennonite Reporter* columns. There are many ways in which the OOMs differ from mainstream society. It is easy enough to describe these different ways. The problem arises when I try to explain the reasons behind the customs. We (and you, dear readers) do not like to accept labels of ignorance and superstition, so I present the reasons as well as I can. If a matter is something about which I feel strongly, I get carried away and sound preachy and self-righteous. For this shortcoming, I sincerely apologize.

When I was asked to write a column, I was prepared to be careful to offend no one. Not so, I was told. They wanted me to write straight from the shoulder: "Let the chips fall where they may." (Naturally, a few flew back into my face.)

The Scriptures tell us to let our lights shine in the world (Matt. 5:14-16; 1 Pet. 2:9; 3:15). I must admit that I am reluctant to follow this through. I am likely to hide my light under a bushel. Why this reluctance? As an OOM, I honestly believe in the truth of New Testament teachings.

Sometimes I comment on the literal interpretation the OOMs place on such texts as the Sermon on the Mount (Matt. 5–7), or on 1 John 2:15-16:

Love not the world, neither the things that are in the world.
If any one loves the world, the love of the Father is not in him.
For all that is in the world, the lust of the flesh, and the lust
of the eyes, and the pride of life, is not of the Father, but is
of the world.

Why should I apologize for such Scripture texts, which are so simple to understand? Am I afraid that someone might blame me, if such Bible references make him feel uncomfortable? Am I afraid of being blamed for having a holier-than-thou attitude? Instead, perhaps I should apologize for watering down such Scripture texts to save face!

This business of apologies can be confusing. Usually when we apologize, we admit that we are in the wrong, and beg someone's pardon for having offended that person. There is a deeper meaning for the word *apology. The Complete Writings of Menno Simons* are chiefly composed of apologies he addressed to his adversaries, in defense of his doctrine. Of course, even ordinary apologies that begin as pleas for forgiveness and pardon frequently continue until they express defense and justification.

Most readers take a columnist's writing with a grain of salt. Columns are usually based on one person's opinion, and are not to be taken too seriously.

On the other hand, there is no point in writing a column, or anything else, unless it contains some ideas or views that can be of value to someone, even if that value consists only in diverting the reader. I trust that my writing will do a little more than just amuse. If not, I hope the reader can bear with me. I may at least be able to prove that Old Order Mennonites are human—very much so!

# Old Order Mennonites in Ontario

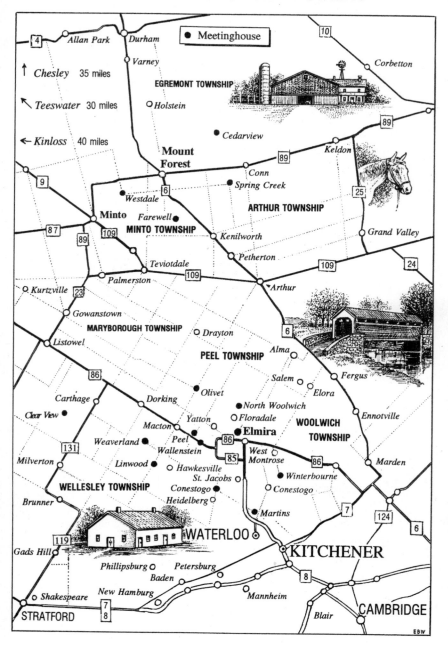

| ● | Meetinghouse |

4  Allan Park  Durham

Varney

↑ *Chesley* 35 miles

EGREMONT TOWNSHIP

↖ *Teeswater* 30 miles  ○ *Holstein*

10

Corbetton

89

● *Cedarview*

← *Kinloss* 40 miles

**Mount Forest**

Keldon

25

89

Conn

○ *Westdale*

● Spring Creek

9

**ARTHUR TOWNSHIP**

**Minto**  *Farewell* ●

87  **MINTO TOWNSHIP**  Kenilworth

Grand Valley

89  109

○ *Teviotdale*  ● Petherton

109

24

○ *Kurtzville*  23  ○ *Palmerston*  109  ► *Arthur*

○ *Gowanstown*

6

**MARYBOROUGH TOWNSHIP**  ○ *Drayton*

○ Listowel

**PEEL TOWNSHIP**  Alma ○

86

Salem ○

*Carthage* ○  *Dorking*  ● *Olivet*  Elora ○

Fergus ○

*Clear View* ●

● *North Woolwich*

131  *Macton*  *Yatton*  ○ *Floradale*

Ennotville ○

*Weaverland* ●  *Peel*  ● **Elmira**  **WOOLWICH**

*Milverton* ○  *Wallenstein*  86  **TOWNSHIP**

*Linwood* ●  ○ *Hawkesville*  85  *West Montrose* ○  86  ○ *Marden*

**WELLESLEY TOWNSHIP**  *St. Jacobs* ○  ● *Winterbourne*

*Brunner*  *Conestogo* ●  ○ *Conestogo*

*Heidelberg* ○

● *Martins*  7

119  **WATERLOO** ⊙  124  6

*Gads Hill* ○  **KITCHENER**

*Phillipsburg* ○  *Petersburg*

○ *Shakespeare*  *Baden*  8

**STRATFORD**  7  New Hamburg  *Mannheim*  **CAMBRIDGE**

8  *Blair*

EBW

# A Bus Tour of Mennonite Country

◆ ◆ ◆

# Left, Write, Foreword!

"Are you Isaac Horst?"

Yes, I am.

"Oh, good! I had a problem finding the place. It was my fault: I made a right turn instead of a left. My name is Jacob Driedger, from Leamington."

Driedger? Any relation to Henry Driedger?

"Possibly. I know two Henry Driedgers around Leamington. A group of us are interested in the Old Order Mennonites. I learned from Ernie Regehr that you are also interested in Mennonite history. Most of our group are history buffs, too. We would like to take a bus tour through your area, if we can find someone to guide us. Would you consider being our tour guide?"

Well, I'm no professional in that field.

"A professional is not what we want. All we want is someone who knows the area, and has an interest similar to ours."

Then I suppose I would consider it.

"While I'm here—or are you too busy to talk?"

I'm never too busy to talk. I'm like a friend of mine who was visiting in the hill country of Virginia. He was riding in the buggy of a friend, whose horse seemed to dislike going uphill. My friend offered to walk, but the driver didn't think it was necessary. At the next hill, it happened again. "I'll get off and walk," my friend insisted. "No, that isn't necessary; but my horse is sensitive about people talking, so if you kept quiet—" My friend replied, "I'll walk. I'd sooner walk than keep quiet." I'm the same. Keeping quiet is not my virtue.

"Good! Ernie also told me that you do some writing. Is that a common thing among your people?"

No, I'm a black sheep.

"Would you care to explain how you got started?"

It all started eighty years ago. My brother, next older than I, had it all figured out in a sort of simile. Our mother had made seven pies, and there was some dough left over—not enough for a pie, but too good to throw away. She rolled it out, spread it with apple butter, and baked it.

"Oh! Were there seven in the family older than you?"

Yes.

"Okay, I'll buy that."

I was a weakling from birth. By school age, I was physically unable to roughhouse with others my age, so I frequently spent my recesses inside, reading.

"A bookworm, eh?"

Quite so. This tendency shadowed me all my life. For the sake of my wife and children, I tried farming but was unsuccessful. I supplemented this income by working in a feed mill for fourteen years, and teaching school two years. The turning point came at my retirement.

"Then you had time to do your own thing?"

Yes, but it came about by accident. I had no intention of writing a book. My uncle had moved to Florida with his family in 1917, a year before I was born, and returned four years later. It was an interesting yet sometimes frustrating experience, the sort of story to tell the grandchildren.

"I suppose you have grandchildren by now?"

Yes, sixty-four of them. Most of them like to read. *Family Life*, one of the Pathway magazines, had a monthly column "Yesterdays and Years."

"Oh, yes! I always enjoyed reading that."

I gathered information on the Florida episode and wrote an article for the *Family Life* column. David Luthy agreed that it was interesting, but it wasn't Amish.

I wasn't ready to give up. I began to gather related material: newspapers, magazines, and Eaton's catalogs, from around 1912-1918, used as oilcloth underlay in an old home I wrecked. A Mennonite diary, 1861-1866; my great-grandfather's letter collection, 1870-1900; the Tweedsmuir history of towns, villages, schools, and churches in Woolwich Township; items on the Depression of the 1930s—oh, I had fun gathering it all together!

When I was finished, I had the hard-cover volume *Up the*

*Conestogo*, with 460 pages. It was *my* book. I didn't want a publisher to tamper with it, so I self-published it: 4,000 copies! How foolish can one get?

As if that were not enough, I allowed myself to be persuaded to publish a 75-page saddle-stitched booklet *Separate and Peculiar*. This describes the customs and tradition of the OOMs. The two books were published simultaneously. The former is sold out; the latter went through four editions.

By now I have written eight religious-historical books, and twice that number of cookbooks. It was fun, but nothing to get rich by. After all, who cares to be rich merely in this world? (1 Tim. 6:17).

## The Mennonite Tour

The tour guide greeted the Leamington bus passengers as they left the Meetingplace and walked toward the bus. The driver, Jacob Driedger, addressed them briefly. "Our tour guide will now take over and tell you something about the village of St. Jacobs."

[Tour Guide:] Good morning, and welcome to *Yakobschteddel*. I hope you learned something about the area Mennonites by viewing the film. We are in the heart of the community here. Just ahead on the right is the Benjamin Restaurant. Joseph Eby, a Mennonite, kept the hotel there 150 years ago. Next to it was the woolen mill. George Eby had a store at the north end of the bridge.

Here on the west side of the street is the old mill. Six generations of Sniders had owned it in the past. Fifty years ago, I worked in this mill, preparing livestock feed for local farmers. Since the mill has been converted to craft outlets, I nearly have conniptions when I see the lovely quilts hanging where the dusty chopper used to be. However, many of my books have been sold here.

Although our time is limited, there will be a few minutes for you to browse through the place. With three floors, the silos, and the warehouses loaded with all kinds of crafts, you likely won't see them all. Good luck!

"Mr. Isaac and I are not so greatly interested in crafts. We think we might learn more through conversation with you."

"Yes, Jake is interested in the history and function of the community. As an equipment dealer, I would be interested in meeting some local manufacturers."

That shouldn't be a problem. After dinner, we'll be touring through the area. After we leave Hawkesville, we'll be in the Martin area. Nearly every farm has a shop of some kind, where they manufacture a variety of furniture, machinery of all kinds, and even do plastic molding. The newest thing is weaner tubs.

"Weaner—tubs?"

Yes, the new concept in farrowing operations is to wean the piglets within a few weeks after farrowing, to shorten the cycle, with less exposure to disease. Weaner decks are raised four feet above the floor, where piggies are fed on special rations. The weaner tub is raised only a short distance above the floor. The plastic is easier to sterilize and keep clean.

"That would be something new for Isaac Equipment!"

"It would be something different at least. I wouldn't mind looking into it."

They also mold hockey sticks, and maple-sap equipment: several sizes of jugs for maple syrup, sturdy sap pails, and sap spouts. In fact, I doubt that there is anything in plastic that they wouldn't try to make.

It looks as though the ladies are finished shopping; so bring your bus to the door of the mill. From here we go south through the village to the lights, where we bend slightly to the right, onto Weber Street.

As we pass through the village, note that the stores on both sides are tourist oriented; generally owned by Mercedes Corporation, if I am correct, as far as the bottom of the grade. Home Hardware had started as a little hardware store in the village. Now Home Hardware is the largest hardware chain in Canada, reaching from coast to coast. If we turned right at Henry Street and crossed the tracks, we would see the Home Hardware wholesale headquarters on the right. You might even glimpse some of the hundred or more trucks if you peep between the homes.

Just ahead we will cross the tracks, which have been restored lately, for a tourist train to run between St. Jacobs and Waterloo. With luck, we might catch a glimpse of it farther on. Here we pass through the traffic light and swing right onto Weber Street. Now the sale barns for the Ontario Livestock Exchange are on your left, and the St. Jacobs Farmers Market on the right. On a Thursday, the parking lot on the left is packed with cars and trucks; on Saturday, the same is true on the right.

Next on your left, watch for the NCR building. That is where the old Peter Martin home stood up to about 1980, when it was moved to Doon Heritage Crossroads, south of Kitchener. Now turn left on Northfield Drive. The farms of Peter's family stretched from the village Conestogo and up the road halfway to Heidelberg.

"There comes the train!"

"Where?"

"Oh, there it goes!"

There is really nothing to get excited about. Recently a man with horse and buggy left Waterloo at the same time the train did. He arrived in St. Jacobs just when the train did.

"Yes, but it is still a real choochoo train!"

"It would be great for watching scenery, too."

As we pass along Northfield Drive, the sale barns can be seen from the rear, at the left. Turn left on old Highway 86. As we travel north, the Martins Meetinghouse is on the right. Let's drive past it and turn right onto the side road for parking.

## Martin's Meetinghouse

[Tour Guide:] This is Martin's Meetinghouse, originally built in the 1830s; the first of the Old Order Mennonite meetinghouses in the area. Since then it has been rebuilt and enlarged several times.

"Is it still in use?"

Yes, but not by the Old Order church. Since 1939, when the Markham-Waterloo Mennonites separated from the Old Order church and began to drive cars, the house had been used alternately by both groups. A few years ago, our people decided that the location, being so close to the city with the increased traffic, was not compatible with horse-and-buggy travel. Since then, the Martin's Old Order congregation worships in the Conestogo meetinghouse, and the Markham group has sole rights to the church, except when an Old Order funeral is held there.

An amusing incident occurred several years ago while the church was still used by both groups. Apparently someone from a distance had been driving north of Waterloo on a Sunday morning. Suddenly he found himself confronted by a procession of horses and buggies—not half a dozen, but hundreds of them. They were all assembling at a long, low, white building at the edge of the city.

Astonished by the spectacle, he pulled over to watch from the roadside. The women, all in dark dress, were unloaded on a porch at one end of the building, where they disappeared inside. After tying their horses side by side in a long row, the men entered by a door at the opposite end. They too were in dark clothes.

Imagining that he had witnessed some sort of pageant, the man stopped at a nearby gas station. Upon inquiry, he was told that he had seen the Mennonites gathering for their regular Sunday morning service. The people were dressed in their usual Sunday clothes.

When the man returned home, he mentioned the matter to his wife. She was quite impressed.

"Why don't we drive up to Waterloo again next Sunday morning?" she suggested. "I'm sure the children would enjoy it, and so would I."

The following Sunday morning, the stranger drove up through Waterloo again, this time with his wife and family. At the edge of the city, he spotted the same long, low, white building, and a procession approaching it—not horses and buggies, but black cars! The dark-robed women gathered on the porch as before. After parking their cars, the black-clad men entered the door at the opposite end.

The man was dumbfounded.

"They came with horses and buggies last Sunday," he defended himself. "I'm sure they did. There was not one car here. Surely they didn't all decide to drive cars at the same time!"

"Maybe you misunderstood someone," his wife suggested. "Maybe they just drive horses and buggies on certain days."

The man shook his head. "I don't think so. Let us go to that gas station and find out."

When the stranger asked about the phenomenon, his informant laughed. "You were at the right place at the wrong time.

There are two kinds of Mennonites using that church on alternate Sundays.

"One kind drives horses and buggies. The other drives black cars."

In this cultural exchange, it's easy to see how surprised the man was, because he interpreted the signs wrongly.

"Yes, there can be such a problem, like that of the blind men and the elephant."

That's one of the lessons we hope to learn from experiences such as this tour provides: we need not be blind, taking in only part of the picture, and be partly right but wrong in our overall concept.

Peter Martin, whose homesite we passed two miles back, was one of the first settlers in this area. Church services were held at his house before the meetinghouse was built. Before we enter the building, let us take a look at the cemetery. Here, just inside the gate, are the graves of Peter and Anna Martin. Do you notice a difference between their headstones and most of the rest?

"Why, yes! Their markers were more ornamental! Why so?"

I think the reason was that the Old Order church had not yet emerged. The headstones were patterned after those of the First Mennonite church cemetery, in what now is Kitchener. Only after they saw where the trend led did the Old Orders draw back to become more conservative.

"Is there really not much difference between the Markham church and the Old Order church?"

To those outside the church, the difference seems trivial. To us, the difference is too great to ignore. Aside from all other differences, ownership of cars is still enough of an issue to warrant caution. In a grade-ten history book of thirty years ago, the author commented on the changing pattern of social behavior in the 1920s:

Quite aside from its use for business or ordinary family purposes, the motor car offered a readily available means of escaping from the watchful eye of parents. American sociologists all agree that it did more than anything else to break down the prewar moral codes and the older, more formalized relationships between the sexes.

The Old Order parents do not feel the need for more of a moral breakdown.

"That sounds like sound advice that we all could use, if it were not too late," responded one thoughtful tourist.

## Introducing the Old Order Mennonites

The earliest Ontario Mennonites are nearly all of Swiss origin. It is not necessary to tell you people the story of persecution through the Reformation, for the Swiss and the Dutch suffered alike, and the Dutch earlier than the Swiss. Nor is there a need to dwell long on the reasons why the Anabaptists were persecuted, or why they were called Mennonites.

For nearly two hundred years our forebears were severely persecuted, moving from place to place, until William Penn offered them asylum and freedom in America. Most of our ancestors came to Pennsylvania between 1710 and 1730.

Seventy-five years later, some of their descendants moved to Canada, to establish a new settlement in Waterloo County and other areas. By the latter part of the century, many of the Mennonites were influenced by modern, evangelistic movements. By 1889, the matter came to a head. Those who refused to accept the progressive practices, which we thought tolerated and encouraged pride and inflated self-esteem, withdrew from the "Old" Mennonite conference. Thus emerged the Old Order Mennonites, who preferred discipline, obedience, and discipleship, rather than the modern Sunday schools, prayer meetings, and revivals.

By 1939, about 40 percent of the Old Order church wished to drive cars and joined a group at Markham, near Toronto. They formed the Markham-Waterloo Conference. The Markham Mennonites drive black cars and are in general a little more liberal than the Old Order church.

Besides these, there are several ultra-conservative groups, both Mennonite and Amish, who have neither cars, tractors, telephone, nor public hydroelectric power. One group, the Martin people, have phones and modern technology, but own no cars, tractors, nor hydroelectric connections.

The main body of Old Order Mennonites are the subject of this study. Hydroelectricity, rubber-tired tractors, and phones are optional, but not used by the ministry. The main body is located in the northern part of Waterloo County (Regional Municipality) and extends about ten miles beyond the boundaries of the county. There are nine meetinghouses for church services.

A daughter colony, established thirty years ago in the Mount Forest area, has four meetinghouses. Total baptized membership in the two areas is estimated at 2,000. Adherents (those under 18) could account for another 2,000. An additional 90 members are located in five new communities: Chesley, Teeswater, Kinloss (at Holyrood), Dunnville, and Lindsay. Of these, only Chesley has a minister and a meetinghouse. The rest have neither so far.

There are three bishops presiding over the whole extended community, working with a total of 16 ministers and 13 deacons. We have 83 teachers in 45 schools.

Since exact membership figures are not readily available, there has been some speculation among historians and writers about the numerical strength of the Old Order churches. In fact, some historians have thought that the Old Order churches were declining and predicted that they may even die out in the near future. A closer look will prove the inaccuracy of this view.

In 1930, before the Markham group withdrew from the main body, there were five meetinghouses to serve all the congregations. Today, there are thirteen places of worship for the Old Order congregations alone, and nine to serve the Markham group. Overall average attendance is over five times as high as it was in 1930, partly because church attendance per person is higher than it was.

Church practices are still maintained at about the same level as they were a hundred years ago. While modern trends do attract our people, the differences between the Old Order church and mainstream society are greater than ever. Today we are applying more efforts to suppress drinking, smoking, and immorality than we did in the past.

However, we still fall far short of our aim. Our desire is to be a chosen generation, a royal priesthood, a holy nation, a peculiar people, as a glorious church, without spot or wrinkle (1 Pet. 2:9; Eph. 5:27). This will take all our efforts and a good measure of God's grace and sanctification.

"How do you account for your 500 percent increase of membership in seventy-five years? Where do you get your proselytes?"

We don't. We grow our own prospective members. My wife and I raised a family of twelve children. My wife came from a family of thirteen. So did her father. But I'm not suggesting that this be taken as a model for every family.

"What form of church administration does your church have: Presbyterian, Episcopal, or Congregational?"

None of those.

"What then? What else can it be?"

You don't like my answer? Would you prefer if I said, all three? I think that would be closer to the truth.

"But the first two are opposites. How could they be the same?"

Christ said, "I and my Father are one" (John 10:30). He also said, "My Father is greater than I" (John 14:28). In the same way, all the members of our ministry are equal. Yet when taking votes or making decisions, the bishop has the deciding vote, or consolidates the opinions of the rest into one. At the same time, it is congregational in a certain sense. The church counsel, representing the members, brings the voice of the congregation to the ministry, upon which the ministry makes the decisions.

"You wiggled out of that one quite well, Tour Guide. I happen to know that those are expressions not normally used among Old Order churches. I think you answered Mr. Parker's question accurately."

Thanks, Jake.

## An Old Order Church Service

Before I introduce you to a church service here, we will discuss the layout (see the sketch). The caretaker has kindly unlocked the door facing the road, which will make it easiest to explain the layout. This door is used by the boys, who sit on the benches to our right as we enter. Young married men occupy the short benches on the extreme right, with an aisle separating the two. On our left is where the girls sit, and for today I'm asking you to sit on their benches.

As you face the pulpit, the benches to the right, facing the end of the pulpit, are occupied by the men; the elder ones in front, the younger ones at the back, according to age. To your left, the women occupy the benches facing the other end of the pulpit, accordingly. Two stoves furnish heat.

Notice the hat racks above the men's section, and their absence above the women. Instead, the women's cloakrooms are on the extreme left, beyond the three doors. The farthest door leads to the elderly women's cloakroom, which doubles as the counsel room. The women's washrooms are found beyond the counsel room, on the right. The men are less favored and find theirs in outhouses.

### Old Order Mennonite Church Layout
Most Old Order Mennonite churches in Ontario have a center door facing the road, for boys and young men. On entering this door, one faces the pulpit. To the left are girls and young women. To the right are boys and young men. On the right of the pulpit are the men; to the left, the women. The left door facing the road takes one into the girls' and young women's cloakroom. The door centered on the left gable end is for middle-aged women, and the one for the older women is at the far corner of the same end.

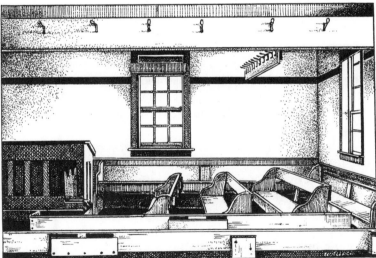

This inside view shows the front two boys' benches in the foreground; beyond that, men's benches face the end of the pulpit. There are about eight benches in each section.

While you are seated here, viewing the whole room, I will explain the procedure and content of a church service, and the related church ordinances. Usually there are at least two ministers and one deacon (all men) behind the wide pulpit for services. There may be more, and occasionally there are less.

The church services usually begin at ten a.m. The home minister or deacon announces a hymn from the German hymnbook compiled in the Berlin (Kitchener) area in 1836, and reads the first verse. Two men are song leaders, and one starts the hymn, without a tuning fork. Every able person joins in to sing soprano. There is no four-part singing in our church services, and no musical accompaniment.

At the close of the hymn, the deacon stands to read the Scripture text selected by the main speaker. This is usually one whole chapter out of the New Testament. When he is finished, the home minister usually makes an introduction, without centering on any particular Scripture text. Usually he gives several remarks inspired by the opening hymn. The main purpose of this brief sermon is to prepare the hearts to receive the message being brought by the main speaker. After speaking for about twenty minutes, he asks the congregation to kneel for silent prayer, especially for the main speaker, that he may be inspired to bring a motivating message. He signals the end of the prayer with an audible "Amen."

At the end of the prayer, the main speaker stands. Let me share one reason why a whole chapter is selected as a text: We believe that "all Scripture is given by inspiration of God, and is profitable for doctrine, for reproof, for correction, for instruction in righteousness" (2 Tim. 3:16). Otherwise, a minister might choose only the verses that appeal to him, instead of opening himself to be more fully inspired by God.

The preacher takes the text, verse by verse, expounding on every detail, trying to bring out the whole thought of the writer. Sometimes he digresses, if the text reminds him of something else, so that it may take him a whole hour before he has touched every detail to his satisfaction.

After this main sermon, he asks the other members of the ministry to share a testimony. The purpose of this is that if they should find his sermon unscriptural, they would set him right and correct his message; but this rarely happens. Instead, they invariably add a few relevant thoughts that have come to their minds, and confirm the points that he has brought out. When they finish, he thanks the others for their testimony, then asks the congregation to kneel, while he leads them in an audible prayer.

After the prayer, the second song leader announces another hymn and leads it in the same way. When all verses are sung, slowly and meaningfully, the minister rises again, sometimes making a few appropriate remarks about the hymn, pronounces the benediction, makes any necessary announcements, and dismisses the church.

"Are visitors welcome in the church?"

Yes, definitely. Although the service is usually in German, the ministers usually preach at least some in English if they realize that there are people in attendance who understand no German.

"Do children and teenagers attend the services?"

Yes; it is a rare thing when anyone is missing, if they are able to go. There are usually at least as many young people in church as older ones.

"What about Sunday school?"

Our Old Order churches have no Sunday school as such. It is expected that parents teach their children biblical stories and principles at home. If the parents do their duty in this, the need for a Sunday school is already met.

## Church Administration

[Tour Guide:] Our church observes communion twice a year. Since we believe that only those who are in unity with each other and the church are compatible with the spirit of communion, two things have to take place first. The first one is counsel meeting, to see whether we stand in peace, love, and unity with each other. On this occasion, the text is Matthew 18, regarding offenses, the lost sheep, and the law of forgiveness.

### Counsel Meeting

At the close of the regular service, the members remain seated. The ministry retires to the counsel room (the elderly women's cloakroom). The elder members follow the ministry: the men in the first group, the women in the second. In a large congregation, there may be two groups of each. One by one, beginning at the eldest, they confess peace with fellow members and God, and express their desire to partake of communion.

If they have any general concerns about problems in the church, this is the time to express themselves. However, if they have personal grievances, they are expected first to reconcile themselves with one another. If they were offended by another brother or sister, they are expected to go and tell that one his or her fault first (Matt. 18:15-17).

When all the elder members in successive groups have been to the counsel room, the results are written down, to be taken to the conference of bishops, ministers, and deacons.

"You mentioned that the elder members go to the counsel room. Do the younger ones not have a voice in church administration? Do they not need to confess peace with fellow members and God?"

That is indeed a thorny question. The reason for this discrepancy is to keep the service from lasting too long. Younger ones are expected to make their contact directly to the ministry at another time, or make their concerns known to and through elder members. I admit that if they were an integral part of the church counsel earlier, they might make a smoother transition into the church administration. However, no serious problems have surfaced because of this seeming discrepancy.

"It seems a pity that these younger people should be neglected because of a lack of time."

I'm inclined to agree with you. Perhaps, someday—

### The Church Conference

The next step toward observing communion is the church conference. Communion is considered too holy to be partaken of by those who are not in fellowship with the church. Generally speaking, counsel meetings are finished before Good Friday in the spring, and in the fall before Harvest Meeting (about Sept. 1). Then the conference is held the Friday following the counsel meeting.

All the members of the ordained ministry are usually present as far as health permits. The conference begins in the morning, at the regular time for church service. It is opened with an appropriate hymn. A suitable Scripture text is read, and a few remarks made, followed by a prayer.

After the prayer, each member of the ministry is individually asked whether he is willing to continue in his office. Generally they all agree to do so, trusting that God can work through human weakness (2 Cor. 4).

Then each spokesman is called upon to bring the results of the counsel meeting in his district. One by one, the results of each meeting are read aloud and discussed. Because members' views vary greatly, and conference members' views similarly vary, a considerable amount of time may be needed for deliberation. Even when all conference members agree on principle, it may still take hours to handle the problems presented by the spokesmen.

"Is the conference open to the public?"

Not at present. The conference proceedings can become embarrassing enough without strangers listening in. In the distant past, lay members sometimes attended, to no good purpose. Elias Eby, son of Bishop Benjamin Eby, wrote some things on this in his diary of 1872-1878:

> **May 31, 1872.** I went with Sem Risser to the conference, where everything passed off peaceably, although many strangers were there, expecting to hear great disputations, and must needs go their ways disappointed. It served them right.
>
> **Apr. 2, 1874.** The conference was held at Ebys, where many ministers gathered to see whether peace and unity might be restored, but all in vain. Many harsh accusations were made, but no one wished to accept them.

"What was the issue at that time?"

The start of the New Mennonites, now called the Missionary Church.

"Is there never any complaint from lay members about the secrecy involved?"

Yes, a few have objected. Human nature being as it is, if the ministry had admitted to barely preserving the peace through endless discussion, the very lay members who complained would have used that information to deliberately destroy the peace.

"I know how it might happen. Why can't Christians learn to act like human beings?"

I must admit that you are right. I have found some church members who can act like spoiled children. They are never happy. They deliberately destroy the peace.

"How long does a normal conference last?"

I can barely remember. It's been so long since we had one. It can take to five p.m. or later. There has been some discussion of taking a second day for the conference, but it might just encourage participants to extend the discussions. As it is, we will continue trying to make the best of it.

## Holy Communion

Communion begins the second Sunday after the conference. This is of necessity a long-drawn-out affair, since the bishops are the only ones who administer communion. With three bishops and thirteen places where communion is observed, it takes five weeks for them to make the rounds.

On communion day, the services begin earlier than usual. The hymns are chosen to fit the occasion: the first refers to the suffering and death of Christ. One deacon (of two present) reads either Matthew 26 or Luke 22. Next the home minister rises and delivers a sermon warning against overconfidence, using the Old Testament like Paul in 1 Corinthians 10. He exhorts members to learn from the stories of creation, the patriarchs, and Joseph's sojourn in Egypt, and mentions incidents related to Christ's life and death. Then the congregation kneels in silent prayer.

After the prayer, the second deacon reads the Scripture following the one previously read: Matthew 27 or Luke 23. The bishop rises, and (you guessed it) takes the Israelite history from Moses' birth to the people's possession of the land flowing with milk and honey. At this point, he reads 1 Corinthians 11:23-29 and admonishes the congregation to self-examination. The bishop and the congregation then again kneel in silent prayer.

After the prayer, the deacon places on the pulpit a plate of bread, precut into long strips. The bishop takes one such strip in his hand, asks the members to stand, and pronounces a blessing on the bread.

When all again are seated, the bishop breaks off a bite for himself, after which he follows the aisles, placing a morsel into the hand of each partaking member. He serves the men first, and then the women. One deacon follows him, carrying the plate. While the bishop is passing the bread, he recites, "Take, eat; this is my body. For we, being one bread, are one body, for we are all partakers of that one bread. This is my body which is broken for you; this do in remembrance of me" (1 Cor. 11:24; 10:17). He repeats similar verses while passing out the bread.

Meanwhile, the other deacon fills a small jug with wine. When the bishop has resumed his seat, that deacon sets a cup of wine before him on the pulpit. The bishop then takes the cup in hand, has the congregation stand, and pronounces a blessing on the cup. When all are again seated, he recites, "This cup is the New Testament in my blood, which is shed for you" (1 Cor. 11:25).

The bishop takes a sip himself, after which he places the cup into the hand of each participant, who takes a sip and returns the cup. Meanwhile, the bishop repeats, "Take this, and divide it among yourselves; for I say unto you, I will not drink of the fruit of the vine, until the kingdom of God shall come" (Luke 22:17-18). A suitable hymn is sung while the wine is passed around by the bishop.

When all have partaken of the wine, the bishop resumes his seat and asks for testimony from the deacons. The bishop leads in an audible prayer, after which a short hymn is sung, the benediction pronounced, and the congregation is dismissed while the members are asked to remain seated.

"Why aren't the Scripture texts explained?"

I have no explanation except that it is a tradition. We have talked of changing it, but we don't want to lose a valuable tradition. The sermons on the patriarchs and the Israelites remind us that we also are part of holy history, God's chosen people today.

## Feet Washing

The nonmembers are dismissed, and the deacons prepare the water for washing feet. Meanwhile, the bishop reads John 13:1-17, which specifically urges church members to wash each other's feet.

This is an interesting account. By his own admission, Jesus was the disciples' Lord and Master, and yet he stooped to wash their feet. Peter wouldn't have it, until he learned that otherwise he could have no part with Christ. After explaining the matter, Jesus said, "If you know these things, blessed are you if you do them" (John 13:17, RSV).

"That's plain talk. How can anyone wiggle out of it?"

I suppose it is too humiliating for today's society. We have never seen a reason for avoiding it.

The tubs are wooden, as made by coopers years ago. The feet are dried with bath towels. The ministers are the first to wash each other's feet, then the lay members, from the eldest to the youngest. The men participants take off their shoes and socks, then come forward to the open area in front of the pulpit, where the deacons have placed the tubs. In pairs they wash and dry each others' feet, and seal their fellowship with the kiss of peace.

The women file out to the women's two cloakrooms, where they shed their shoes and stockings. They likewise wash each other's feet in pairs and share the kiss of peace. While feet washing is in progress, a special hymn is sung, signifying humility and respect for others.

After all have finished with feet washing, and the women have returned to their seats, the bishop reads the conference proceedings and resolutions. He admonishes the members to conform to the conference decisions and to obey them.

"How long have the Mennonites practiced feet washing?"

It is prescribed by article 11 of the 1632 Dordrecht Confession of Faith, which we accept and teach. I believe it has always been practiced among Swiss Mennonites in Canada, although some modern churches may have dropped the practice.

## Youth and the Church

The public has conflicting views on Old Order youth and conversion to a new life. Some hold the opinion that the parents and the church wield a big stick, thus intimidating the young people into church attendance and ultimately forcing them to join the church.

Others find this theory unlikely, because what they know from their acquaintance with the Old Order young people does not support such rule by coercion. They seem to be a fun-loving and happy group, although not beyond the potential for mischief.

On the matter of the young people's church attendance, we are well satisfied with them. We know that sometimes they may get into mischief. Yet we also know that it would be beyond our powers to bring them into the church services if they had no desire to attend.

As a group, we believe in bringing up our children "in the nurture and admonition of the Lord" (Eph. 6:4). This is certainly commendable. Thus there is not such an obvious and drastic change when they finally surrender themselves to conversion and consecration, as there is among those who have grown up undisciplined. As a result, even the youth themselves find it difficult to point to a certain day and hour when they were converted.

We have a number of examples in the holy Scriptures of those who experienced a sudden and dramatic conversion. Saul was struck to the ground on his way to Damascus (Acts 9). He heard a voice from paradise rebuking him, so that he knew not whether he was in the body or not (2 Cor. 12:2-4). The Philippian jailer was another one who was converted on the spot, through remarkable circumstances (Acts 16).

These were definitely exceptions to the rule. If we expect to be converted in such a way, we may be deceiving ourselves. Satan may be deluding us if we imagine and wait for circumstances we think would be convincing.

"I have often wondered about this phenomenon myself. The strongest supporters of a dramatic conversion are often the ones who, after conversion, still live in a worldly fashion, yet claim to have eternal security."

As a result of their upbringing, most of our young people are converted at about the same age. The fifteen- and sixteen-year-olds are inclined to get into mischief, in spite of their parents' admonitions. They love their parents and wish to please them. Gradually, they grow dissatisfied with such a life, especially since their peers are going through the same experience. Besides, they realize that they are nearing the age when others are usually baptized.

All these factors combine to create an atmosphere of guilt in their minds. As a result, they eventually surrender themselves to instruction, conversion, and finally baptism as they become members of the church.

To those who have been raised in an emotional and charismatic atmosphere, such a conversion may seem insipid. However, it is a well-known fact that a person will usually react as his peers do. It is easy to be exuberant when everyone else is on cloud nine.

Hence, when our young people are nearing the age when their peers are ready to join the church, they would be hard-hearted indeed if God's Spirit did not move them as well. They may not have experienced conversion when they start instruction classes, but chances are that the environment will turn on the heat. In this respect, they experience the same emotions as those who attend revival meetings.

Some time during the spring, an "altar call" is made by the ministry. The young people are encouraged to make application for baptism well in advance. When they do approach the ministry to make such an application, the ministers question them on their motives. If the minister has reason to doubt their sincerity, perhaps because of recent unruly living, they are advised to defer the matter until later. In any case, they are admonished to renounce sin and self, and begin a new life in Christ.

There are usually about seventy-five candidates for baptism in one summer. The names of the applicants are publicly read several times, beginning at the end of May. This gives church members an opportunity to acquaint themselves with the applicants.

On six consecutive Sunday afternoons, instruction meetings are held for the applicants. These begin about mid-June and are held at various churches throughout the Old Order communities. The instructions are based on the eighteen articles of the Dordrecht Confession of Faith, drawn up by Dutch Mennonites in 1632, and later also adopted by other Mennonites. Three of the articles are discussed each Sunday.

"That sounds familiar. Except for slight variations, we still go by them."

"Is shunning still practiced among you?"

Only in two respects: at communion, and at functions such as weddings and funerals.

### Baptismal Rites

Instruction meetings begin about the middle of June and continue every Sunday afternoon for six weeks. The meetings begin at three p.m. The applicants sit at the front of the church, on benches usually occupied by the elderly men and women. Thus the young women and the young men face each other—we still call them girls and boys, even though typically they are around eighteen years of age.

The first hymn, translated to English, begins:

Halt! tender child; where do you haste?
Consider your destruction!

After the opening hymn, a deacon reads Hebrews 11, the faith chapter. A minister gives a discourse on the text, which encourages the young people in faith. Then all kneel in silent prayer. Next, the second preacher reads the first Dordrecht article of faith, regarding God and the creation. He explains the article, reads related Scripture verses, and instructs the applicants. Then he asks whether they understand and believe the contents of the article. Each applicant replies in the affirmative, first the boys, then the girls.

Another preacher follows the same procedure with the second and third articles of faith, dealing with the Fall of humanity, and the restoration promised through Christ. After these two articles have been affirmed by each applicant, the preacher invokes God's blessing on their promises, and asks for testimony from the other ministers. After an audible prayer and another hymn, the service is closed. This lasts about two hours, the same as a regular service.

For the next five weeks, the services follow the same pattern: two appropriate hymns, a suitable text, and the next three articles: on the coming of Christ, the gospel of the New Testament, and the need for repentance. The next Sunday's articles are on baptism, the communion of saints, and the appointment of church leaders.

The fourth Sunday, the articles deal with communion, feet washing, and marriage. The fifth is about our duty to the higher powers, nonresistance, and the swearing of oaths. The last three cover excommunication, shunning, and the last judgment.

By this time, a lot of young heads are swimming, and yet there's more to come. On the Saturday afternoon before baptism, the applicants gather at the meetinghouse with the ministry, to review the articles of faith and receive counsel in faith, charity, and forbearance.

The following morning the applicants gather in an overflowing house. The first preacher expounds on the text for the occasion, John 1:1-36. After a silent prayer, the bishop exhorts the applicants as he stands in front of the pulpit, with the class in a semicircle around him. He asks them three questions:

• Do you believe in God, who created heaven and earth; in Jesus Christ, the son of God and Savior; and in the Holy Spirit, flowing from the Father and the Son?

• Have you repented from sin, and are you willing to forsake your own will and the works of Satan?

• Do you promise, through God's grace and guidance, to follow the teaching of Christ unto death?

After each has responded affirmatively to all three questions, the applicants kneel forward while the congregation kneels in the benches. The bishop offers a vocal prayer. The class remains kneeling while the congregation rises from kneeling and is seated. A deacon steps forward with a pail of water and a cup.

Over each applicant's head, the deacon pours water into and through the bishop's cupped hands, who pronounces each person baptized in the name of the Father, Son, and Holy Spirit. For the girls, the deacon's wife lifts the prayer covering from each girl's head for the bishop to baptize her, after which the bishop's wife replaces the prayer covering.

When all have been baptized, the bishop returns to the first young man. With his right hand of fellowship, he clasps each youth's right hand in turn, raises him to a new beginning, and salutes him with the kiss of peace. Then the bishop greets each of the young women with a handshake, and the bishop's wife salutes them with a kiss. They are all welcomed as brothers and sisters in the congregation.

The young people take their seats, and the bishop takes his place behind the pulpit, reads Romans 6, and expounds it. A prayer ends the service.

"Are these young people supposed to know all those articles of faith by heart?"

We expect the parents to make sure that each applicant has a copy of the *Christliche Gemütsgespräch*, or its English counterpart, *Saving Faith*. Besides the eighteen articles of faith, these books have an extensive "catechism" of questions and answers on matters important for the instruction of youth. The applicants are encouraged to study this book.

### Ordinations

There is one more church ordinance that I wish to describe before we move on. We consider it one of the most serious undertakings, because we want to feel assured that it comes from God and not simply from human beings. This is the ordination of ministers, bishops, and deacons from within the congregation.

The need may arise through death or disability of ordained leaders. It may come through community expansion and the establishment of a new congregation. Whatever the reason, the congregation is admonished to prayerfulness several weeks in advance. A week or two before the proposed ordination, the counsel of the church is taken, to assure that there are no objections to the ordination.

The system which we use for choosing ministers is the one described in Acts 1:21-26. There is no scriptural injunction that we should use this method. We use it because there is the least danger of human preference being involved. We feel most comfortable in leaving the matter totally in God's hands.

On the Sunday before the proposed ordination, the text may be Luke 10: "The harvest truly is great, but the laborers are few. Pray therefore to the Lord of the harvest, that he would send forth laborers into his harvest" (10:2).

The bishop is usually in charge at this time. Sometimes ministers or bishops from a distance are present and take part in the ceremonies. During this service, the congregation is again admonished to prayerfulness.

At the close of the service, the bishop retires to the counsel room (the elderly women's cloakroom). One at a time, usually beginning with the eldest, members go to the counsel room to nominate others for the office to be filled, and the bishop writes down the names recommended. This is voluntary, and usually from five to fifteen men give their counsel. Some may go out to offer their blessings without nominating anyone.

After a period of time, if no more members go out to give counsel, the bishop returns to the pulpit. He reads off the names of those nominated, speaking clearly so that there may be no danger of naming the wrong person. Then he asks the candidates and their wives to appear at the church the next afternoon for examination.

This meeting of examination is begun as a regular service, with a hymn, Scripture reading, a short sermon, and a prayer. The candidates are examined to see whether they conform to the requirements of the office to be filled. They are asked whether they are willing to make any changes that may be required. If despondent, they are comforted and otherwise encouraged to prepare themselves for the calling if it should fall to their lot.

The following morning, the day of the ordination, the church is usually crowded. Relatives and friends of the candidates will attend from a distance. The candidates sit on a bench directly in front of the pulpit and facing it, according to age. Their wives sit on the front bench, where the aged women usually sit.

The order of the service is the same as for an ordinary church service: a hymn, Scripture reading, introductory sermon, and silent prayer. However, all of it is keyed to the occasion.

After a sermon measuring up to the occasion, the bishop instructs, admonishes, encourages, and comforts the candidates. Two deacons then take as many identical hymnbooks as there are candidates. The bishop prepares a slip of paper bearing the words (in German): "The lot is cast into the lap, but the whole disposing thereof is of the Lord" (Prov. 16:33). He places the slip in one of the books, which the deacons take to the counsel room and shuffle until no one knows which carries the slip. Then they bring them in and set them in a row on the pulpit, in front of the candidates.

There is total silence in the church. The bishop announces a prayer for God's blessing and leading. The congregation kneels.

After the prayer, the bishop asks the candidates each to take a book. Again, he comforts and encourages the candidates. Then he asks them to return the books, one by one, beginning with the eldest. He thumbs through the book; if he does not find the slip, he returns it. When he does find it, he reads it aloud: "The lot is cast into the lap, but the whole disposing thereof is of the Lord."

The bishop asks the chosen one to come forward and kneel at the end of the pulpit. Placing his hands on the head of the elected one, he intones the consecration and ordination rites. This is found in 1 Timothy 4:13-16.

After testimony and prayer, a suitable hymn is sung, during which the other ministers in turn embrace and kiss their new fellow laborer.

"I could tell by your description of the event that it is a high-

ly emotional experience. Is there any difference between an ordination for a minister, deacon, or bishop?"

A bishop is always chosen from among the ministers. Of
course, the Scripture texts vary somewhat. Otherwise there is little difference.

"Is a good education a point of qualification?"

No. Paul was an educated man before his conversion; yet he
counted that all as loss or dung when compared to the knowledge
of Christ and the work of the Spirit of God (Phil. 3:8; 1 Cor. 2).

## Schools and Education

[Tour Guide:] With the church behind us, our next main stop
is at the school. First, as we travel northeast along Country
Squire Road, we will pass many historical farms, cleared by the
pioneers. After the first crossroad, on our left is the farm on
which Deacon John Weber settled when he moved to Canada in
1825. He was ordained to the ministry in 1833.

John and his wife were the parents of the fraktur artist, Anna,
or Nancy Weber. "Indian" John Weber, a son, took over his father's farm at the latter's death. He was only there about ten
years when he sold out, acting as his own auctioneer. At one time
he lived in West Montrose, where he had only a small barn, and
no straw for his horse and cow.

At one time a son-in-law had more straw than he needed, so
he told his two young sons to take a load of straw to their grandfather, and they could have whatever he gave them. The boys
were happy. After the straw was unloaded, "Indian" John told the
boys, "Thanks for the load of straw—or is there a charge for it?"

At least, the boys had their grandfather's thanks to take home!

Apparently, John earned his name because he preferred the Indians' way of life: the men hunting and fishing, and the women
doing the farmwork.

We will stop a moment at the next crossroad before we turn
left. Half a mile down Lexington Road, to your right, were two
pioneer homes. On the right side was the home of the pioneer
Henry Weber, who moved to Canada in 1816. In 1824 he was

ordained minister for Schneider's (Bloomingdale) church. For many years a log bridged the Conestogo River, by which he crossed to attend to his church duties.

His only son, Samuel, was ordained for Schneider's and Martin's in 1864. His only daughter was married to Joseph Weber, who became a deacon and lived a half mile straight ahead. Many of our ministers today are descended from this line, including two of our three bishops.

On the left side of the road is the home where my great-great-grandfather settled when he moved to Canada in 1820. The farm stayed in the family until it was recently sold for city development.

As we turn to the left, our first stop is at the South Woolwich school, one of the first Old Order Mennonite schools, established in 1966. Beside it is the brass foundry, where harness parts are cast, for selling to harness makers far and wide.

A short distance ahead at the farm on the left, was the pioneer home of Daniel Weber, brother to Henry, mentioned above. He moved there in 1820, to be close to his brother. This farm, too, has remained in the family ever since. On this farm is located a woodworking shop, where quality furniture is made for an elite trade.

If anyone would rather go to the brass foundry or to the woodworking shop instead of the school, you can either walk to the foundry, or Jake can take you to the woodworking shop.

"Not right now! It's recess, and there's a ball game going!" protested Jake.

"Tour Guide, Linda Regehr is with us. She teaches school at Leamington and would like to hear something of your school beginnings."

"Yes, if you don't mind; I can still keep one eye on the ball game."

Certainly. There is no problem on my part. Let me start at the beginning. For about a hundred years, the public school system worked satisfactorily in rural Ontario, even among the Mennonites. A three-man school board was elected from among the ratepayers in each school section. They were responsible for hiring teachers, obtaining any supplies the parents didn't buy, and keeping the school in satisfactory running condition. They were aware of individual needs, and they knew the ratepayers. There was little interference by the provincial department of education.

Over forty years ago, some ratepayers in the country felt rural pupils were entitled to the same advantages that pupils enjoyed in the city. In some areas, a majority of ratepayers had no desire for these "advantages," but that was beside the point.

"That would have been in the late fifties."

Yes. Consequently, larger school areas were designated, with larger, paid school boards. Parents and board members were strangers to each other. Consolidated schools replaced the one-room schools.

"If I remember correctly, the ones who desired such changes were those who had moved out from the city 'to get away from it all.' "

Right. Ironically, they still wanted their children to have the urban outlook. They did not wish their children to be farmers. All these changes were created with urban designs. Buses took the pupils to and from the schools. Gymnasiums had to be erected to provide the exercise formerly acquired by walking to school.

"Yippee! The shortstop caught Mr. Driedger out!"

"Yes, I guess I'm too old for such exertion. I'd better go to see the brass foundry, if I can find someone to go with me."

Now, where were we? Oh, yes, about walking to school, and the changes in the school system.

"Yes, isn't it amazing? Yet those were people who considered themselves a cut above the local farmers."

There was no point in local people fighting the issue. The die was cast. Yet all those developments combined to form an atmosphere unfriendly to the Old Order people.

The Amish who settled in Ontario had already been operating their own schools in the USA. They looked askance at the new developments and voiced their suspicions to the Old Order Mennonites. As a result, a delegation from the two groups visited the ministry of education.

"The fact that the Amish and the Mennonites were willing to work together was commendable in itself. That helped to

strengthen their approach with a united front."

They questioned officials about future policies, and received honest but startling answers. At this point, school policies were turning toward permissiveness. Teachers were allowed a freer hand. The trend was toward evolutionary doctrine; biblical authority was relegated to the background.

"Such permissiveness has a tendency to replace authority."

Right. The delegates were alarmed. They immediately called meetings about establishing parochial schools. In their zeal, a slight misunderstanding developed between them and those who were not involved, who had no firsthand information. The latter felt that they were being railroaded into something without their consent. Eventually this misunderstanding was reasonably resolved.

In the spring of 1966, a meeting was called at an area home. Some of the Amish from Aylmer, Ontario, were present. The key figure at this meeting was a qualified young public school teacher with Mennonite background. He was personally acquainted with the Old Order Mennonites and interested in the project. Therefore, he offered his services as a teacher, as supervisor of the system, and as unofficial representative to the ministry of education.

"What a break! In my opinion, that was probably the key to a successful operation. It represented a strong link with the ministry of education. It supplied a pattern for other teachers to copy. At the same time, he was there as a supervisor for the inexperienced teachers, as well as the school board."

He agreed to conduct a two-week crash course in teaching, with seven pupils. With this encouraging offer, the proposal went ahead.

In September 1966, eight parochial schools opened their doors under Bauman's supervision—seven among the Mennonites and one in the Milbank Amish district. The teachers were Bauman, two older men, one young man, and four young women. Bauman was the only one with more than eighth-grade education.

"Here is an interesting sidelight. In the public school system, another eight years are required, after grade eight, before a teacher is qualified. With sixteen years of education, a teacher should be able to teach the pupils the basic language skills. Yet so many leave school without a knowledge of basic English. Your "unlettered" teachers, with no more than grade-eight education, could hardly do worse with their pupils."

Maybe so, and maybe better. In spite of adversity, the schools flourished. Dedication made up for education. It soon became obvious that the results in academic skills proved as satisfactory in these schools as in public schools. Indeed, in one-room schools, younger pupils learn much by listening in on upper-grade classes.

Today there are 83 teachers in 45 schools, some with several rooms. Bauman has retired as supervisor. Through a division of labor among those who have taught for twenty years or more, his post has been filled. In addition, the beginning teachers are paired off with more-experienced ones, who periodically visit the younger teachers' schools and offer advice and encouragement.

The greatest problem continues to be the availability of suitable teachers. However, so far the doors have always opened with a teacher behind the desk. The increase in teaching aids is a great advantage. Most of the schools are well equipped and equal to the challenge. Such teaching aids were conspicuously lacking during the first years.

Sometimes, even in the most difficult situations, interesting incidents turn up to brighten the day. During the first year, a young girl who entered the teaching field too late for summer school seemed to be in need of moral support. The supervisor spoke to another young man, one of the teachers. "Someone should encourage her," he said. "I can't, since she is afraid of me. Would you try it?"

Although she was also a stranger to him, he tried it—and ended up marrying her!

### After Grade 8

"I understand that in your parochial schools, the pupil finishes school at the end of grade 8, or when he turns fourteen. Can he do that legally?"

Yes. We make use of an escape clause stating that a child must attend school until turning sixteen, unless the minister of education is satisfied that he is receiving a satisfactory education elsewhere. One such avenue of escape is through our system of apprenticeship.

The system of apprenticeship was established for our school system in about 1965, shortly before our schools began. Under this system, at the end of grade 8 or at age 14, pupils are apprenticed to their parents until their sixteenth birthday. If the parents do not have enough work to keep them busy, they are apprenticed to another farm family, by mutual agreement, where they can be gainfully employed until their sixteenth birthday. The children are not to receive any pay for their work, but shall work for their board.

"What would you do if your child wished to seek other employment?"

If I were a full-time, successful farmer, there would be a small chance that he would not want to farm. Besides, if my son did not wish to be employed in a farm-oriented environment, the chance is small that he would be an Old Order Mennonite. That would mean that he would be leaving all his former friends and would need to establish an entirely new circle of friends. Under such conditions, we naturally would not encourage such a move.

"Is there a special reason for not sending your children to high school?"

Definitely. We have valid reasons for this. In our parochial schools, our children are to a certain extent sheltered from worldly influences. It would be the height of folly if, during their most critical and formative years, we would send them to high school, where the environment is more worldly than in public elementary school.

On top of that, higher education would tend to draw them away from the farm and toward the city. Since there is a scarcity of good farmers, it would be equally foolish to give them an education which would automatically draw them away from the farm.

After our children reach the age of sixteen, if they are not needed at home, both boys and girls are hired out by the year to Mennonite families who need help. They receive board and lodging and a minimal wage, and are treated as members of the family. Their wages are low, but so are their expenses. They gain a varied experience, which stands them in good stead when they start on their own.

Eventually, some do turn to other vocations. There are many cottage industries among us. This builds a diversity of trades within a rural environment. It also strengthens the community by making it more self-sufficient.

"Would there not be an advantage in a farmer having his son go to an agricultural school?"

"No." One farmer is reported to have said, "I wouldn't mind letting my son go to college, if he were willing to learn when he gets home!"

Have you ever worked on a farm?

"No, but think of the advantage of having enough education that he could do your own repair work—"

Have you ever milked ducks?

"What do you mean by that?"

Old George Steiner had been ringing the church bells for years. A young chap tried to tell him how it should be done.

George replied, "Don't try to teach your father how to milk ducks!"

Higher education cannot hold a candle to the method of passing on knowledge from father to son, especially as far as farming is concerned.

We took up quite a bit of time here at the school. With my single-track mind, I didn't even notice whether anyone went to see the brass foundry or the furniture shop. I feel sorry for not giving Linda more time with the teachers here. Instead, I wanted to supply the background information.

"If you'll excuse me for saying so, through your single track-mind, you didn't notice that I did sneak a short interview with the teachers. I found out that they have thirty-one pupils in two rooms, and verified that the school was built in 1966."

Checking up on me, were you? That's okay; I do make mistakes. Now, is everyone on board, Jake?

"We are back from the brass foundry, but I left two couples at the furniture shop. That foundry was worth going to visit. We were lucky enough to see them pour the molten brass into the molds."

Then we're off to the furniture shop. I hope we have no bureaus or sideboards to load. Anyone else wish to take a peek?

"I think we should load up and move on. I'm getting hungry."

"Here you are! I'm glad you came. I was afraid we might need a trailer to take everything home!"

"Oh, come now; all I bought was a little silverware chest."

"And we didn't get anything except a calendar and a business card; but oh, I could have just looked and looked!"

"*Gloated* would have been a better word."

Now, with everyone on board, here we go down the hill, around the bend, and over the bridge. Conestogo lies before us at the top of the hill. *Blockschteddel* is the German name.

"A logging town, in other words."

Turn left at the top of the hill, and drive on for a block to the bakery. I wouldn't call it a logging town, although Peter Musselman had a sawmill and flour mill here, 150 years ago. We shall stop at the bakery for a few minutes. There will be room for a few people to go in.

"Let's go. A Mennonite bakery is too good to miss. We'll tell the rest of you about it."

This bakery was started by a Mennonite couple who were vendors at the farmers' market. Now the next generation of two single girls sell everything over the counter.

"Wonder how soon they'll be back. I'm still hungry."

"Here they come. Ah, the aroma!"

"Now who's gloating? All right. There won't be any peace until we share with you. We bought a dozen cream buns and a dozen donuts. We even borrowed a knife to cut them in half, so there will be enough pieces to go around."

"How thoughtful of you."

"Don't forget, we are on our way to a Mennonite dinner. Jake and our tour guide, the hardworking ones, deserve a whole pastry one of their choice. I'll serve, if you return the knife."

"No, no! A half is enough for me. I want to enjoy my dinner, too."

Yes, I'll just have a half like the rest. Take home what we don't eat. Now we drive on toward the west. Next on the left was Ludwig Koch, a Mennonite minister of 150 years ago. To the south, on adjoining land, was my great-great-grandfather Reist. Ludwig's wife was his sister. In 1821, they were building a bridge a mile down the river, and the Reists' single brother, John, was drowned.

"How long since they had come to Canada?"

Only about a year. It was quite a shock to the rest of the family.

"Was pastor Roy Koch a descendant?"

Yes, a great-grandson. His wife is my first cousin.

"I promised we'd tell about the bakery. It's hard to describe.

They have a large oven and a dough mixer—the whole bit. At busy times, such as Christmas, they hire extra workers, and they often hire our tour guide's granddaughters!"

I could have told you that, if it had occurred to me. Up ahead, at the lights, we cross Highway 86. St. Jacobs, or *Yakobschteddel*, is on the left, at the bottom of the hill. From here, we make a right and a left and a right again, then travel west.

After we cross the railroad tracks, on your right is the farm my great-grandfather carved out of the woods in 1844. In a letter written November 24, 1891, he reported that the railroad passing through their farm was almost finished. On Monday it would be opened to traffic. They could see the St. Jacobs station from their door. Three trains would pass through daily. Then passengers could take breakfast here, and the next morning in Pennsylvania. That's traveling fast!

At the crossroad, on our right, is the old Conestogo-St. Jacobs cemetery. The new Conestogo meetinghouse is on our left.

## Mennonite Dinner at Mary's

Here we are at Mary's Kitchen. Because we were late, we flew low over the Three Bridges, past my former home, and over the hills to Hawkesville. This place is designed to accommodate those with a taste for elegance. It nevertheless smacks of homey, old-fashioned cooking. That was why we picked this place for our dinner. Mary was born an Old Order Mennonite and knows the customs and traditions. Here you may experience Old Order cooking, table manners, and customs, without feeling awkward, as you might for a meal in a private home.

When all are seated at the table, the host (in this case, the tour guide) leads in a silent grace. The only indication of its finish is the rustle, shifting, or creak of the host's chair.

In most cases, you will find the knife and fork on your plate, and the teaspoon on your saucer. Then, if you watch me, you may be in for a surprise. Seventy-five years ago, I learned that a knife is for cutting, a fork for stabbing, and a spoon for eating with. You can't teach an old dog new tricks. I have adhered faithfully to this principle ever since, especially because I like my potatoes with lots of gravy. I choke on dry food. I also dunk my cake; but more of that later.

"Hey! I've found a kindred spirit! My wife has been trying to break me of that habit for fifty years!"

The bread plate is usually passed first. Butter and apple butter are strategically placed within everyone's reach. Before the first course starts, it is customary to eat a slice of apple-butter bread. A word of caution here: leave the crust, as you may need it to wipe your plate clean after your first course. This is the only plate you get, so it must be ready for the second course.

Traditionally, you will be offered a second helping, to which you are welcome; but the host (meaning me) will likely watch. Don't take more than you can handle, because food left on the plate is considered wasteful! So relax and enjoy your meal. Let us bow our heads in silent prayer. . . .

Now, the bread: Linda, you're about the closest.

"Which way?"

To the left of the dealer, of course!

"This must be Wellesley apple butter."

There's a good chance it is, although a lot is made locally. Sad to say, butter is likely margarine, yet the taste is much the same now.

"It is good!"

"No doubt about it. I'm looking ahead for the mashed potatoes and gravy."

"To say nothing of the pork sausage."

I suppose at Leamington you have been eating fresh peas for some time. Likely strawberries, too.

"Yes, peas and strawberries are pretty well over, but they nevertheless taste good."

"My, that was a delicious meal, even if there was no borsch! What happens if I can't get behind the wheel?"

Without your Russian soup, you didn't eat all that much. Did you even touch the apple pie and ice cream?

"No, but I didn't want to make a pig of myself."

Hawkesville was a thriving village 120 years ago. It was

named after the Hawke brothers, pioneers of the village. When the time came to pick the county seat, Berlin, Shade's Mills, and Hawkesville were all in the running. When the votes were counted, Shade's Mills (Galt) was behind. Berlin and Hawkesville were tied. One of the Hawke brothers cast the deciding vote in favor of Berlin (Kitchener)!

Hawkesville had five blacksmiths, two wagon makers, two harness makers, two shoemakers, two carpenters, two masons, a weaver, a tailor, a cooper, a butcher, a druggist, a doctor, and a schoolteacher. There was a general store, a flour mill, a woolen mill, a tannery, three churches, two hotels, and a school.

Today, there is a general store and a sawmill. The owner of the threshing machine shop is now 88 and can no longer carry on alone. His helper, 84, sometimes works alone.

As we travel westward, past the sawmill, Countryside Mennonite Fellowship church and school are just around the corner. Straight ahead, the large farmhouse was the home of the Warkentin family over seventy years ago. They were the parents of blind Peter Warkentin. Anyone know him?

"We sure do! Everyone knows Peter! We should have brought him along!"

There is some more history connected here. I think Katie Isaac, Herb's wife, was somehow related.

"Herb Isaac of St. Catharines? Herb is a cousin of mine! We'll have to ask Peter about that. I'm sure he'll know."

From here, we will take the lane just south of the house. It leads to Matthias and Nancy. I'm sure you'll enjoy this visit.

## A Runaway

I called Matthias and Nancy from Mary's place. I'm sure you would enjoy a visit there, but our time is limited. Matthias' bells come from all over the world, and so do Nancy's spoons. Matthias also collects books and other memorabilia.

"Is that the man who helped to prepare the history for the Meetingplace in St. Jacobs?"

I think so. We will stop long enough to sign the guest book, which reads like a who's who. I persuaded Nancy to let her father join us on the bus.

"Hello! I'm Nancy. Your tour guide tells me you are too busy to come in, so I will pass my guest book through the bus. I do want all your autographs. Daudie thinks he can get on the bus. I'm sure he would enjoy it. He likes to tell people all about what happened long ago. Do you really think you can get on, Daudie?"

"Oh yes. I'll push my walker against the steps, so—then I'll grab the handle—see? Nancy always worries about me. She thinks I'm old. I'm—91 years young!"

"Thanks for signing the guest book. You'll bring Daudie back again."

Oh, yes; no problem.

"Are you ready, Matthias? Oh, excuse me. I'm Jake Driedger, your driver. Just behind me is Harry Isaac, of Isaac Equipment. We're all from Leamington and Wheatley. We are eager to hear anything you have to say."

"Well then, I must tell you a little story. When I was still a boy, Alvin Ottman's father was here, just where we are now, and looked across the field on our left. 'When I was a boy,' he said, 'I learned to mow grass in that field. Doctor Lackner's father lived here then. He hired day laborers in Hawkesville for mowing grass with the scythe. He asked my father if I could help.

'I was proud of being asked, and hurried over here with our scythe. I hadn't cut much grass yet. Four men were already at work, following each other around the field, each cutting a three-foot swath. I started in, and it wasn't long before that smart aleck, Keller, caught up to me. I mowed furiously, but he was right behind me. I was afraid he would cut my heels.

'Just before noon, Lackner came home and saw what was happening. He called to Keller to take it easy. Right after dinner, Lackner came out and showed me how to handle the scythe. After fifteen minutes he was satisfied that I could really handle it now. I started in a short distance behind Keller. It wasn't long until Keller complained. He was afraid I would cut his heels!' "

We are heading out the south lane now, turning right, toward Linwood. A widow has a store here on the left—

"Hey, is that horse not stopping? There's no driver on the buggy!"

Can you pass him? Drive on a quarter mile and let me off!

"Watch he won't run over you!"

"I'll turn left and see if I can crowd him—"

"The lines are dragging—He missed them!"

Whoa boy! Easy now!

"He's slowing down. Hey, the lines are wrapped around the hub!"

Easy, boy! Whoa, boy! You're all right. You stopped yourself.

"Someone's coming arunning!"

"You caught him, did you?"

Yes. The lines were wrapped around the hub. Everything okay?

"I think so. He broke loose from the tie rail. Thanks for stopping him."

No problem. Now let's get going. There's a shop on the right where they fabricate stainless steel. Up ahead on the left is an organic farmer who also has a welding shop. See those long rows of manure in the field? That's where he composts his manure. The latest thing is manufacturing compost mixers. What do you say, Harry? Would that be something for Isaac Equipment?

"I was thinking about it. Let me off. I shouldn't be long."

That's what he thinks! When that man gets started talking compost, you can't get away. Let's drive in and look around.

"Okay with me."

Back here in this shed is the mixer he uses to make his own compost. The idea is to mix organic waste with stable manure, to get more value out of it. After mixing, the compost is lined up in long rows and turned occasionally. The idea is good, if it is practical. It's intended to replace chemical fertilizer.

"Here Harry comes with an armload of paper. Are you ready to go?"

"Yes, I'm taking home some literature to see what happens."

# Barn Raising

What do you think, Matthias: should we drive back to the sawmill and sugar bush now?

"Ah, yes, that would be nice; but I thought of something else. You know that barn that was struck by lightning on the other side of Linwood? I hear they're getting ready for a barn raising soon. With this good weather, they might just be ready by now. It's only about three miles from here."

Say! That's a good idea! Let's head over there now. Meanwhile, I should brief you on barn raisings, and what leads up to them. Immediately after a fire, a committee of three men, besides the deacon, is appointed to assess the damages and make arrangements for rebuilding. The committee arranges for the services of a head carpenter.

There are usually good barns near the city to be taken down. The carpenter and the owner of the barn contact Wrecksall Demolition of Unionville. Several barns are available there, for taking down. Wrecksall trucks deliver the building material right to the building site. When the most suitable barn is selected, arrangements are made for sending a busload of neighbors and friends to dismantle the barn. In one day fifty men can dismantle a barn and load the material on trucks to be sent home.

"Is there no problem with the Department of Labour, or Health and Welfare, when unqualified men work at such a dangerous occupation?"

Not as long as the men wear hard hats and safety boots, and are at least sixteen years old. Because no money is involved, the company is not held responsible for accidents. No one is paid for the work, so Workman's Compensation is not involved either.

"Have there been any serious accidents as a result of such work?"

Yes, we have two young men among us who are paralyzed from their waists down through accidents related to farm-building demolition and erection. Such accidents occur as part of our occupation. We accept the risk and take responsibility for caring for the injured.

It takes about a week to prepare the frame for rebuilding. The volunteer crew may be almost ready to raise this barn. Sometimes a raising is planned for a certain day, but then enough volunteer help appears that the barn can be raised a day earlier.

"Is this the place? The yard is filled with buggies!"

"Oh, look at all the people! The place is swarming with them."

"Should I drive in the lane?"

Just hang on a bit, Jake. I'll go talk to Aaron, the carpenter boss, and then be right back.

"I wouldn't be surprised if they would be ready for raising today. What do you think, Matthias?"

"I think so, too. Look, they're carrying timbers up the bank."

"Here comes our tour guide."

How many of you would care to help raise a barn?

"I think we all would. What about the women?"

This is not exactly work for women. They are free to watch at a safe distance, or they may stay in the bus. Jake, you can park the bus where they have a good view. Matthias will stay in the bus, and he might explain the work to the women. Aaron says he can use all hands, so take orders from him.

"This way, everybody! Bring bars to carry timbers. Twenty men for this timber. Push your bars underneath. Walk right up to the barn floor! Twenty more men over here! Take this one to the opposite side!

"Now bring in the plate and the girths! A brace here and pegs. Get the brace in! Now the pegs! Drive them home! Got them all in? Now everybody; come on Leamington! Gather round the bend!

"Grab ahold! Ready? All together: yo, heave! yo, heave! Get your shores in! Yo, heave! Rest a second.

"Ready? Yo, heave! Get your pike poles! Yo, heave! Walk right up! Heavy on the ropes! Yo, heave! Tie the ropes both ways. Now pull tight! Straighten up that corner. There!"

"Bring in the timbers for the next bend. Twenty men here. Joe, tell them where to put it. Twenty for the next one. Walk right in. Now the plate and the girths. Now the tie girths. Get the ropes ready to hoist them up.

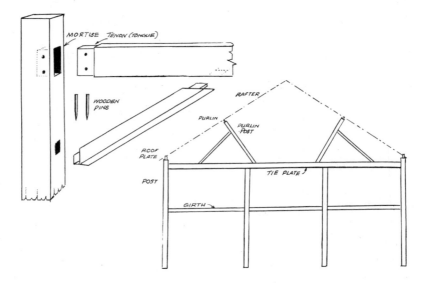

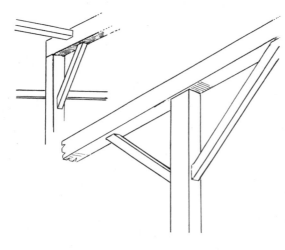

"Get the braces in and peg them. Got them all in? Now, gather round the bend! Ready? Yo heave! Yo heave! Get your shores ready. Rest a second. Ready? Yo heave! Get your pike poles! Yo heave! Yo heave! Walk her right up! Tighten the ropes! Steady!

"Get your ropes on the tie girths. Hoist away! Got your braces? Send a brace up there with the rope. Drive in the pegs. Now the level. It's an inch out of whack. Drive the post to the east with the sledge. Give it another bang. There!"

Well, Aaron, can you manage without our help now?

"I think so. It gave us a good start. Part of the barn is free-standing now, so the rest is easier. Thanks for your help."

Thanks for letting us help. Good-bye and good luck!

Jake, too bad your cousin Henry wasn't on this load. He would like to see a barn raising some time.

"I'll tell him about it. He might be jealous, though."

## Sweet Dreams

Next, we head south for the sugar bush and sawmill. Here on our left is the concrete tile works. I think they make septic tanks as well. On our right, we pass the house and barn for the farm with the sugar bush. From here, we wind through the sugar bush. The evaporator building comes first, but we drive on to the sawmill. The mill doesn't seem to be running, so the men are likely nailing pallets. Here is Menno at the door.

"Hello, Matthias! So you brought us some strangers."

"Or at least, the strangers brought me. We were at the barn

raising on other side of Linwood."

These people are from Leamington, and wish to see a bit of this area. I see the sawmill is not running today.

"No, we're putting pallets together. We have quite a few pallet orders, and quite a pile of pallet lumber is ready."

"Do all these pallets go to one buyer?"

"Oh, no; they go to many different manufacturers and distributors. This lot goes to a wood machinery distributor, for handling drill presses, band saws, table saws, sanders, and routers. Most of these are loaded with one machine per pallet. They also use pallets for skill saws, saber saws, hand sanders, and routers. These are packed in cartons, then put on pallets for loading."

"We use pallets for dairy and stable equipment, too. I sell and install such equipment in the Leamington area. Here's my card."

"Well; Isaac Equipment. That's your last name."

"Yes, I'm Harry Isaac."

Is anyone in the evaporator building?

"No, I think the boss is in the maple syrup room, over near the house."

Are any of you ladies interested in maple syrup?

"Are any of us *not* interested? At least we want to see it, and find out how it's made."

Jake, we might as well drive back there, then see the evaporator on our way out.

"Good enough. Want to ride along? You'll have to guide us anyhow."

Sure. It isn't far, though.

"Hello. I just waited on a customer, so now I'm ready to wait on you. We have five sizes, from $40 down to $4.50.

"What we want mostly is to have a taste of it, and maybe have some with doughnuts and pancakes."

"If a number of you want the small size, why don't you take a case of 12, and split it between you? A case is $50, so you save $4."

"Sounds alright to me. Here's a fifty; then I'll have to see how I get my money back!"

"Why don't we take another case, and make it an even hundred? I might be able to sell a few at the shop. I'll put up a sign and tell my customers that if they put a bottle of syrup under their pillows at night, they'll have sweet dreams! So, here is my fifty."

Would you have time to show us the evaporator and equipment? If not, I can give them some idea about the equipment and how it works.

"Maybe that would be a good idea. You know how it works; at least, you used to. I should get back to my men. When the cat's away, . . . you know."

I feel rather foolish in explaining this operation to you, not knowing more about it than I do. I think he has between two and three thousand taps, with about half on pipeline, and the rest with pails. He probably harvests around 700 gallons per year.

"How much sap does it take to make a gallon of syrup?"

That varies with the season. I always figured on forty gallons of sap to make a gallon of syrup.

"How much can he cook in a day?"

My guess is that he averages fifty gallons a day. He has one of the larger-capacity evaporators and a finishing cooker besides. With this setup, the evaporator does not need to slow down when a batch is ready to be taken off.

"How does he handle the sap that runs through the pipeline?"

Not everyone does it the same way. With his contoured woodlot, I presume he has several holding tanks in low spots. He likely pumps the sap into a tank wagon, which he draws to the evaporator.

"Do they make any other products here, besides maple syrup?"

Yes, but I'm not sure to what extent. Maple sugar is made by most maple syrup operators. I think they make maple butter and taffy cones besides. Those extras all run into money. A sweet tooth can be quite expensive.

"And hard on the waistline!"

# Doggie Baths

Two more things are on our agenda. First, a quick tour through intensive farm and shop country in general, and finally the plastic establishment.

As we travel on this ten-mile circuit, you may find it interesting to observe the differences between these farm settings and the average farms in southwestern Ontario.

You will notice that nearly every farm has a windmill. No doubt the reason is because few of the farms have hydroelectric power. The homes are generally not elaborately built, yet there are extensive roofs. Many of them seem to be two or three homes joined together.

"What would be the reason for that?"

Most of them shelter large, extended families. Besides, since many of them have large shops, more people are employed than on the average farm. Presumably, some are "boarding houses" for employees. The barns, of which there may be several, generally have square ventilators on top. Since numerous cattle are housed in these barns, lots of ventilation is necessary.

Near the house and barns, nearly every farm has a shop. This is not just a shop for repairing the farmer's machinery, but for commercial manufacturing of farm gates, cattle and hog feeders, farm wagons and racks, cattle squeeze chutes, stabling, floor slats, harness and harness parts, buggies, feed carts, and furniture.

In the fields, one sees teams of six or more horses pulling tractor discs and cultivators with apparent ease. In grass fields, one sees teams of horses pulling mowers and siderakes on one farm, and haybines and mower-conditioners on the next. However, when the hay is dry, there is a tractor and baler in nearly every field, and the baled hay is put on wagons and drawn in by teams of horses. These tractors and balers appear on the scene as an exchange of labor with neighbors who own tractors and tractor equipment.

At harvesttime, the grain is cut by horse-drawn grain binders and *stooked* [sheaves set into shocks] by hand. The crops are surprisingly good, considering that the farmers' time is divided between farm and shopwork. The work ethic is quite strong.

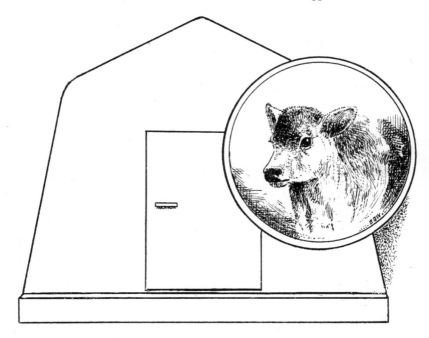

"How is it that this extraordinary display of industry is so uniform in such a large area?"

This is an intensively cooperative effort, passed down for generations by the farmers of this particular area. The ability and desire to operate such shops and manufacturing concerns is likewise hereditary.

As we are nearing the end of our tour, we shall visit the plastic works as the climax to our travels. I assume Harry would appreciate having an audience with the owner and manager. We can spend some time in the yard where the plastic fabrications are on display.

Those white huts resembling igloos are calf hutches. The problem with starting young calves, especially in winter, is not so much in keeping them warm, as in keeping the air dry. A poorly ventilated barn, where the walls are damp and the calves are alternately sweating and shivering, is almost certain to cause pneumonia. These individual calf hutches are cool but dry. They seem to be the best solution for raising small calves.

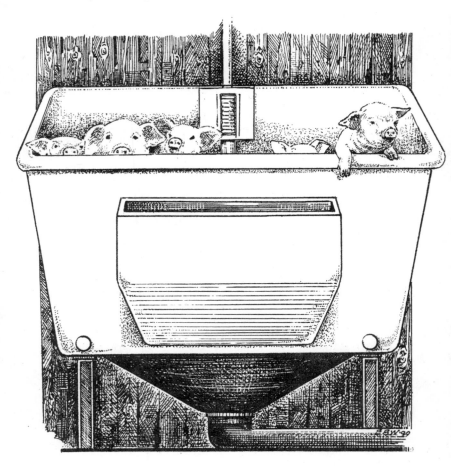

The little upside-down hutches are called weaner tubs. The new concept in farrowing barns for sows, is the weaner deck, a pen raised to shoulder height, where the piglets are placed when from two to four weeks old. These pens are dry, because any moisture will filter through the floor of the pen. Weaner tubs are a new variation of the weaner deck. Being constructed of plastic, they are easier to keep clean and sanitary, therefore less inclined to harbor disease. At least, that is part of the concept.

It appears as though this establishment caters to the maple

syrup trade, too. Those sturdy plastic sap pails can expand and contract from frost without bursting. That roll of plastic tubing looks like sap pipeline to me. Those tall buckets are for gathering sap. I've also been told that they manufacture various sizes of maple syrup jugs as well.

"Here comes Harry. So is Isaac Equipment going to sell doggie baths now, too?"

"Doggie baths? Now what do you mean by that, Helen? You mean the calf hutches?"

"No, she's talking about the piggy banks."

"Curiouser and curiouser. Whatever are you girls talking about?"

I think she means the weaner tubs. You know, the Americans call a wiener a "doggie," and of course a tub is a bath.

"Sure enough. How did you figure that out, Tour Guide?"

Elementary, my dear Watson. I've been married for a long time and have learned how to put two and two together. I think, though, that my portrayal of this agricultural equipment may have been too vague. I'll explain a little more about farrowing and raising pigs, so that Sherlock Holmes need not get the information for you by sleuthing.

See that long building over there near the barn, labeled NO ADMITTANCE? That sign on the door is to prevent visitors from spreading disease. So we can't go in and see the setup. One end of the barn has individual dry sow stalls, where the sows are kept from the time their piglets are weaned until they are ready to farrow again.

The farrowing crates, where the sows give birth to their litters of piglets, are in the other end of the same stable. These crates are so constructed that the sow can nurse the piggies without any danger of lying on them. When the little pigs are several weeks old, they are placed in the weaner decks, suspended above the farrowing crates. There they are fed a special formula in creep feeders, with waterers alongside. Within a month or six weeks, they are ready to be placed in larger pens.

The plastic weaner tubs made here are a new concept that may replace the weaner decks because of better sanitation. Seriously though, Harry, did you have any success with the plastics?

"Sure did. I've got all the info I need. I just might be back with the truck shortly."

Now are you still taking Matthias and me home?

"Of course we will. We'll have you home in fifteen minutes."

"If you ask me, this was a full day. I can't remember everything we learned."

"It was worth it all, though."

# Elderhostel, Part 1

◆ ◆ ◆

# The Call

Hello. Isaac Horst here.

"Hello, Isaac. This is Lorna Bergey. How are you tonight?"

Oh, I'm quite well for the shape I'm in. And you?

"That goes for me too. I hear you served as tour guide on a Leamington bus tour recently. Two of the people on that bus were so impressed that they are planning to come to our next Elderhostel. That's what I'm calling about. You've spoken to those groups before, and we were pleased with the results. There's no better way to bring our point across, in telling them about the Old Order Mennonites, than by letting them listen to someone who is familiar with the group from the inside out.

"I'll just repeat some of the purposes of the Elderhostel, to refresh your mind. As you know, it offers a course of lectures on the history and character of the Mennonites, especially the local group known as the Old Order Mennonites. Most of those attending the lectures have a vague idea who the Mennonites are and how they live. The majority are seniors, and they are usually quite receptive and open-minded in learning all they can.

"Would you be interested in speaking to them again?"

I suppose I could. I have always enjoyed it. Since most of them are elderly people, like myself, we find it easy to identify with each other. Will it be at the Conrad Grebel auditorium again?

"Yes, but wait. This time it will be different. There are so many things these seniors wish to learn about the Old Order Mennonites; and the best way to learn is from someone who knows all the answers. Are you quite busy?"

You know how busy we seniors are. We can put in a lot of time, without getting much done.

"Yes, I know all about that. What I'm trying to say is that one day is not enough. We could spend a whole week without covering every subject. Would you be available to speak for a whole week?"

A whole week! You mean—

"Well, not all week. It would be Tuesday, Wednesday, and Thursday, 9:30 to 12:00, and 1:30 to 4:00."

Hmm. I suppose we could come down to St. Jacobs on Monday evening with the bus, stay with our daughter, and go home Thursday night. Then I wouldn't need to go back and forth every day. At least, it wouldn't be so far. Let me check. Mom! Would you like to spend a week with Hannah?

"When would that be?"

June 9, 10, and 11.

"Sounds good to me, Pop."

I suppose we could make that, Lorna. It isn't difficult to get her to stay with her daughter.

"Good! And while we're at it, what about August?"

What *about* August?

"You see, there's another Elderhostel in August. We won't finish in one week."

Oh!

"Now what's wrong?"

Should we move down to Waterloo?

"Oh, now, it's not that bad!"

The same thing over again in August?

"Yes. August 11, 12, and 13."

I'll be over eighty then, if I live that long.

"You're still good for another ten to fifteen years. Here's what your talks are supposed to be about:

| | | |
|---|---|---|
| June 9 | a.m. | the church: growth, social patterns, expansion |
| | p.m. | child rearing, discipline, obedience; home and raising families |
| June 10 | a.m. | courtship, marriage, peaceful married life |
| | p.m. | the role of women, their work, keepers at home, and raising families |
| June 11 | a.m. | our heritage, church issues |
| | p.m. | various views and changes |
| August 11 | a.m. | biblical principles |
| | p.m. | pensions, social security, insurance |

| August 12 | a.m. | swearing of oaths, photography, Sunday schools |
| | p.m. | foreign missions, voting, shunning |
| August 13 | a.m. | organic gardening and farming, the environment, occult and eastern mysticism |
| | p.m. | nonresistance, the German language, our economy |

"This is only a rough sketch. You can have a free hand to regulate that as you see fit. A little deviation here and there is fine. We want you to address the people however you feel they will get the most out of it. We'll count on you then."

We'll try to make something of it, and I'll let you know if things don't work out.

"Good! We won't ask more of you than that."

## Growth of the Old Order Church

Good morning. I hope you are enjoying this Elderhostel.

"Yes, we are. We are eager to hear about your people. Thanks for coming to speak to us."

One hundred years ago, the Old Order Mennonite Church came into existence in Woolwich Township. There were only four places of worship in the community then: Martin's, Conestogo, Elmira, and North Woolwich.

The services alternated in a four-week cycle. Each meetinghouse was used just once every four weeks, and most people attended church every two weeks. The other two Sundays were reserved for visiting within the home church district.

Ten years later, the Peel meetinghouse was built in spite of a storm of protest. Why build a meetinghouse away out in the middle of nowhere, when only two families lived beyond it?

The argument was unfounded. There were still no more than ten miles between it and the most distant of the older meetinghouses. Besides, the Peel meetinghouse is now practically in the center of the community. Today, a new meetinghouse stands on the same grounds.

The four-week cycle remained, with Peel inserted on a three-week cycle. Every three weeks, there were meetings at two places. This system continued until 1932, with the worshipers usually crowding into the meetinghouses. Leaders then worked out a system for having two places of worship every Sunday, alternating locations so it was possible to visit any meetinghouse at some time, without missing the service at home. This five-week cycle worked out well, although some people objected because it interfered with visiting!

Seven years later, about 40 percent of the members favored the use of the motor car as their transportation. This group united with the Mennonites at Markham, who had been driving cars for about ten years, to form the Markham-Waterloo Conference. They alternated with the Old Order church in using Martin's, Elmira, and North Woolwich meetinghouses. As a result, conditions were less crowded.

This condition did not last long. The Olivet meetinghouse was built in 1955. It was inserted on a three-week cycle. Linwood was built in 1962, and Winterbourne in 1965. This time the system was changed to have three places of meeting on each Sunday. Since then, Weaverland and Klear View were built toward the west, and Spring Creek, Farewell, Cedarview, and Westdale in the new Mount Forest district. Today, there are from six to eight places where services are held on any one Sunday. Still, the houses are frequently filled to capacity.

Few farms are available in the Woolwich community. The

boundaries are continually being pushed farther west, over fifteen miles beyond the Peel church that people had thought was "in the middle of nowhere"! Some families are separated by twenty-five miles, yet are still in the old community, now extended. Regular communication by horse and buggy is out of the question, except by taking more than one day to the trip.

Regular bus routes have been established between Woolwich and Mount
Forest. Early Monday morning, a bus
starts at the edge of Waterloo, zigzag-
ging northward through the area, shut-
tling people around and gathering a load.
Then it circles through the Mount Forest area, picking up and dropping off
passengers as it goes, taking three hours
one way. At four o'clock it returns along the same route. Thurs-
days, the same route is traveled in reverse. These routes also loop
through the western areas, providing service to draw the two
ends closer together.

We still cherish our unique system of unannounced visiting.
When we have services in our home district, we may expect up
to thirty people for dinner. We may also have none. It means
being prepared for visitors who may or may not show up. It can
mean eating leftovers for a week!

The problem is rarely critical because a family has shelves full
of canned fruit, vegetables, meat, and pickles in the basement for
such occasions. To round out the meal, the women usually bake
a cake or two during the previous week.

To reduce this uncertainty by half, some of our church districts
are now divided in two. This gives one side the opportunity to
visit the other, without fear of missing visitors. That means being
prepared for visitors only every other home-district Sunday.

There is satisfaction in knowing that the welcome mat is always out on designated Sundays. Friends whom we did not expect will continue to drop in. Such hospitality and fellowship
must be experienced to be appreciated. Because of this system,
we have been accustomed to visit one another throughout the
communities. As the areas enlarge, this becomes more difficult.
However, we cherish it so much that we will continue to keep
such a system viable.

"I don't grasp what you were saying. Where does the increase
come from? How can the community expand so fast?"

By mathematics. We do not simply add to our community: we

multiply. We even divide now and then, but we keep on multiplying. Church attendance is more regular than it was when I went to school, and that accounts in part for the church expansion. Since our families are considerably larger than the Canadian average, the increase is greater.

"When was the Mount Forest community started?"

Thirty years ago. Our family moved July 1, 1968. One family had moved the previous fall. This new community's growth has been far beyond our wildest expectations. Apparently the timing was right.

## Advantages of Rotation

Some people find our Old Order Mennonite customs difficult to understand, or even foolish. For example, especially during the summer, our places of worship are usually filled to capacity, yet about five meetinghouses stand empty. More meetinghouses will be built rather than using all existing houses at the same time. Observers ask, "Why not have services at every meetinghouse every Sunday? It would save the expense of building, and less driving would be involved."

The answer lies in our age-old social pattern. When we have no services in the home community, we attend church in another community. After the service, we have dinner in one of the homes, then spend the afternoon in fellowship or just plain visiting. Usually we go home at about 4:30, in time to do the chores. Those currently milking usually go home earlier. Occasionally we have supper at a second home, if the young people do our chores.

This pattern is entirely different from that practiced among Old Order Mennonites across the border. Among them, all visiting is by invitation. At those meetinghouses shared with the Horning church, they meet on alternate Sundays only. Yet they would never consider visiting a home in another community without an invitation.

Our system seems haphazard to them. They likely think, "What if we have more company than we can accommodate?

What about leftover food? Why set the whole house in order, when perhaps no one will come?"

To us, the advantages of this system far outweigh the disadvantages. Not the least is the surprise element of not knowing whom to expect. The hospitality shown by the hosts and the warm fellowship with others—both are very rewarding. By visiting in other communities alternatively, we maintain a close fellowship with all the other communities.

One of the greatest advantages of this system is the automatic exchange among the ministers. We have visiting "evangelists" almost every Sunday. Because services rotate among the various communities, the ministers likewise rotate. We never know who will be preaching before we arrive at the meetinghouse. We are ready to agree that variety is the spice of life.

In Ephesians 4:11, we read that Christ gave some to be apostles, some prophets, some evangelists, others pastors, and still others as teachers. In 1 Corinthians 12:4-11, we read of diversity of gifts. We can endorse that.

Since no two of our ministers are the same, we have this diversity at our disposal. Some of them are more inclined to be evangelists, others pastors, and still others, teachers. This gives us a vast scope in the administration of God's Word. If only we would make better use of this advantage!

"This system comes as a surprise to me. I understand the Old Order Mennonites to be frugal. You are careful about wasting money. Yet you operate five meetinghouses more than you need. How can you explain this?"

Everything you say is true. I find it hard to explain, myself. The best answer I can give is that it shows how extremely high we value our rotating meetings, and our social system. If it helps to strengthen the bonds of love and fellowship, who can put a price tag on that?

"Oh, yes, you are definitely right in that respect."

There is another angle to consider. Even though we are frugal and all that, we are also very slow to change. This system is so deeply ingrained that no one gives a thought to the foolishness, financially.

"Is it common practice for two ministers to speak every Sunday?"

Yes. Sometimes it happens that one minister is alone. It does not spell a hardship, as far as the congregation is concerned. Yet one can tell that the minister feels rather burdened, to carry the load alone.

"Do the deacons never help to bear the burden of speaking?"

They might give a longer testimony than usual near the end of the service, but that's about all. It would indeed be permissible for them to speak longer. But again, doing so would mean a change from the normal custom.

"Are your ministers installed for life?"

Yes, at least for as long as they are able to carry out their duties, depending on their age and health. When they are replaced, they still exercise their office as much as health allows.

## The Church Flourishes
## in Daughter Settlement

In our imaginary visit, I welcome the Elderhostel to Mount Forest. We have just passed a milestone. The Mount Forest Old Order Mennonite Church is now thirty years old.

Compared to our forebears' move to Waterloo County 175 years ago, our 35-mile move northward seems insignificant. They moved 500 miles over rough roads, in covered wagons, from Pennsylvania to the wilds of Canada.

For several generations we lived in the Waterloo area. We could visit each other at our pleasure. To break this chain by moving away seemed quite an undertaking. How could a horse-and-buggy community survive, separated from friends?

We had several reasons for wishing to move: high-priced farms, overpopulation in the old community, and a desire to make a fresh start, with hope of evading some problems in the old community.

A few daring souls bought farms near Mount Forest in 1964, after about a year of window-shopping. Since we were firmly resolved not to move without the assurance of others following, we waited three more years. Nothing happened. Obviously, someone had to take the plunge, or we would have to abandon the project.

On November 1, 1967, the first family moved to their farm. Our promise to follow the next summer, after school was over, was their only assurance of church fellowship. Two more families followed us the next year, and seven in the next.

At first, we held occasional services in our homes. We built our first meetinghouse in 1972 and ordained a deacon and a minister soon afterward, with the help of church leadership from the Waterloo area. More families followed. We built churches and schools.

Today, over 160 families live in the area, served by four churches, a bishop, four ministers, and three deacons. Our schools have fifteen classrooms in operation. So our families and churches are well established.

The objections of our former neighbors were well-founded. We might not have survived a church division, had one occurred. Motor travel has indeed increased to maintain contact with the home community. (Of course, such travel has also increased in the home community, because of expansion there.) Yet the traditional standards are honored and supported. The unrestricted use of cars would ultimately lead to more social interaction with those of lower moral standards, and a weakening of the nonresistant, nonconforming faith.

After thirty years in a smaller community, we find the advantages outweighing the disadvantages. Farmland continues to be available for future generations. The greater distance from urban centers means less inducement to worldly pleasures, less opportunity to earn high wages, and less to lure youth away from a quiet, Christian life.

In a smaller community, all members are needed; in large communities, some members sit back and fail to participate in church affairs. The greatest and most edifying benefit is the close fellowship among a smaller group. This fellowship is something we have learned to cherish. We would never wish to forfeit it.

I conclude that it seems advisable for large communities to

spread out into smaller groups. Certainly, with a bit of effort, there is a greater opportunity for witnessing to those around us, by letting our lights shine.

May the lower lights continue to shine, and not go out.

"Did you anticipate such growth when you first planned to move?"

By no means! We would have been well pleased with half of this increase. Of course, we are well pleased that it has worked out so well. The fact that it did work out well encouraged others to try the same thing again, at Chesley. However, the financial situation is not as favorable as it was when we moved.

"From what you mentioned at the beginning, I gathered that support of the mother community was not too strong. Has that changed through the years?"

Definitely. The next generation of those who dragged their feet are now eagerly looking for available farms—not necessarily in this community, but at least in one of the other new communities. The course of action has proved itself, so the road is clear.

"You mentioned a desire to make a fresh start in hope of evading problems in the old community. To what are you referring?"

There had been some conduct among the young folks of which we disapproved. While our community was small, there had seemed to be some improvement along this line. There is a possibility that if growth had not been quite so dramatic, the problems might have been easier to control. When a town grows fast, the same is inclined to happen. People give up the slow pace, and a lot of things change. To some extent, we sacrificed quality in favor of quantity.

## Mennonites Moving Out

Some time ago, a local newspaper published an article about Old Order Mennonites who are moving out of the Waterloo Region. The article was well written and not unduly biased. Yet viewed from the inside, the article seemed to present several views that could be wrongly interpreted.

The article states, "After almost 200 years in Waterloo County, Old Order Mennonites are moving out." To those unfamiliar with the area and the Old Order Mennonites (OOM), that sounds final, doesn't it? It implies that, given time, there will be no OOMs left in the Waterloo region.

What the article really says is that "OOMs are moving out." It doesn't say "all the Mennonites" or even "the OOMs." Nor does it say what has happened to the farms they left behind.

Generally speaking, those who left were beginning farmers, who left no vacant farms behind. A few who moved out had been farming before. They either
  • left their farm to a son,
  • sold it to a Mennonite neighbor, or
  • sold it to developers.
Except for the gradual encroachment of the city on farmland, there will be no fewer Mennonites in the region than before.

A second misleading statement was made in the article: "The first migration from Waterloo County was in 1968, when about 100 families moved to the Mount Forest area." Can you imagine that? Two families per week, for a whole year? What did we do with the families we turned out of their Mt. Forest homes: throw them into immigration sheds?

Had the article stated that the first migration *began* in 1968, it would have been closer to the truth. In fact, the first family moved in 1967, three in 1968, and so on, until there eventually were about 100 families in twenty years, and 160 in thirty years.

Nor did those migrants leave a vacuum in the mother settlement. Most of them only began to farm on their own after they moved. Those who had been farming generally sold to a Mennonite neighbor.

It is unfair to blame the scarcity of farms all on the encroachment of the cities. During the past fifty years, the internal growth of the OOMs has been phenomenal. Even without the expansion of the cities, the Waterloo Mennonite community would have become congested.

In most cases, one of the sons takes the home farm; but what of the other three or four? Most of the neighboring farms are already possessed by Mennonites. The only alternative is to seek farms on the open market, where and when they are available.

Another point to consider is that moving out of the county is not necessarily moving out of the community. The Waterloo Old Order community has long ago spilled over into five other townships, in neighboring Wellington and Perth Counties. At present, it seems that the Old Order community knows no geographical boundaries. It continues to expand in every possible direction. Yet it is still one community. When the pot overflows, there's no knowing where it ends.

In the above article, mention was made of the Mennonites being "aggressive" and "shrewd." There is a possibility that some will use unfair tactics when buying farms. The problem is that, when some do this, all will be tarred with the same brush. It is regrettable that some people will resort to greed and rudeness for the sake of financial gain.

When the Amish moved into a certain area, they were surprised how many reasonably priced farms became available in such a short time. Later they learned that after they had purchased a few farms, a real estate salesman went around telling the farmers how odd and peculiar these "Mennonites" were.

He told them that the Amish had their own church and school, did not associate with the "English" neighbors, and would not help to pay school taxes (which, of course, was not true). As a result, the locals were only too glad to sell their farms rather than live among such odd people!

"Maybe your people should use such tactics when buying farms in Perth County. Then it might be easier to afford the farms."

I think a better solution would be for those who live in the new areas to show a friendly and agreeable spirit toward their neighbors. It certainly would be more scriptural.

"Besides, you might even make some friends."

I would hope so. Of course, some of the statements are partly true. The presence of the Mennonites will affect the schools, but it's not all negative. The Mennonites do pay school taxes but do not reap direct benefit thereby. They cause no expenses in teachers and equipment. They do not support service clubs and do not create a need for them, either. They do not support the other local churches; yet these are on the decline anyhow. The farms and homes of the Mennonites will increase in value; that is an asset to the community.

# Child Discipline

The subject of child discipline is not very popular today. In fact, it is well to tread softly when discussing it. Yet the Old Order Mennonites believe so strongly in child discipline that I am willing to take a chance. I feel confident that among more elderly people, it can still be discussed without being booed and catcalled into silence.

In a recent article on child training, the author claimed that there is no such thing as a "good spanking," implying that all forms of spanking are evil and a form of child abuse. Such a view is contrary to the teachings of the holy Scriptures, even though we agree that there are limitations to the value of spanking.

What comes to mind first are several quotations from the Proverbs, written by one who was purported to be the wisest mortal who ever lived on earth. In spite of the masculine pronouns, these precepts apply to all children:

He that spares his rod hates his son; but he that loves him chastens him promptly. (Prov. 13:24)

Foolishness is bound in the heart of a child; but the rod of correction shall drive it far from him. (Prov. 22:15)

Withhold not correction from the child; for if you beat him with the rod, he shall not die. You shall beat him with the rod, and shall deliver his soul from hell. (Prov. 23:13-14)

The rod and reproof give wisdom; but a child left to himself brings his mother to shame. (Prov. 29:15)

This evidence might be discredited by saying that the teachings of the Old Testament are no longer in effect. On this question, however, the New Testament supports the Old.

My son, do not despise the chastening of the Lord, nor faint when he rebukes you. For whom the Lord loves, he chastens, and scourges every son whom he receives. If you endure chastening, God deals with you as with sons; for what son is he whom the Father chastens not? . . . Now no chastening for the present seems to be joyous, but grievous: nevertheless afterward it yields the peaceable fruit of righteousness unto those who are exercised thereby. (Heb. 12:5-7, 11)

Obviously, the type of discipline to which the article refers is spanking in anger and frustration. Such discipline can indeed be harmful. It also refers to spanking without making it clear why the child is being spanked. In fact, one exception to the "no-spanking" rule is given: in cases where a quick smack can avert a great danger, such as for playing with fire, or dashing across the street. If physical danger merits an exception to the rule, surely spiritual danger should do the same!

The article gives the following reasons why children should not be spanked:

• It teaches children that problems can be solved by violent measures.

• It teaches them that the bigger you are, the more right you have to hit others.

• It can lead to children having a poor image of themselves, fostering the idea that they are inherently bad.

• Most parents come to the conclusion that spanking is ineffective.

However, these four reasons for not spanking children show that the parent-child relationship is already out of joint. Before spanking can be effective, the child must realize that the parent (or teacher) is loving, as well as being in charge. The person administering punishment must be worthy of respect and authority. Regarding the third reason, we as Anabaptists maintain that babies are innocent at birth. We also admit that evil is manifest in growing children, and we make strong efforts to bring them above such a level.

In all these objections, the important point remains; the child must learn to know why he is being spanked, and learn that as young as possible. He must know that the parents hate the sin

but love the sinner, just as God does. After being spanked, the child must not be allowed to go to the other parent for sympathy. The sin which he has committed must be painstakingly explained to the child, so that he learns to understand the importance of the lesson, just as in the case of playing with fire.

Setting certain limits for conduct, strict and consistent adherence to the rules, and punishment for disobedience—these are important. However, with the best of discipline, there will be cases of willful disobedience. Christ himself did not exercise force on his children. We are all creatures of choice. As Paul told the Thessalonians, "Not all people have faith" (2 Thess. 3:2).

"What forms of spanking are applied by Old Order Mennonites?"

Various means are used from one family to the next. Among small children, the most common is probably the bare hand applied to the seat of the problem.

The strap is rarely used. Every school is expected to have a strap. Every pupil knows that the strap is there and will be used when necessary. This fact is often all that is needed to bring the mischief-maker to terms.

"At what age would you spank a child?"

That depends on circumstances. If a child has temper tantrums and is lying on the floor and kicking, he should be given a few slaps, regardless of age. However, the parents must be wise as serpents, and harmless as doves, to discern and analyze the circumstances. On the other hand, if a child is fourteen and has not yet learned obedience, spanking at this age will not be effective either.

### The Old Woodshed

During the past ten years, many new houses have sprung up in our neighborhood. Some of them are quite impressive, but one thing they have in common. There are no woodsheds attached. Instead, most of them have two-car garages

I can understand that older people desire to get away from a woodshed. Splitting wood, carrying it in, and carrying out the ashes—these are things that elderly people like ourselves can well do without. With younger people, it is different. The woodshed had an indispensable role in raising children.

Most people of our age have a distinct memory of filling the woodbox every evening, after walking home from school, and before helping with other evening chores. I mention the latter because they went right along with woodbox filling. They were also a part of the concept.

I find it difficult to identify with the pent-up youthful spirit of a boy who rides home from a day at school, to sit down in front of a TV set for the rest of the evening. He may not have developed the muscles as most farm lads of our day did, but the emotional verve is there all the same. Without a creative outlet for this energy, he is inclined eventually to give vent to his feelings in a violent or destructive way. This is especially true if he watches violent programs on TV and other shows. This is possibly one of the chief causes of juvenile delinquency.

The woodshed is also a symbol of another concept of child training. If the youthful spirit remained untamed by woodbox filling and other chores, and revealed itself in disobedience or defiance, a trip to the woodshed for a spanking was in order. Naturally, this administration of discipline did not produce the desired results if applied in anger. There needed to be a mutual understanding that discipline was required, and that after repentance, no ill will remained. If at all possible, a heart-to-heart talk was the best method to foster understanding.

Perhaps it is already too late to return to this concept. A generation has grown to maturity since the day of the woodshed. In the summer, the father arrives home from his air-conditioned office in his air-conditioned car. The electronic door opener makes it unnecessary for him to set foot outside his car before he reaches his air-conditioned home. In the winter he follows the same procedure, except that all the facilities are heated. It will be difficult for him to identify with the woodshed.

No doubt the mother's circumstances are similar. I am so far out of step with this life, that I will not pretend to understand her schedule.

The woodshed is gone, likely never to return. It fell victim to so-called progress. Let us remember, though, that change is not progress unless it changes for the better. For the better of what: our present comfort and ease, or our future welfare? In many homes, discipline and obedience have been replaced by permissiveness. The results are often frustration, a breakdown of a line of communication between parents and children, a disruption of family relations, and even divorce.

In the churches, conditions are similar. Discipline, obedience, and discipleship are often replaced by progressiveness, Sunday schools, theological colleges, and other institutions. Christian humility is no longer considered a virtue.

"I agree that something is lacking in a school system that has pupils riding in buses to and from school, and then finds it necessary to spend a fortune in building a gymnasium, to give the pupils the exercise they no longer get by walking to school."

"Would you have any suggestion on how people in the city should or could handle the situation, in the absence of the woodshed?"

Because the situation is so foreign to me, I am hardly able to answer that question appropriately. What comes to my mind would be for the children to read a good book instead of watching TV. Get them to wash the car, mow the lawn, hoe the garden, or fix Widow Brown's garden gate, and pile up her wood.

The question is somewhat redundant, in the light of some of our beliefs and practices. Facilities for providing creative exercises to blow off steam are not available in the cities. That is one of the reasons why we wish to raise our children on the farm. If I wished to be nasty, I might say, That's where you made your bed; now you will have to lie in it! As for me and my house, we will stay in the country.

## Coping with the Wayward Ones

Considering the problems faced by many churches, we of the Old Order Mennonites have reason to be thankful. Our young people attend church on a fairly regular basis. There are times when some of the teenagers need to be reproved for not giving the sermon their undivided attention. Sometimes there is enough whispering to cause a disturbance. Still, they are present and will obviously absorb some of the message.

Even so, there are always a few who are not content to grow up in the Old Order faith and practice, for various reasons. Some just fail to see any value in our confined or restricted way of life. Some hanker after the world of entertainment and immorality. Others seek a more aggressive form of religion, with Sunday schools, revivals, and prayer meetings. Yet in the majority of cases, the main drawing card is their desire to own and drive a car.

Strangers learn that the Old Order teaching of youth centers chiefly around discipline, obedience, and discipleship. They are inclined to wonder how we deal with disobedient young people. What relationship do we have with those who fall under the censure of the church? Are those who leave the church treated like heathen and publicans?

If the disobedient ones were already members of the church, they can no longer partake of communion. What relationship has righteousness with unrighteousness? (2 Cor. 6:14). They are not ignored, but neither are they totally accepted in the social circle. They are made to realize that the church is still concerned for them, and they must make amends if they expect again to "belong."

Since such cases occur infrequently, there is no cut-and-dried form of relationship between such young people and their parents. In the past, there have been cases in which the transgressors were totally disowned by their parents. In some areas, this is still practiced, but it is rare among us now. There are also some parents who make no distinction, and ride along in a disobedient son's car at every opportunity.

Our own way of life has changed enough to modify the general attitude. We believe that there are times now when using a motor vehicle is almost a necessity. We do not object to their use when necessary. Our concern is to discourage their abuse or misuse.

At the risk of being repetitious, I will quote a Canadian history textbook. In the chapter on social behavior during the 1920s, the author makes the following statement about the increased use of automobiles at that time:

> The motor car offers a readily available means of escaping from the watchful eye of the parents. . . . It did more than anything else to break down the prewar moral codes, and the . . . formal relationships between the sexes.

We do not wish to offer a readily available means for escaping from the watchful eye of the parents. We do not wish to break down the moral codes, nor the older and more-formalized relationships between the sexes.

As long as no car stands at the door, beckoning to be used, these temptations are much smaller. For this reason, perhaps the most common method is to allow the disobedient one to live with his parents, provided that the car is not stationed there.

This is especially important in homes where there are younger brothers and sisters who might be influenced to follow the same course.

When a reasonably lenient attitude is maintained, there is a possibility that the wayward one may be won back. Even if he doesn't come back, the lines of communication are still open. On the other hand, if the parents ride in their son's car too readily, it gives the lie to their convictions.

With those who are old enough to make their own decisions, there is little point in being too harsh. We can suggest and advise, but the best teaching is through a good example. If we have failed to impress on our children the value of a humble and God-fearing life, we have likely failed earlier.

"What is the name of the book you quoted from?"

*Decisive Decades*, for grade 10, possibly written about 1950-60. I wish the history books had been so frank when I went to school. There are other equally pertinent statements in the book, which I cherish.

"I agree that what you quoted is quite frank and honest. Too often our schoolbooks, especially history texts, are glossed over to make our own actions seem right, while others are all wrong. We hear and read so much about propaganda, at least in wartime. Yet no mention is ever made about the fact that in wartime, propaganda is deliberately spread, to make our enemy seem so evil that our soldiers will hate them."

### The Age of Accountability

At the dawn of the Mennonite church, 475 years ago, the Swiss Brethren were called *Anabaptists* (Rebaptizers). They baptized persons on their confession of faith and did not recognize any earlier infant "baptism" in a state church. After a generation passed, that name was not as appropriate except with reference to baptizing converts from a state church.

The Anabaptists did not have a certain age for those being baptized. Applicants needed to be mature enough to be converted, affirm belief for themselves, and leave the state church. In a sense, it is still the same. We baptize our young people after they have come to a realization of their sinful state, and have gone through a series of instruction meetings.

However, there is a certain age when most of our young people usually come to baptism. As they approach this age, circumstances draw them toward conversion. When their peers lead the way, a great deal of soul-searching takes place among the majority. Only the most callous and obstinate ones do not surrender their self-will to prepare themselves for the baptismal class.

Within the Old Order church for the past 75 years, the median age for baptism among the boys was 18 to 20, and for the girls 17 to 19. A hundred years ago, the girls averaged 18 years at baptism, and the boys 21. There was less difference in the age for baptism between the sexes before the church divided in 1889. At that time, there occasionally were men who were much older at baptism. Frequently some married first and were baptized much later. Bishop Abraham Martin did not condone that. He married none who were not baptized.

In 1918, when the conscription scare brought the boys to terms, ages of the boys ranged from 18 to 25. In at least one family, four boys were baptized in one year. Some had delayed too long, while others were baptized much earlier than usual, because they were rudely awakened by the war. In that year, 83 boys were baptized. The year before there were 20, and the year afterward only 3!

Among the more liberal Mennonites and Baptists, children are generally baptized at a younger age. Among such churches, the average age may be 12-15 years.

The Old Order churches consider the age of accountability as the ideal age for baptism. This can vary according to the individual's rate of maturity, the response to the encouragement of the parents, and the example of their peers. One point is obvious: individuals must realize that if they are old enough to make their own decisions—too old to be told what to do and what not to do— then they are old enough to be accountable for their actions.

It is well to consider what King Solomon has to say in this respect:

> Rejoice, O young man, in your youth; and let your heart cheer you in the days of your youth; and walk in the ways of your heart, and in the sight of your eyes; but know that for all these things, God will bring you into judgment. (Eccles. 11:9)

Just what is Solomon saying? In my opinion, he tells us that there is nothing wrong with young people enjoying themselves and being cheerful, if they control their lusts. For God will judge all these things, whether they be good or evil. Childhood and youth are vanity, in the sense that childish actions are not fitting for grown people.

In all these records, the girls are usually younger than the boys at baptism. There may be several reasons for this. It seems that girls mature faster than boys. They are sooner ready to settle down. This may possibly be more pronounced among the Old Order churches, since girls are constrained a little more than boys. For instance, girls are discouraged from riding bicycles, possibly dating back to the time when all bicycles had crossbars, which was considered immodest for girls.

"When you talk about the age of baptism, you mention nothing of the new birth. Don't you believe in the new birth?"

Yes, we do; but in my experience, conversion and the new birth did not come in such a dramatic form. Some have "sowed their wild oats" and lived in open rebellion and all manner of sin. Such persons might experience and demonstrate more of this visible conversion. Even among those who have experienced a flash conversion, there is a vast variation in what visible form it takes.

"Could you tell me the time and day when you experienced your conversion?"

No, I can't. I did have several experiences that gave evidence of the new birth, with weeping and praying and finally relief.

My first thoughts were not of marking the date on the calendar. Because the experiences were not so dramatic (or traumatic), it was more like a continuous growing process.

"I hear what you are saying. If those with whom we associate have an emotional experience at conversion, that is likely the way we will act. If we are among a group where emotions are bottled up, we will respond in the same way."

There is possibly little difference in the actual conversion of different people. But there is a great difference in the outer forms of conversion.

## Decency Pays Off

Thirty-five years ago, J. Edgar Hoover, the chief of the Federal Bureau of Investigation (USA), made a strong statement regarding obscene literature. He called the propagators of filthy literature "sewage salesmen." The following points are still pertinent today, as condensed from a statement he made to the public to awaken the need for watchfulness.

Hoover said it would be naive to assume that there is no relation between the increase in obscene literature and the increase in immorality and assault cases. Too often, the purveyor of filth reaps a rich reward at the expense of youthful minds, because the public is too preoccupied with other matters to pay attention.

He urged parents, school authorities, and all law-abiding citizens to share the duty of reporting sources of obscene material to the proper officials. Hoover called for cooperative effort between police and the public to assure that local bylaws against obscenity are fully enforced.

That was thirty-five years ago, before the full impact of television was felt. At that time it was not unusual for filthy magazines and books to lie by the roadside. That has changed—not because obscenity has decreased, but because it is no longer of prime importance to dispose of such material. In many circles, the language of the *Playboy* magazine has entered coffee-table conversation. Television has brought it into the homes, where it is available for anyone at the shift of a channel.

This, of course, does not diminish the point that Hoover tried to make clear. No one can honestly claim there is no relation between such obscenities and the increase in immorality and assault cases. Such cases, currently being reported in newspapers, are indeed a direct result of the indecent attitudes in both marital and extramarital relationships.

This is, of course, nothing new. Christ rebuked the Pharisees for their unbiblical views on marriage. Paul warned the Romans and the Corinthians about those who worshiped the creature more than the Creator, so that God gave them up unto vile affections and a reprobate mind (Rom. 1:18-32). Many of these things are creeping into the churches today.

Common sense and our own human nature teach us that the purpose of marketing obscene literature and television programs is to stimulate a desire in the human mind and thereby make a profit. James, in his epistle, puts the case clearly:

> Blessed is the man who endures [does not yield to] temptation. for when he is tried, he shall receive the crown of life. . . . Every man is tempted, when he is drawn away of his own lust, and enticed. Then when lust has conceived, it brings forth sin; and sin, when it is finished, brings forth death. (James 1:12, 14-15)

Note well that if it were not for his own lust, he would actually not be tempted, drawn away, and enticed. Then the time comes when he will pick up obscene literature or watch a filthy show. Lust seems to be an innate but latent part of youths' nature. If they are not exposed to obscene material, they may outgrow it. Even better, they may have their minds filled with more worthwhile thoughts and interests.

How much better to endure temptation and receive the crown of life, than to conceive sin, which brings forth death!

That is the payoff.

"Do you have any evidence that your young people buy obscene literature at book or drug stores?"

No. In a small town, where our people know the store clerks, it is doubtful that they would. Of course, since our children are grown, we are not as well posted on that matter. It is obvious, though, that inquisitive young people would pick up such obscene literature if it were lying by the roadside.

"When you mention coffee-table conversation, I assume you are not talking about your own people."

No. I was referring to the general public. *Playboy*, coffee tables, and television are not found in our homes.

"Obviously, today's unbiblical views on sex and marriage do lead to vile affections and a reprobate mind."

Yes. And then the door is wide open. Where there are vile affections or lust, obscene literature or a filthy show are bound to follow. At first, out of respect for parents, they will hide everything along this line. But if such a track is followed, they will be hardened to the point where they no longer care.

"Exposure: that is the key word. If we can guard against exposure, through keeping our own literature and language pure, we have come a long way."

## They Twain Shall Be One

In speaking to various groups about the Old Order Mennonites, it is sometimes surprising how vague their ideas are, and even what warped opinions they entertain. For instance, one person in a church group asked me whether we believe in marriage! Naturally, I had the feeling that there would have been more justification for asking such a question of a society in which divorce is the order of the day.

I am calling this address "They Twain Shall Be One" since that is what marriage is all about (Mark 10:8). Before marriage, there is usually a period of courtship. And courtship begins with dating, right? According to the dictionary's definition of dating, yes. But according to common practice in dating, no.

The dictionary says a date is a social engagement between two persons of the opposite sex. In common usage, dating means having a random date with anyone of the opposite sex. Among the Old Order Mennonites in Ontario, it is not common practice to have a date with anyone just for fun. The only kind of date our young people traditionally have is with the "object matrimony," in Marryin' Sam's words.

Of course, two young people might start off with good intentions, only to find after some time, that they are not compatible, and they would stop seeing each other. Generally speaking, if their courtship is agreeable, they will continue for two or three years, depending on their age, before they think of marriage.

Under favorable conditions, they usually discuss the matter of marriage with the parents on both sides. When all have agreed on a tentative wedding date, the young man pays a visit to the bishop, under cover of darkness, to have the wedding date approved. The bishop is then responsible to see to it that the young couple is published in church, on the three Sundays preceding the wedding day.

If the date is approved and the first Sunday's announcement has been made, preparations for the wedding begin in earnest. The bride-to-be must cut and sew her wedding dress, if she has not been able to do so earlier without arousing suspicion. She also wishes to do as much of her own baking and preparing for the wedding dinner as possible. The home of her parents, where the wedding is traditionally held, must be cleaned from attic to basement.

She will also be responsible for writing the wedding invitations on a single sheet of the size used in a typewriter, and folded in half. The names of relatives on the bride's side are listed in one column, and the groom's relatives alongside. The rest of the guests are all grouped as well. A couple composed of close friends precedes the bride and groom, and another four or five unmarried couples follow. After these come the chore boys or hostlers, then the waitresses. Last of all come the children of school age and under.

When she has written out one copy of the invitation, she will run it through a photocopier to make as many invitations as needed. Most of the guests are personally invited on the weekend following the first public announcement. The young couple travels from place to place with horse and buggy to deliver the invitations personally to those who are local. They mail invitations to guests living far out of the community. Frequently they will need to change horses, as there are many miles to be covered.

According to the invitations, the wedding begins at 9:30. However, most of the guests arrive quite a bit earlier. If they come too late, they might miss out on something. Two of the young men move around among the guests, passing out cookies and little shot glasses of wine. These are rationed to one per guest, with no refills. It is the only liquor that is served.

As the guests arrive, the hostlers meet them with numbered tickets in sets of three: one for attaching to the buggy, one for the harness, and one for the driver. The hostlers stable the horses and line up the buggies. When a guest is ready to leave, he presents his number, and the hostlers hitch the horse to the right buggy.

In the main room of the house, the ministry has the center stage. Usually several ministers are invited. On either side are the parents and grandparents. In front of them, seats are reserved for the bridal party, with the bride and groom directly in front of the bishop. Two young men act as ushers, directing the guests to the seats reserved for them. The bridal party remains upstairs until everyone else is seated.

In Pennsylvania, the Mennonites have the same system, except that the ushers announce the young man's name, adding "and friend" for the partner. A visitor misunderstood them to say "end to end." He was greatly relieved when they came down step by step, rather than head over heels.

"Yes, that would have been an awkward situation, especially at a wedding!"

"Why does the young man go to see the bishop under cover of darkness?"

Tradition. Before the public announcement, no one except the immediate families are aware of an upcoming wedding. Of course, there is some guessing and teasing going on when someone suspects an approaching wedding. In addition, the couple planning to marry does not attend church or other functions during the time when the announcement is made and up to the wedding day. This too is an old tradition without a current explanation.

### The Marriage Vows

When all the guests are seated in their proper order, the ceremony is ready to begin. All the guests take part in singing a wedding hymn. Then the bishop makes an exhortation on Mark 10:2-12, "What God joined together, let no one put asunder."

After a silent prayer, the bishop continues another fifteen minutes and then asks the bridal pair to come forward. He asks them whether they are free from all others as far as marriage is concerned; whether they confess that marriage is an institution of God, confirmed by Christ, that must be approached in the fear of God; and whether they take each other as their marriage partner, through thick and thin, so to speak.

He asks them to join right hands, and clasping them in his own, he intones, "The God of Abraham, the God of Isaac, and the God of Jacob, be with you, to help you together, and bless you. Go forth as man and wife. Fear God, and keep his commandments" (Tobit 7:15, Luther's *Bibel;* Eccles. 12:13).

By turns, the other ministers exhort the young couple on Ephesians 5:21-33, on submissiveness; 1 Tim. 2:8-15, on praying, adornment, modest apparel, not wearing gold, and so on; 1 Pet. 3:1-7, on having a meek and quiet spirit, and being joint heirs together; and 1 Corinthians 11:1-15, on headship, women wearing a prayer veiling, and not cutting their hair.

In conclusion, there is an audible prayer, another hymn, and the benediction. All this takes about two hours.

As soon as the young people have gone back upstairs, there is a banging of chairs and a pushing of tables, as the ushers set up the tables. For safety, the guests squeeze into some corner or go outside until the tables are set up.

There is no lack of good food at such a wedding. For example, scalloped potatoes, pork with gravy, stuffing (actually, the whole meal is stuffing!) with mixed vegetables, jellied salad, coleslaw, carrot and celery sticks, two kinds of pickles, and catsup, for the first course. Fruit salad, cake, two kinds of squares, ice cream, and coffee round out the dinner and the stomachs.

After dinner, there is an hour or so of fellowship, while the dishes are being washed, and then an hour and a half of four-part singing from the *Christian Hymnal.* Meanwhile, we are served with lemonade. The little girls and boys come around selling oranges and popcorn bags for 25 cents each. (The young couple has supplied the oranges and popcorn, but the children pocket the money.) On a wedding day, everyone feels generous and gladly adds to the enjoyment of others, especially children.

Then the bride and groom come around to give each guest a candy bag, a chocolate bar, and a sample swatch of the bride's wedding dress. During this time, we sing wedding hymns for their benefit.

At about four-thirty, the guests start getting ready to go home. First, they must bid good-bye and give best wishes and God's blessings to the young couple. Then they send the buggy ticket out and prepare for a hassle with the hostlers, who kid around and try to extract every possible dollar for their services. Generally they settle for two or three dollars.

The immediate family, and the young people, remain for supper, enjoying another feast. With the older people gone, there is sometimes a bit of reciprocal mischief. Sometimes the bride and groom must eat from one meat platter, with a meat fork and butcher knife as the only cutlery. Yet all this passes in high spirits.

"What about a shivaree? Is anything of the sort practiced now?"

In the past, shivareeing had gotten out of hand, with damage resulting. Now church members who are involved are required to make a public confession or risk being excommunicated, depending on the extent of involvement or the damage caused. Shivareeing is rare now.

"What do you do when marriage does not work out?"

In my seventy years of experience, I have never really encountered a case that did not work out. The point is that if there is no escape valve open, it can and will work out, with commitment and some adjustments. After all, if marriage is approached in the Lord, the Lord will also be there to fulfill it.

### Divorce Not the Answer

About thirty-five years ago, Judson F. Landis of the University of California conducted a study on the effects of divorce on college students. As a result, all of the 330 students from divorced homes who were interviewed found themselves handicapped. A fourth of them felt they were different from other children. Some suffered from shame. Others felt inferior or embarrassed. Still others felt that their parents' divorce injured their pride.

The divorce rate continues to increase. Those whose marriages are successful to the end will soon be in the minority in North America. Disillusioned couples seek an alternative to real life in

Harlequin Romances or in movies. Instead of remedying the situation, such unrealistic fiction only aggravates the problem.

By personal experience, I know that divorce is not necessary. In the Old Order communities, divorce is virtually unheard of. Because there is no escape valve of divorce as an alternative, we try harder to make our marriages successful. Right at the beginning, during courtship, the object among us is matrimony. No causal dating is practiced. All dating is intended to lead to marriage and a lifetime partnership.

However, even with the best of intentions, not all partners are totally compatible. This need not be a serious problem. If both are true Christians, it need not be difficult to spend a lifetime together.

Professor Landis's findings come as no surprise. Instead, they are the obvious result of a natural sequence of events. Yet with the prevalence of divorce, the actual feeling of being different will eventually subside, to be replaced by a general deterioration of respect for parents. The Christian home environment will be broken through disagreements and conflict. Children will turn more to their peers for security instead of their parents. Street gangs will result, partly because of a lack of discipline. Even organizations that try to step into the breach have a difficult time where home teaching is lacking.

How can such situations be avoided? The Scriptures do have an effective answer: "Whoever puts away his wife, and marries another, commits adultery; and whoever marries the woman who is put away from her husband commits adultery" (Luke 16:18). Casual dating, for pleasure only, leads to one of the pitfalls. Lust must not be mistaken for love.

If the time of courtship is spent in becoming better acquainted, and marital pleasures are reserved for after marriage, the chances of a successful marriage are much greater. There are two reasons for this: The couple will have time to learn how compatible they are by nature. There is more to look forward to after marriage.

Even if there were no moral obligations in this respect, common sense dictates that this is the natural and elementary order. It works. Why would anyone settle for less, when so much is at stake? How could any other marriage be considered as marrying in the Lord? (1 Cor. 7:39).

"You mentioned a study showing the effects of divorce on college students. It should be interesting to know how those 330 students reacted to the divorce issue a generation later. Did they learn from their experience, or did they throw up their hands and run with the crowd?"

If this was followed up, I didn't hear about it. However, with no encouragement from their parents and peers, and likely none from the church, with which they likely had no contact, where could they go for guidance?

"What methods do you use to enforce the rule of no casual dating?"

Did I mention anything about a ruling against casual dating?

"Come to think of it, I can't say you did. I just figured there would have to be. How else would your young people adhere to such a standard?"

I can give only one answer to that: tradition does deserve a place of honor among us. Those traditions, passed down from generation to generation, are not all bad. Some good traditions are firmly entrenched in the minds of young and old. If we throw them out just because they are nothing more than traditions, we may well be throwing out the baby with the bathwater. We must remember that such customs probably started with a good reason, even though we may not remember what the reason was.

"In other words, if there are things among the Old Order churches which we fail to understand, we would do well to dip deeper and find the source."

That's why you're here, isn't it? The pathetic part is that you may ask our own people why we do as we do, and they are unable to give a rational answer. We would do well to make sure that our own people understand the reasoning behind our customs.

"You certainly have given us something to think about. Even though you don't have all the answers to our problems, apparently we have fewer answers. It all boils down to what Jesus tells us: 'Search the Scriptures; for in them you think you have eternal life; and they are they which testify of me' " (John 5:39).

# The Role of Women

They tell me I have a full agenda in describing the various forms of Old Order Mennonite living. Because there are so many misconceptions regarding the Old Order Mennonites, and because the Mennonite women are often greatly misunderstood, that is where we will start this afternoon. What is the role of Old Order women? Are they being discriminated against? Do we, like the cavemen, drag them home by their hair, and club them into submission?

This reminds me of a city man who moved to the country to get away from it all. He realized double returns from his venture. He personally built his own classical stone house. Then he made a tidy fortune selling the book he wrote, describing the house-building venture.

His friends failed to grasp what he was accomplishing. After looking about the place, they invariably asked, "But what do you *do* away out here?"

When he explained that he was building his own house, single-handed, the usual response was "Oh, so you don't really work?"

This is a common attitude among city people. No one works unless he receives a paycheck. It may be only a choice of words, but I do wish to impress on you the fact that Old Order women do work, whether or not they bring home a paycheck. There is an old saying, "Man may work from sun to sun, / But woman's work is never done" (anonymous).

## Unpaid Workers

The working mother thinks nothing of hiring a babysitter, paying a cleaning lady and a laundress, serving only prepared foods (except when the family dines out, at exorbitant prices), and buying ready-made clothing for the entire family, ad infinitum. She figures she can afford it because she works out at good wages. Yet she wonders why she can't save money.

The Old Order mother and housewife does not consider an alternative to the old ways. A babysitter is a poor substitute for a devoted mother. Her farmer husband deserves to have a wife in the home who prepares a decent meal for him at noon. She serves a nourishing, hot, home-cooked meal, besides the genial sociality of a shared meal at home. She does her cleaning and washing in between mealtimes and caring for the children.

The newly married farmer's wife finds herself in her kitchen, preparing meals, and keeping the house in order. During the summer she tends the garden and puts up fruits and vegetables for the winter. When necessary, she drives a team or tractor in the field, taking the place of a hired man. Usually she helps with the chores, to give her husband a longer day in the field.

When children appear on the scene, the mother has less time for outside work. Not only does she have the extra care of the babies, but she is responsible for their early education. Generally, if she is in good health, she struggles along on her own until she has her third child. From then until the eldest daughter is able to help, she needs a hired girl.

In the case of the urban working mother, this state of affairs has progressed for two generations or more. Many young wives and mothers have not been educated in the art of housewifery and mothering. For this reason, they may find it necessary to serve prepared food and buy ready-made clothing, in spite of domestic science courses in high school.

To my way of thinking, the financial aspect between the two methods of housekeeping can't vary greatly. However, there are two other important factors to consider. First, if there are children, no babysitter can be a true substitute for a mother, who imparts motherly love. A mother's guidance supported by tearful admonition can often soften the heart of a wayward son or daughter.

The second factor to consider is the influence on the family when husband and wife, or father and mother, work together as a team. Later, the combined influence of father and mother working with the children can make a lasting impression on youth, in rearing them in the "admonition of the Lord" (Eph. 6:4).

How can we expect children to grow up to be law-abiding, God-fearing citizens, if these elements are missing?

"Would you say the Mennonite mother considers her work at

home important enough that she can afford to stay at home?"

She certainly does. In fact, she would, even if she had less money in the end. What about the command to women to be

"keepers at home"? (Titus 2:5). Besides, what sort of a mother would she be, if she were not willing to make sacrifices for her child or children?

"Do situations never arise in which the Old Order mother feels she needs to go out and work to make ends meet?"

Not if she has children. Even those who don't have children would rather do piecing, quilting, or sewing, than to work outside the home.

"Your approach to this subject makes sense to me. I agree that the mother's place is in the home."

### Appreciating Our Women

After spending so much time in commending our women for their role as keepers at home, I must propose another, similar subject. Some observers assume that we discriminate against our women. They have seen our children on their way to school, with the boys riding bicycles and the girls walking. Why this difference?

The church has always discouraged our girls from riding bicycles. This counsel dates back to the time when all bicycles had crossbars. Dresses would have slid up enough to cause indecent exposure, in our view.

In general, we discourage our girls from acting in a boyish, brazen, flippant, or immodest manner. Does this mean we discriminate *against* them? Is it discrimination if we discourage a child from playing with fire? Flippant girls are in the gravest danger of being molested. If they are dressed to attract attention, especially when bordering on exposure, they are in much greater danger of falling prey to those with evil intentions.

That we should even think of discriminating against our girls is ridiculous. We esteem our women too highly for that. There is less disobedience among the girls than among the boys. The boys are the ones who create the most discipline problems. They cause disturbances in church by whispering. In the boys' section, sometimes hymnbooks are defaced and candy wrappers found on the floor. Nothing of the sort is ever found in the girls' section.

It is also among the boys that disturbances are caused at singings. Some boys refuse to help with singing and seek other entertainment. Girls usually are ready at an earlier date to submit themselves and come to Christ. Even later in life, when a family leaves the church, the young husband is usually the one who takes the initiative.

Our girls and women are not perfect. There is possibly a greater show of vanity among the fairer sex than among men. Perhaps they have more to be vain about. It is also possible that the worldly practice of dressing to attract the boys is not altogether lost among our girls. However, there would likely be more of this if the mother's hand were not present to steer the girls away from such dangers.

Can anyone believe that we intimidate our women into submissiveness? Those who believe that, give us credit for more virtue than we deserve. Chastening our children is a Christian virtue; but our boys are chastened more than our girls, because they need more of it.

Why is this the case? Perhaps boys do mingle more with the outside world. A limited number of both young men and women do find outside employment: Girls who do housework in non-Mennonite homes come into closer contact with TV and similar attractions than boys. Some young boys experience an urge to drive a car. All around us, today's women drive cars as a matter of course; hence, our girls might just as easily experience this urge.

The women's liberation movement has been hard at work to create equality between the sexes. This movement falls far short of being commendable from a Christian viewpoint. As far as is evident, our Old Order society is still free from it. Seventy-five years ago, the movement was quite militant, bombing government buildings and private homes. When arrested, they literally fought tooth and nail, like wild beasts.

Such difficulties do not stem from the denial of freedom. The fact that they do have the freedom to act or react encourages them to assert themselves in aggressive ways. As is often the case with dissenters and protesters, in their emphasis on liberty, they enslave themselves to license, and renounce the blessings promised to women in the Scriptures.

Women are not second-rate creatures. Through the gospel of Christ, they have opportunities equal to those of men both now and hereafter (Gal. 3:26-29). They have a unique and, in a way, enviable position as mothers of posterity. We appreciate them for that, and rejoice with them in the promise given to them: "Notwithstanding, she shall be saved in childbearing" (1 Tim. 2:15). Men have no greater promise than that.

"Since most of us here are women, I would like to thank you for singing our praises. I'm wondering, though, how well you know women."

Isn't that sort of an embarrassing question?

"No, I didn't mean to get personal. I was just wondering whether you may be overestimating women and girls."

Well, we raised nine daughters. We have thirty granddaughters and four great-granddaughters. We enjoy them all. Does that answer your question?

"All right. I'll take it all back!"

## Wife Abuse

There has been quite a stir lately on the subject of wife abuse. We are told that the problem is much more widespread than one would imagine. Many women are afraid to admit that there is a problem for fear of retaliation.

We as nonresistant Mennonites are inclined to think that our church may be free from this scourge. I certainly hope this is true. Yet there are people who feel that we are guilty of a type of wife abuse in an entirely different form.

As a church, we take the greater part of the Holy Scriptures literally. When we read 1 Peter 3:1-6, we believe that Peter meant exactly what he said:

> Likewise, you wives, be in subjection to your own husbands; that, if any obey not the word, they also may without the word be won by the conversation (lifestyle) of the wives. . . . For after this manner in the old time the holy women also, who trusted in God, adorned themselves, being in subjection unto their own husbands; even as Sara obeyed Abraham, calling him lord.

Peter says twice that the wives should be in subjection to their own husbands, even as Sara obeyed Abraham, calling him lord.

Paul also wrote to Timothy: "Let the woman learn in silence with all subjection. But I suffer not a woman to teach, nor to usurp authority over the man, but to be in silence" (1 Tim. 2:11-12).

Paul told the Ephesians to submit themselves to one another in the fear of God. He counseled the women, "Wives, submit yourselves unto your own husbands, as unto the Lord. For the husband is the head of the wife. . . . Let the wife see that she reverence her husband" (5:21-23, 33).

As we follow the commands in these three quotes from the Scriptures, some may think that we are intimidating our wives into being submissive and in subjection to us. There may indeed be men who take advantage of these texts for selfish reasons. I hope not. We do not demand obedience and subjection from our wives. They observe these commands of their own accord.

In 1 Corinthians 11, Paul clarifies the matter: "The head of every man is Christ; and the head of the woman is the man; and the head of Christ is God" (11:3). That is the divine order: God, Christ, man, woman. It is no more degrading for the woman to be subject to the man, than for Christ to be subject to God.

All through the Bible we notice that when men were counted, the women were not included. When Jesus fed the multitudes, five thousand or four thousand men were satisfied, "besides women and children" (Matt. 14:21; 15:38). No doubt the fact that women were not counted in ancient times was because a country's strength lay in the number of their men of war, or men of valor. The men were also usually the ones making decisions, teaching, and ruling. Regarding headship or ruling power, Paul wrote to the Corinthians that God is the head of Christ, who is the head of man, and man of woman.

If Christ was willing to be subject to God, why should woman not be willing to be subject to man? After all, man and woman are one, even as Father and Son are one (John 10:30). All are equal in the sight of God, but not all have the same mission in life.

If wives, through their chaste conversation, can win their husbands who obey not the word, their mission is just as commendable as that of the man who teaches. If wives are adorned with the ornament of a meek and quiet spirit, how much more good they can do than by outward adorning or by fighting for women's rights!

We Mennonite men certainly love our wives and give ourselves for them, as Paul instructs us (Eph. 5:25-33). Yet in some ways we do not show the same courtesy to women that modern etiquette dictates. We sit down to the dinner table before the women do, and we do not open doors to allow the ladies to go ahead of us. When we sign our names, mine comes before that of my wife. She is well satisfied to be Mrs. Isaac R. Horst.

We could reasonably assume that in a society where "ladies first" is a common slogan, there would be no wife abuse. It makes no sense whatever for a man to show all the social graces to his wife, and then turn around and beat her up.

One might think that those of us who do not show those little social graces to our wives, would be the first to abuse them. The records show otherwise. In fact, divorce and wife abuse seems to go hand in hand in the same society.

Perhaps the answer lies therein. In today's society, men may feel compelled to show those social graces, and their deference may be superficial. If this is the case, then wife abuse can actually be a direct reaction to their feigned courtesy. They may be retaliating to save face or because of resentment.

Our social etiquette may seem crude, but the basic scriptural way works out quite satisfactorily, from our viewpoint.

"Where does the Old Order church stand regarding divorce?"

When I say that we have no divorce, it could be misleading. We do have at least one man whose wife divorced him. The man is still a member of the church. His wife left the church before divorcing him. We have a son whose wife divorced him, but neither he nor his wife ever belonged to the Old Order church. There are a number of similar cases, but all had left the church before being divorced.

There have been cases where a man and his wife did not live together for some time; but I don't think that at present we have a married couple separated from each other.

### *Caveman Treatment?*

Generally speaking, the longer it takes to prove that someone else is wrong, the more reason there is to believe that he is partly right. For example, a tractor salesman was trying his best to sell a tractor to a farmer. He spent a whole hour criticizing a competitor's tractor. When he had finished, the farmer said, "Now I know which tractor to buy. If it is worth the time to spend a whole hour in running down a tractor, it must be really good."

If I need so much time to prove those wrong who claim we take advantage of our women, there must be something to it. In part, the problem stems from the fact that it seems as though the Scriptures were discriminating against women. Since we know that we must "let God be true, and every man a liar," we realize that we must dig deeper for the answer (Rom. 3:4).

Even when we try to explain that our women are satisfied as matters stand, such people are inclined to believe that we intimidate the women into submission, and that they are afraid to express themselves on the subject. They probably imagine that we use caveman methods, dragging women home by the hair and clubbing them into submission.

It would be difficult to prove them totally wrong. Maybe among us there are indeed women who harbor ill feelings against men in general, and against their husbands in particular. Perhaps some are even justified in such feelings.

On the other hand, in homes where harmony reigns, it is doubtful that such feelings endure for any length of time. The wife who watches her husband as he struggles with his income tax forms, spends hours in treating sick cattle only to find them dying in spite of treatment, or trying to hold the banker at bay— that wife is not too greatly inclined to covet her husband's position. If such feelings actually did exist to any great degree, we would become aware of them. At least, we feel certain that the women's liberation movement is not alive and well within our society.

There is considerable evidence that our women in general are satisfied with the existing relationship. The women themselves are responsible for the restrictive rules regarding women's dress standards, and not the men. More of the young men leave the church, or fail to join it, than women. If the younger women were indeed dissatisfied with conditions within the church, more of them would likely leave it. Besides, the girls are inclined to have believer's convictions at a younger age than the boys, and they are generally baptized sooner.

The whole matter can be summed in a few words. The scriptural order is for women to be subject to men, without in any way being inferior to them.

> For after this manner in the old time the holy women also, who trusted in God, adorned themselves in a meek and quiet spirit, being in subjection unto their own husbands; even as Sara obeyed Abraham, calling him lord; whose daughters you are, as long as you do well. (1 Pet. 3:4-6, adapted)

Because our women take this as a scriptural order, they do not find it difficult to submit themselves to it. They receive a spiritual blessing by submitting themselves to their husbands. On one hand, the woman is not to teach, nor to usurp authority over the man, but to be in silence (1 Tim. 2:12). On the other hand, the wives are to be

> in subjection to their husbands, that if any obey not the word, they also may without the word be won by the conversation (lifestyle) of the wives; while they behold their chaste conversation coupled with fear. (1 Pet. 3:1-2).

This shows clearly that both sexes have their respective fields of labor in which to discharge their duties. Neither is more important than the other; yet the higher authority lies with the man.

"You mentioned that the women are responsible for the restrictions to women's dress standards. How does this come about?"

Through the church counsel. It is the older women who defend conservative dress standards for girls and young women, when giving their counsel before communion. They are the strongest supporters of such Scripture texts as Mark 10:2-12, on commitment in marriage; Ephesians 5, on wives submitting to husbands; 1 Timothy 2, on modest apparel instead of outward adorning; and 1 Corinthians 11, on women's prayer veiling and hair not being cut.

"You quoted from 1 Timothy 2, that the woman is not to teach, nor to usurp authority over the man. How do you interpret this?"

Paul mentions two related but separate injunctions, both regarding the relationship between woman and man. The woman is not to teach a man, nor to usurp authority over man. If a woman is ordained as a minister for a mixed congregation, she would be teaching men. Paul says he would not permit that, nor would he allow her to usurp authority over man. The reason? Like it or not, because the woman, being deceived, was first in the transgression (1 Tim. 2:14; Gen. 3).

Yet, she shall be saved in childbearing! (1 Tim. 2:15). Then what will save those who refuse to bear children? A sobering thought!

"What about women who teach school?"

Those women who teach elementary schools, and mothers who teach their own children, are not teaching mature men, old enough to be ministers or to occupy other offices of authority.

## In Praise of Families

A professor of German at the University of Waterloo recently wrote a column on the above subject. He presented the traditional extended family of the past: Father sitting in his armchair and reading, with the children playing around the fire, while Mother prepares the evening meal. Grandmother sits in her rocker, knitting.

During the past fifty years, the family picture in the larger society has greatly changed. The extended family—an expression coined in 1935—has disappeared in Canada. The nuclear family, first heard of in 1947, is seriously threatened. Grandmother now lives in a nice, comfortable nursing home. In many cases, Father and Mother do not even live together. If they have any

Edwin B. Wallace '99

children, there are generally no more than one or two.

There is something contradictory about today's views on family size. We are told that large families are now out of the question, because of the insecurity of the national food supply. Yet, the Canadian government has agreed to bring in more immigrants to supplement our aging generation. There are just not enough children.

Now, here comes the interesting part. We are told that the cost of raising a family is prohibitive. A recent study indicates that it costs $54,000 to raise a child to eighteen years. We raised twelve of them, without child allowance. $54,000 x 12 = wait a minute! Something must be wrong here! I must have counted wrong! Yes, the figure says $648,000! And here I always thought I was a failure! Of course, we did not give them a college education.

Although we did not spoil our children through overindulgence, none of them ever went hungry. None of our family, including myself, had more than an eighth-grade education, officially. Whatever we gained besides that came through correspondence courses, independent study, and experience. Generally, the potential would have been there to go on through college. Later in life, this has stood us in good stead. Our cumulative terms of teaching school have added up to over twenty-five years.

Another contradiction surfaces here. Our children supposedly should have had a higher education to compete for the lucrative though precarious job market in the cities. Unemployment is already high there. Here on the farm, there is no unemployment. Our schools provide at least as satisfactory an education for potential farmers as the public and high schools do.

I was never a successful farmer. Both my interests and my physical ability pointed in a different direction. Because we felt the need of a rural environment to raise our family as we wished, we made the best of it. Several of our children are traveling a similar course. Yet I am convinced that our combined experiences have taught us at least as much of practical economics as we would have learned in high school.

Even though we raised our family far below the assumed poverty level, they were not deprived of the essentials of life or the pleasures of life that lead to lasting satisfaction. I am also convinced that as a group, they and their children will not be a greater burden to society than today's average, whether through lawlessness or as financial burdens.

Since ours is still a traditional extended family setting, the foregoing indicates the effectiveness of this obsolete arrangement. The ingredients are still at hand to create it on a larger scale with the extended family, where social benefits from the government are not needed. With no social insurance (security) payments to drain the coffers, the national deficit could disappear like magic!

However, we are aware of the fact that it would not work on a large scale. The general public has been pampered too long. They want their social insurance, even though they know that it all comes out of their own pockets!

"You mentioned raising twelve children. Is that a usual number among your people?"

It is not unusual, although the average might be from six to eight.

"Do you accept no social assistance whatever?"

No. The only assistance we accept from the government is in the form of rebates, which we regard as discounted prices on purchases.

When we consider the motor traffic on our highways, especially during the summer, it is reasonable to assume that the cost of highway travel is substantially to blame for the cost of living among Canadians in general. Whether we like it or not, we are a spoiled nation, living far beyond our means.

"I commend you people on your attitudes in this respect. I agree that our problems would be much less if we all tried to follow this course."

"Yes, we might even be healthier and happier if we were able to live more like you do."

## Are Church Divisions Scriptural?

"Every one of you says, I am of Paul, and I of Apollos, and I of Cephas, and I of Christ. Is Christ divided?" (1 Cor. 1:12-13).

It is generally accepted that church divisions are unscriptural. J. C. Wenger strongly endorses this view. He claims that there was no excuse for expelling Christian Funk in 1778, John H. Oberholtzer in 1847, Jacob Wisler in 1872, and Jonas H. Martin in 1893.

"Why was brotherly love at so low an ebb?" he asks (*Bishop Jonas H. Martin: His Life and Genealogy,* Gateway Press, 1985).

If all church divisions were unscriptural, then the Anabaptists would likewise have been wrong. However, Paul warns against being unequally yoked together with unbelievers. The Lord calls believers to come out from among them and touch not the unclean thing (2 Cor. 6:14-17). Thus, if a church has deteriorated to the point where its members may rightfully be called unbelievers, a division would be scripturally justified.

We know that in many cases the differences consist in varying interpretations or applications of the Scriptures, rather than in actual doctrine. Often they consist chiefly in material matters, which should be easily resolved if love and tolerance were exercised. Such virtues too often fall by the wayside. Neither side honestly attempts to see the others' point of view.

We are inclined to look back at earlier church divisions and decide that the results were favorable. The Old Order churches became even plainer after the 1889 division in Ontario. The liberal group forged ahead with more revival meetings, educated ministers, more elaborate churches, and less restraint in worldly apparel and furnishings.

We fail to consider that, if they had remained together, the liberals would have benefited by the restraint of the conservatives. Likewise, the conservatives would have absorbed some of the liberals' religious zeal.

For example, Abraham Martin, a conservative bishop, expressed a willingness to withdraw his objections to evening meetings and English preaching, if the Sunday school question were dropped. There is even reason to believe that he would have tolerated the Sunday school if it had been operated with a lower profile. This proves that the differences were minimal, within a range where reconciliation was possible, if more of an effort had been directed toward agreement.

No one knows how the situation would stand today if such measures had been fully carried out. Actually, twenty years after the 1889 division, when the Ontario Conference Mennonites leaned heavily toward fundamentalism, the possibilities for reconciliation would have been much more favorable, except that the automobile had appeared on the scene to widen the gap once more.

One point is obvious: if all the members on both sides of a divisive situation would look to Christ for answers in all cases of disunity, a division would be impossible. Selfish interests and unyielding obstinacy prevent harmony. Invariably both sides have those who are at fault.

Sectarianism must not be confused with true Christianity. When the day of reckoning comes, Christians will likely be found among all denominations. No doubt there will also be some among every denomination who will hear the words, "Depart from me, you workers of iniquity, I know ye not" (Luke 13:27).

In J. C. Wenger's words, "God, give us leaders who can enable us to follow Christ and his apostles."

Elias Eby, son of the pioneer Bishop Benjamin Eby, wrote in his diary: "On Apr. 2, 1874, the semiannual conference was held at Eby's, to see whether peace and unity might not be restored, but it all seemed in vain. Mutual love and confidence have gone too far astray; many harsh accusations were made, but no one was willing to accept them."

Therein lies the essence of the matter. Different views and opinions can be worked out, if the line of communication remains open. Harsh accusations are much more difficult to excuse and condone. If no derogatory remarks were made by anyone during the five-year period prior to a church division, it is doubtful that a schism would occur.

One might argue that the differing views would still exist. True. Yet first, they will not be as irritating. Second, in the absence of slander, there is more brotherly love and unity. There is less desire to offend, thus narrowing the gap.

Over 150 years ago, Heinrich Balzer, a Mennonite minister in southern Russia, made the following statement:

Above all else, one must be on guard against uncharitableness and contempt toward each other. Love promotes unity. Unity creates stability. Stability guards against [spiritual] shipwreck.

Where this is fully exhibited and practiced, there is little danger of schism.

### Our Early-Church Heritage

When we as Mennonites refer to our church forefathers, we generally think of those since January 1525. At that time, a small group of believers met to discuss the issues on which they differed from the state church. The outcome of the meeting was that Georg Blaurock and Conrad Grebel rebaptized each other, and Georg baptized the rest of the group. Thus these events mark the beginning of the first Anabaptist church.

More recent discoveries and translations of writings originating with Christians of the first few centuries shed more light on our history. These indicate that we may rightfully trace our faith back to the time of such early Christians. Tertullian, a native of Carthage, was one such writer. He lived during the latter part of the second century and into the early third. Among his extensive writings are many that strongly support Old Order Mennonite doctrine today. Here are some quotes from his writings.

"The blood of the martyrs is the seed of the church." Unpopular and revolting as this statement may seem, it is painfully true. The church is at its strongest during persecution. This does not mean that we should pray for persecution. Christ himself prayed, "If it be possible, let this cup pass from me; nevertheless not as I will, but as you will" (Matt. 26:39).

Tertullian explains his position further in this quotation:

It is not by being merely in the world that we fall from the faith, but by touching and tainting ourselves with the world's sins. To go to the circus or theater as a spectator is no different from sacrificing in the temple of Serapis. If we keep our throats and bellies free from defilement (by food offered to idols), how much more should we withhold our ears and eyes from such enjoyments.

We have nothing to do, either in speech, sight, or hearing, with the madness of the circus, the impurity of the theater, the atrocity of the arena, the emptiness of the wrestling gallery— tragedies and comedies, the bloody and lascivious tormentors of crime and lust.

Abstain from these condemned things: hair twisted, curled up, fluffed up; wigs, turbans, paints, dyes, cosmetics, rouge. Lay aside the diseases of the desire of wearing ornaments; for they who rub their skin with medicaments, stain their cheeks with rouge, make their eyes prominent with antimony, sin against God. Whatever is plastered on is the devil's work. What reason can you have for going about in gay apparel when you are removed from all with whom this is required?

How shall a Christian wage war: nay, even how shall he be a soldier in peacetime, without the sword which the Lord has taken away? For although soldiers had come to John and received the form of their rule, although even a centurion had believed, the Lord afterward, in disarming Peter, disarmed every soldier.

I owe no duty to forum, campaign, or senate. I make no effort to occupy a platform. I am no office seeker. I shun the voters' booth, the jurymans' bench. I break no laws, and push no lawsuits. I refuse to do military service. I have withdrawn from worldly politics. My only politics are spiritual.

In all forms of entertainment, worldliness, immodesty, politics, aggression, swearing, and war—Tertullian's views seem to run parallel to that of the Old Order Mennonite views today. Is this merely a coincidence, or are we indeed directly descended from the early church fathers?

"Who was Tertullian?"

Tertullian (ca. 155-220+), was an elder in the church at Carthage, North Africa. He wrote numerous apologies, works against heretics, and exhortations to other Christians.

"What—I don't know how to ask this, but—was he directly connected with the apostles of Christ?"

No doubt he was. Most of the early Christians were directly or indirectly connected with the apostles. Polycarp of Smyrna and Ignatius of Antioch were disciples or companions of John. Several church leaders were associated with Peter and Paul. The rest were generally pupils or disciples of the earlier ones. All of them were leaders of the Christian church before the time of Constantine. After that, the church and the state were no longer separate. Whenever this happens or has happened, the church loses out.

"This is indeed the first time I have heard of any church group that so definitely endorses the Old Order Mennonite and Amish doctrine. Since there is every reason to believe that Tertullian received his doctrine in direct lineage from the apostles, it is reasonable to assume that this was indeed the way the apostles taught. It appears from this that the Old Order Mennonites and the Amish are indeed closer in teachings to the apostles' doctrine than any of the mainstream churches today."

Perhaps there is another point to consider. Regarding entertainment, worldliness, immodesty, politics, aggression, swearing, and war—might it be that some of the churches would agree with Tertullian's views in principle, but then find them too difficult to put into practice?

"I wouldn't argue the point."

## *Our Anabaptist Heritage*

"You seek me, not because you saw the miracles, but because you did eat of the loaves, and were filled. Labor not for the meat that perishes, but for that meat which endures unto everlasting life" (John 6:26-27).

Many people today, especially young people, are seeking for an alternate lifestyle. They are sick and tired of the rat race, and they gaze longingly at the pastoral scenes in the country. Then they find the Mennonites and the Amish, who seem to live such a quiet, reserved life, far removed from the turmoil of the city. Surely this must be what they are looking for! Thousands have already purchased farm homes and sometimes whole farms, where they spend their weekends. They hope someday soon to make their homes there permanently. Many more are dreaming of eventually doing so.

Throughout Canada and the United States, tourists flock to the Mennonite and Amish areas all summer, to see the quaint

people, buy souvenirs and crafts, and gather as much information about the people as possible. Many students and others
come for interviews, because they have decided to write their
theses or term papers on this subject.

To a certain extent, this is good. The Mennonites and Amish
do indeed have something of value that could be incorporated
into the lives of society in general, to their benefit. Country living does have its advantages if properly applied. Granted, certain
sacrifices must be made before those advantages can be fully realized. However, most of such seekers find the simple life too de-
manding. Besides, by looking at the Mennonites superficially,
they miss the main point.

They admire the Mennonites for their plain dress, their simple
lifestyle, and their antiquated mode of travel. This may be compared to admiring an apple tree for its blossoms. True, an apple
orchard in full bloom is a sight to behold; but it is the fruit that
rewards us for our labors. In this case, the end justifies the means.
This is the point that Christ tried to get across to the people at
Capernaum (John 6:26). "You seek me, not because you saw the
miracles, but because you did eat of the loaves and were filled."

The people missed the point. We too will miss the point if we
look to Christ as a source of cheap food. Likewise, the plain
clothes and simple lifestyle are not at the heart of the Mennonite
faith. Instead, they are the outward evidence of the inner conviction.

Few of those who show curiosity about the Mennonites are really interested in the foundation of their faith. They do not realize that the Anabaptist-Mennonite church was the first to
emerge from the Reformation as separate from the state churches. They do not know that both Luther and Zwingli, the German
and Swiss reformers, agreed with them on the principles of baptism, the swearing of oaths, and nonresistance. The only reason
that they changed this policy was because they wished to unite
church and state. This the Swiss Brethren could not conscientiously do.

Through two hundred years of persecution, under constant
threat of martyrdom, most of the early Anabaptists adhered to

their nonresistant doctrine. Several thousand died the martyr's death, rather than to compromise their faith. With most of them, their faith never wavered. In fact, the church prospered during that time as never before or since. They "labored not for the meat that perishes, but for that meat which endures unto everlasting life" (John 6:27).

This is our priceless heritage. Yet we must feel pangs of guilt about it. Are we, who live in comparative ease and comfort, really qualified to claim those martyrs as our forebears? Can we truly claim to be joint heirs with them?

"You mention that few people are interested in the foundation of the Mennonite faith. What is the foundation of your faith?"

First, "Other foundation can no one lay than what is laid, which is Jesus Christ" (1 Cor. 3:11). This is the foundation that is built on the rock, Jesus Christ.

Second, our faith is built upon the foundation of the apostles, Jesus Christ himself being the chief cornerstone (Eph. 2:20).

Third, we lay up in store a good foundation against the time to come, not being high-minded, nor trusting in riches, but trusting in the living God, to do good, and be rich in good works (1 Tim. 6:17-19).

Fourth, that Christ may dwell in our hearts by faith, that we may be grounded in love (Eph. 3:17) and ready to speak of the hope that is in us, with meekness and fear (1 Pet. 3:15). That we may continue in the faith, grounded and settled, and not moved away from the hope of the gospel (Col. 1:23).

In short, Jesus Christ is our foundation, through faith, hope, charity, love, trust, and meekness. The Sermon on the Mount is an exemplification of the Christian life that the Old Order Mennonites endeavor to follow (Matt. 5–7).

"That makes sense to me. However, living up to this example is not so easy."

### A Tribute to Our Swiss Forebears

In the expanded German edition (1890) of his *History of the Mennonites* (1888), D. K. Cassel reports on an event of fifty or sixty years earlier, around 1830-40. A renowned Swiss writer,

Heinrich Zchokke, traveled through the Jura Mountains and described the bishopric of Basel and its inhabitants. Zchokke's interesting account of our forebears is drawn from Cassel's German book:

◆ ◆ ◆

Over a hundred families of Baptists live here. They are scattered on solitary farms or feudal holdings, in valleys and on
mountains. Through their diligence, they squeeze production out
of an unproductive region. They are a sturdy race of good blood
lines, faithful, peaceable, conscientious, and kind. They are
loved by their neighbors; Catholics and Protestants of the area
trust them farther than they trust one another.

These upright people were banished from their homes in the
seventeenth and eighteenth centuries by the Bernese government
(Calvinistic church and state) because they would not swear an
oath or bear arms. The sovereign bishops of Basel, more prudent
and tolerant than the Protestant government, accepted the rejected disciples of Menno into their temporal domain at that time.

When among them, it seemed to me as though I was living in
the early Christian times; so serene, so God-fearing and without
dejection, so hospitably and diligently they live in their patriar-
chal simplicity and pious manners. There are no drunkards
among them, no gamblers, no night-revelers, no liars, no jealous
neighbors. If a quarrel or dispute arises, which is seldom, it is
settled in a friendly way by a deacon or bishop.

They help each other with their work, free of charge, at haying, harvest, and wherever needed. Their temperance and moral
purity preserves their health to a high, vigorous age. An old man,
over seventy, who is one of their teachers (they have no pastors),
led me briskly over hill and vale, like a vigorous youth, to the
rest of their brotherhood. What true love among married couples, what tenderness among brethren, what attentiveness of
children towards parents—all these I saw there!

The whole upbringing of children consists in the example that
grown-ups set for youth, and in a few words: "Keep God in

sight!" Yet they enjoy a nurture more precious than the richest in the world. What people, what Christianity, that needs no lawyers, no priests, no judges, yes, barely a doctor!

On Sundays they gather to perform their devotions, sometimes with one teacher, sometimes with another; sometimes in the open, in a barn, or in a large room. The teacher preaches according to his impulse or the need of his audience, or he reads out of an old, edifying, book. He baptizes, passes out communion, performs marriages, and yet is a farmer like the rest. When the service is over, those from a distance are entertained at neighboring homes, free of charge [really!], and the hosts can expect to be invited by their current guests at other times.

Equipment and clothing is neat and yet unadorned, like the modest homes. Yet just as other church groups in the Christian world, the Baptists have their own pious vagaries and peculiarities. It is commendable that the married men let their beards grow. But the short gray coat, the short pants, and the stockings pulled over the knees are not compatible with the majestic beard.

The women are just as simply clothed. No gold, no velvet, no silk, not even a bright or light-colored silk band may flutter around a girl's straw hat. In spite of this, the girls have ways and means without endangering their religion. Just look how pert these slim, blossoming mountain dwellers know how to set their hats, and how the delicate bows and flowers of the woven straw float and nod! Yet everything is so modest.

◆ ◆ ◆

All of the above sounds so familiar, just like our own practices and ways, and our people are still the same.

"Isn't it interesting that after 150 years, there is still so much in common between the Mennonites here and the mountain dwellers in Switzerland?"

Actually, it is more like 300 years since our ancestors left Switzerland. Of course, clothing styles are far different from what they were then, but the purpose is still the same: to wear simple, unadorned clothing, of the type rejected by the world. It is espe-

cially interesting that the Swiss at that time had the same practice of visiting each other as we have.

"I do believe that such a heritage is worth preserving. By this
means, the social circle is kept intact, and the brotherhood maintained."

## Our Double Standard

If strangers were to question us about our ministry, they would
possibly root up some peculiarities of which we are barely aware
ourselves. The conversation might run something like this:

"What do you call your ministers?"

Usually we call them preachers. The bishop and the deacons
are also members of the ministry.

"I mean, how do you greet them?"

With hand and kiss.

"No, no! If you talk to your preacher, do you address him as
Preacher Jones, or whatever his name is?"

Oh, you mean his name? We call our ministers Elam, and Melvin, and Wayne. We don't say, "Preacher Melvin" if we speak to
him. Our ministers are just ordinary people, just as we are.

"How is your minister dressed? Does he wear a surplice, or a
vestment?"

I don't know exactly what that means, but our ministers are
dressed just as we are. Well, unless they are wearing their overcoats.

"Their overcoats?"

Yes; the ministers' overcoats have a cape attached to them,
over their shoulders.

"Does your minister live in town?"

No. Why would he live in town? He couldn't make a living
there. He's a farmer.

"Can't he make a living by preaching?"

I guess not! Who would pay him?

"Don't the members of the congregation pay him?"

No. Why should they? He lives by farming, the same as the
rest of us do.

"You mean to say he doesn't get paid for preaching?"

No. The rest of us don't get paid for working on Sunday either. The Scriptures tell us that the ministers should tend their flock willingly, not for shameful gain, but eagerly.

"Aren't you afraid they will go some other place to preach, where they get paid?"

I doubt it. So far that has never happened. When they are ordained, they are told to attend to reading, to preaching, to teaching, and hold to that. If their health allows, they continue in this until death.

"Do your ministers go to college before they are ordained?"

Oh no. They preach as the Holy Spirit moves them.

"How are your ministers chosen?"

They are ordained by lot. But before they are ordained, they are examined to see whether they qualify, and whether they are willing to submit themselves to the rules of their office. The ministers are required to come up to the standards of the older men. This includes the round haircut, a plain and wide-brimmed hat, shoes without toe caps, and broadfall pants.

"Can you explain that? What is a round haircut?"

The hair is unparted and cut right around the bottom.

"What are broadfall pants?"

They have a buttoned-up flap instead of a fly. Besides that, he must have steel lugs on his tractor, instead of rubber tires, and he can have neither hydroelectric power nor telephone.

"Wow! And he doesn't even get paid for his work?"

No. Of course, his wife also has to measure up to the standards of older women. In addition, they are expected to visit the sick and the aged, and cheer up the depressed. Naturally, he also needs to spend lots of time in reading.

"Oh my! I pity the poor man whose lot it is to be a minister!"

I'm not sure whether that is necessary. There is a great spiritual blessing awaiting faithful ministers. Paul wrote to Timothy, "Elders who rule well are worthy of double honor, especially those who labor in preaching and teaching. The Scripture says, 'You shall not muzzle an ox when it is treading out the grain,' and, 'The laborer deserves his wages' " (1 Tim. 5:17-18, RSV).

"Right there Paul says, 'The laborer deserves his wages.' Doesn't that refer to a paid ministry?"

Not necessarily. In Luke 10:7 we see Jesus' instructions to the seventy, who are sharing the gospel of the kingdom of God: "In the same house remain, eating and drinking such things as they give, for the laborer is worthy of his hire." Jesus tells them to accept what is offered but does not tell them to ask for anything (10:8). Yet I admit that we may be guilty of not offering enough to help our ministers.

Paul also calls ministers to live out the faith and teach it steadfastly: "Take heed to yourself and to your teaching; hold to that, for by so doing you will save both yourself and your hearers" (1 Tim. 4:16, RSV).

"What a glorious promise for faithful ministers!"

## The Telephone Issue

To be fair to you, I will explain circumstances surrounding the telephone in our Old Order church. When the church divided in 1889, the telephone was still something new. Peter Sherk had a phone in his mill, and yet he sided with the Old Order group. He was a brother-in-law to Bishop Abraham Martin, the Old Order leader, and was a staunch supporter in opposing innovative methods of worship and personal adornment.

At that time, the Old Order Mennonites decided that the phone would be tolerated in business places, but not in homes. For a hundred years, this system was supported by the church. Nevertheless, changing farming methods were not compatible with this rule. For several years, a system of semiprivate phone booths were set up at intervals throughout the communities. This was fine for outgoing calls, but not for calls coming in.

It came to the point where a slight majority favored allowing phones in homes, if it could be done while still maintaining the peace. Apparently this was stretching a point. A few conference members objected but gave in enough that it seemed to work out. In the conference decisions, it was announced that the phone was "tolerated."

After quite a few phones had been installed, it turned out that this change was not unanimous. We lost several members and injured several others. It is regrettable that such things should happen. The church was caught between a rock and a hard place. However, to ease the situation, firm lines were laid down. Phone sets were all to be black. No accessories would be allowed, such as fax, Internet, memory, call hold, and so on.

It is not surprising that something of the sort should happen. With such a large community and several smaller ones, we cannot expect that there would be no differences of opinion. Telephones now appear in over half of the homes. If nothing is done to further aggravate the issue, the matter will heal, to a certain extent, but it will never be quite the same again.

"Does the telephone issue follow the same course as the one on personal adornment, modernism, and worldliness?"

Not really. There are some farms and homes right up front in modernism, where there is still a thumbs-down attitude toward the phone. Other homes are much plainer, with farming methods less progressive, where the phone has found a ready place.

"Why do you think the telephone is so strongly opposed by some individuals? After all, farming practices have changed greatly during that period. Grain binders appeared on the scene about the same time as the telephone did. Yet for thirty years, binders have been obsolete or nearly so. Threshing machines have followed the same course during that time."

There always has been a certain stigma attached to the telephone for our people. A hundred years ago, there was still more superstition among us than there is today. If superstitious people heard someone talking into the box on the wall, and were told that the answer came from someone twenty miles away, it seemed like ESP or telepathy to them. In bygone years, we commonly heard remarks about the telephone being "the devil's mouthpiece" and a sign of being bound to the world.

"I'm ready to admit that the telephone had been a nuisance at one time. People with time on their hands sometimes talk for hours and tie up party lines. All right, Jake, don't look at me like that! With private lines, that problem has evaporated."

We're not asking to be excused in that respect, either. With most of our family living at a distance from us, we do run up phone bills. However, it is still cheaper than driving that far.

In Indiana, the Wisler group accepted the telephone and separated from other Old Order Mennonites in 1907. Yet by now, telephones are common in homes of the Indiana OOMs. In Pennsylvania and most of the daughter colonies, phones have been in OOM homes for as long as I can recall. Yet in all our communities, there are still some who do without, as is also the case with other conveniences.

## An Old Order Frankenstein

One hears much criticism these days regarding the inefficiency of Canada Post. It seems that the less insight we have about a matter, the better we know how it should be operated.

Many options seem to be open for improving mail service: a deluge of letters to the newspaper or the Member of Parliament for our area, a march on Ottawa, a boycott, or a royal commission of investigation.

Deep down we know that none of these methods would be effective. In Canada Post, we see a political hot potato, a labor-management stalemate, and a complex bureaucratic administration. It has turned into a Frankenstein that may eventually devour itself.

Happily, it is not our responsibility to reform the government in all its complexities. Yet we are finding similar situations in our churches. Many church organizations are growing so unwieldy and the administration so complex that they are like Frankenstein's monster. Things happen in the churches over which we seem to have no control. We have issues such as Salman Rushdie threatened by the Muslims, gay preachers in the United Church of Canada, women in the Mennonite ministry, and the telephone issue among the Old Orders.

To outsiders, the answers seem so simple: Appoint a royal commission. March on the capital. Fire the union. Boycott the church!

As with Canada Post, the churches have internal problems that are not solved by political means or aggressive methods. They are only aggravated by intolerance. Besides, in the Mennonite church, any violent measures are totally at variance with our historic nonresistant doctrine.

We ourselves have created most of these problems. We have winked at acts of inconsistency. We have become bureaucratic, applying pressure on our administrators to act in our personal favor. By being selfish, jealous, and envious, we have caused stalemates in our labor-management relations. We have not loved our neighbors as ourselves.

In the depths of our hearts, we know the answer. We need no royal commission to find it. If we humble ourselves to a Christlike attitude, we will see plainly where the trouble lies. We will not like what we see, that we are the ones who have sinned.

Telephones are now being tolerated in Old Order homes. This will largely eliminate our earlier practice of encroaching on the privacy of neighbors to use their telephones, which almost seems to be trespassing. Yet the problem is not solved. This reversal of policy has infringed on the deep-seated convictions of some members. We have an even greater need to demonstrate forbearance and respect toward each other.

"When you say, 'We, ourselves have created most of these problems,' I assume you are referring to the whole church. I can see where those who pressed for slightly more liberality may be considered at fault. Yet there will naturally come a time when others must shoulder part of the blame if they are inflexible and refuse to give any concessions and make allowances for those whose needs are different."

It all depends on how we look at it. I felt the time had come when we should no longer inconvenience our neighbors by entering their homes. Others still felt strongly opposed to allowing phones in our homes. If the issue had come up regarding the automobile, about allowing it to be placed at everyone's doorstep, I would have been just as inflexible. I see a much greater danger in what it would do to our young people, letting them "get away from the watchful eye of the parent."

"I can see your point there, although I still would not be ready to forfeit my 'car at the doorstep'!"

"These problems you mention, have they increased in step with the phenomenal growth of the church?"

Definitely yes! This is natural. Partly it is caused by the distance at which some members are separated from each other, and as a result have little acquaintance with each other. Partly it is because of numerical abundance, causing the congregation to grow unwieldy. We can write it all down to growing pains!

"I suppose you are still glad for the growth of the church."

By all means. We want the church to grow. I would be quite reluctant to use an expression I heard from an American friend. He suggested that there is usually a church division every thirty .years, and remarked that it was time for another schism. Since we look on schisms as an evil, we want to avoid them as much as possible.

"Do you see a solution for your problem?"

Yes, if we are all willing to do our part. Whenever differences of opinion arise, there are rarely any serious consequences, as long as tempers are controlled and nothing is said or done to belittle, degrade, or insult one another. Differences of opinion can be tolerated, but derogatory remarks are never forgotten. They are ready to cause trouble whenever an issue arises. If we could all control our tongues, those unruly evils, we could possibly tolerate the differences (James 3).

## One Small Voice

On February 1, 1992, the *Mennonite Reporter* celebrated its twentieth anniversary. As one of the contributing writers, I was asked to participate in the program and present the Old Order voice: one little voice among many.

When the *Mennonite Reporter* was established, it was to present an overall review of Mennonite churches in Canada. I believe the aim was to present news, views, opinions, and suggestions of a greatly diversified Mennonite population.

If those views and opinions did not always correspond with

each other, it was perfectly natural. Why would there need to be so many Mennonite denominations if they agreed on everything?

One of the guests sensed that I did not agree with all the voices and activities during the celebrations. He suggested that the anniversary activities were no more alien to me than the Anabaptists' meetings were to the Catholic and Zwinglian state churches. He implied that this celebration could be compared to an Anabaptist meeting, and I to an outsider from the state churches.

I can see at least a slight parallel. Wilmer Martin and Sue Steiner of the planning committee opened the meeting, offering thanks and invoking a blessing on behalf of those present. This could be compared to the opening by Georg Blaurock and Conrad Grebel, at the meeting on January 21, 1525.

However, to make a comparison, we must visualize a meeting taking place twenty years later. Since the early leaders had already met their fate, Menno Simons and Dirk Philips might have been the leaders. Like Dave Kroeker, they could have mentioned the joys, sorrows, life, and death during this period.

Like Kathy Shantz and Reg Good, they could have described their journeys. They could have mentioned their peace movement, as Ernie Regehr did, or plans for the future, as Ron Rempel did. But—who would have provided the entertainment?

When the associate editor asked me to write a monthly column in 1988, I had no desire to offend anyone. I told her that I would try to be discreet in my writing. Not so, she said. The column is intended to present Old Order views. Let the chips fall where they may.

I participated in this twentieth-anniversary program by talking of the milk can shipping controversy in 1977, as it affected the Old Order community. I could justly and gratefully pay tribute to the *Reporter* staff, especially Dave Kroeker, editor at that time, for going to bat for the Old Order groups.

If this column is somewhat confused, it is because I am still struggling to recover from culture shock. The entertainment was too overwhelming for me. I was not with it. This Old Order voice is one among many. The drumbeats of this age are too loud for it to be heard.

Recently I had occasion to attend the funeral of a nephew. Actually, I think they called it a memorial service. A number of "witnesses" spoke, recalling his youth, some of which was not exactly uplifting, at least not in the spiritual sense.

We grieved for and with the parents. They may not have grieved as those who have no hope, yet they grieved (1 Thess. 4:13). When Lazarus died, Jesus stood beside the grave and wept. We know that he did not grieve as those who have no hope, for he had more than hope. Standing beside the grave of a loved one, even attending his memorial service, is no laughing matter.

To me, the closing words of Theron Schlabach's book, *Gospel Versus Gospel*, seem appropriate here:

> Had they listened to stiller, smaller sounds, they might have gone forth not quite so much to the drumbeats of Anglo-Saxon Protestantism. Had they listened more to Jesus' low-key rhythm, to the modest congregations of Christians of Paul's time, to the Anabaptists, to the best words of their Mennonite forefathers . . . ah, but what was, was.

The show must go on.

"Are you suggesting that some of those 'witnesses' did not hear the 'low-key rhythm' that goes with mourning?"

It did make me wonder, yes. Elijah discovered that the Lord was not found in the deafening drumbeats of the wind, the earthquake, or the fire; but in the still, small voice (1 Kings 19).

"You mentioned Kathy Shantz, Reg Good, and their journeys. What was that about?"

Some time earlier, they had traveled across Canada in the Menno van, witnessing for the Mennonite church as they traveled. I presume that part of the purpose was to show the diversity of the Mennonite churches.

## The Modern Age

When World War II began, the Canadian economy improved. Almost 10 percent of the Canadian workforce was absorbed into the armed forces. Another significant number were employed in military manufacturing. Farmers, already shorthanded, were assured of a ready market overseas.

When the war ended six years later, certain controls were necessary to assure a rational transition to a peacetime economy. The government put in place subsidies, quotas, and other forms of stabilization. However, for this system to work satisfactorily, officials should have gradually phased out such stabilizers, to let the economy find its natural level.

Greed prevented Canada from finding such a solution. Even though farmers and others were doing remarkably well, they were not about to give up this windfall. If the government was able to help thus far, why not continue? Surely we all deserve a break!

However, with assistance being rendered to almost every form of enterprise, its value was doubtful. This assistance came out of taxpayers' pockets, even while they were receiving assistance.

I can recall a report of over fifty years ago, that the welfare state in Great Britain had all but caused the country's bankruptcy. I told myself this would never happen in Canada. How wrong I was! We are now in about the same shape as Great Britain was then. We have unemployment insurance, disability insurance, workman's compensation, old age pension, and almost every form of financial assistance imaginable. Yet our country is almost literally bankrupt.

Taxpayers obviously have to pay for all these benefits, whether they like it or not. Besides, they have to pay the bureaucrats who administer all these benefits. How much cheaper and easier it would be if we paid our own benefits, while helping others in distress. Of course, this would be contrary to our selfish natures.

We are also in about the same situation as the Americans were after the First World War. Canadians are certainly not far behind in their pursuit of pleasure! Even with the recent recession, few Canadians have been willing to sacrifice their pursuit of sports and entertainment for the sake of economy. They have come to consider their pleasure as a God-given right.

A prominent national figure states that our prosperity involves selfishness, moral relativism, the emphasis of the individual at the expense of the community, and the belief that technology can dominate everything. People have become so involved in the pursuit of things that the sense of inner being has been lost.

We are living in a privileged country. We have never faced starvation. We have unprecedented freedom. Yet we undoubtedly abuse it. If we are willing to live simply, we can be assured of three meals a day. Supposedly this is the attitude of the Old Order Mennonites; but is it? Slowly, gradually, we are following the general public in the pursuit of happiness at the expense of survival.

If we wish to live the life of Riley, we may become disappointed. Our government does not have the funds to supply all our wants. If we demand wages high enough to pay for all our whims, we will be priced out of a market. We have been heading in that direction for a long time. It is time for us to wake up to the facts. Someone has said, "Enough is what would satisfy us if our neighbor didn't have more."

The choice is ours: to be satisfied with the funds available, or demand more and lose all.

"How was the Old Order Mennonites' financial situation at the end of World War II?"

They were sitting pretty. Many of them enlarged their barns and stables, for there was a ready market for all farm produce. The poultry and egg situation was at its peak. It was possible to sell yearling hens, replace them with ready-to-lay pullets, and have a dollar left per bird. That was too good to last.

"Were you living on a farm at that time?"

I had a little farm, with a few sows and laying hens, while I was employed at a feed mill.

"Wow! Did you say a few thousand laying hens, and you were working out besides?"

No! I said, "A few sows, meaning pigs, and laying hens!"

"Wages were not too high then, were they?"

I started at the mill for fifty cents an hour. But of that, I paid twenty-five dollars per month to the Red Cross, as part of an alternative to military service.

"Didn't you serve at an Alternative Service camp?"

No, I was too old for that. Those who were six weeks younger were drafted into camp service, though.

"It surely is a shame that when we are doing well economically, we fail to appreciate it. Instead, we blow it on entertainment."

"If we were to save it for a rainy day—but that isn't human nature. How did you put it? 'The emphasis on the individual at the expense of the community.' That is our problem to this day."

I'm thoroughly convinced that we are headed for deep trouble. We are already priced out of a market for many of our products.

## Rural Christian Communities

The Old Order Mennonites have their own ideas about what they believe, how they wish to live, and what they ought to do or not do. Since the majority have a limited education and no experience in public speaking or writing, they find it difficult to express their beliefs, motives, and views of life in general.

As a result of this lack, I have found writings of others that expressed my own views better and clearer than I could do so. The writings of J. C. Wenger in his book, *Separated unto God* (1951), are a case in point. In the chapter on management-labor relationships, he expresses the general views of Old Order Mennonites today. (One reason for that may be that at the time of his writing, the Mennonite General Conference was in much the same position as the Old Order Mennonites are today.) We would not support the views of the labor unions, nor those of capital represented by most large corporations.

Wenger frequently refers to the writings of Guy F. Hershberger, who fifty years ago wrote extensively on Mennonite community life. Wenger and Hershberger dreamed up a utopian Mennonite community that sounds too good to be true, yet which would not be without merit, if it could be achieved.

They didn't like Mennonites working for the established industrial corporations in the cities, where labor and management are continually clashing. Instead, they suggested that Mennonites establish their own strong communities, totally consecrated to Christian principles. There would be a Mennonite business community within the farming community, operating in a rural atmosphere.

The two communities, business and farming, would be integrated to such an extent that one would complement the other. The business community would operate mainly in the interests of agriculture, processing farm commodities, marketing farm produce, and supplying agricultural needs.

Although the whole concept savors of Hutterite ideology and practice, this should not discredit the plan. If the Hutterites have a strength in an area where we are weak, we should be willing to learn from them. If such a plan could be carried out, it would certainly improve business and community relationships. There would be no class struggle, no unchristian economic rivalry. What a joy it would be to live and work in such a community!

On second thought, would we miss something in such a situation to which we have become accustomed, and which we secretly enjoy? Do we get a twisted satisfaction out of driving hard bargains, beating others at their own game, and bearding the lion in his den? If this is even partly true, we would do well to examine our Christian principles and business ethics.

It might also be wise to examine the problem closer to home. Is our church free from class struggles, rivalry, contentions, and abuse of power? If not, there would be little hope for the success of the larger community. Let us examine ourselves, and make sure that our business ethics are beyond reproach. If we allow our-

selves to be governed by the golden rule, our good attitudes are likely to be reciprocal (Matt. 7:12). Perhaps, then, we will not find it necessary to establish our own business community.

At present, the suggestion made by Wenger and Hershberger is being seriously considered in Wellesley Township, a twenty-mile drive from Kitchener. There would be certain variations and adaptations, of course.

An area of nearly half the township has highly productive and prosperous farms, using horses exclusively, except for custom tractors and balers used in haying time. In the same area, a pattern of cottage industries has also emerged, with a shop on almost every farm. Metal fabricating, machining, and woodworking developed so successfully that a Frankenstein monster seems to be at work.

Two of the chief problems confronting the township council seem to be zoning and business tax. Unless these issues are fairly met, city industries have reason to complain of unfair competition.

Township officials met several times with the industrialized farmers, proposing clusters of farm-oriented homes, each with its stable and shop, with up to seven units. There have always been some objections on the grounds of discrimination.

"If these shops are doing so well, they will surely be paying business tax?"

I assume they are, though I have no evidence to prove it.

"If they are, what grounds would city industries have for complaining?"

Possibly that income from the farm would lower production costs for the industry and enable "unfair" competition with city businesses.

"I suppose that could indeed present a problem."

### What Do We Have to Offer?

There are times when we grow discouraged and disillusioned. Our cherished ideals seem to collapse around us. We don't seem to measure up to what we expect of ourselves. When that happens, it is time to take inventory of our assets.

Sometimes we wonder about our churches. We are gradually

losing some of our cherished values. Our farming practices are becoming more modern, so that our overhead is almost as high as that of our neighbors. We tend to squabble and bicker among ourselves. Do we still have something worth preserving?

Let us take a look at our inventory. How do we measure up when compared with the world around us? Is our position any more favorable than average, in relation to current national issues?

There is reason for grave concern about our country's astronomical national debt. One wonders if there is any possibility of ever breaking even again. The public has become so dependent on social security that they would be lost without it. We as Old Order Mennonites contribute our share to support these social benefits, yet we reap little of the returns. We accept no Old Age Pension, no Child Allowance, no Hospitalization, Unemployment Insurance, Workman's Compensation, or Child Tax Credit. We accept no government grants or stabilization payments.

We contribute our share to the mounting costs of education, yet we independently maintain our own schools and take no advantage of the public educational system. This is as we desire to have it, so that we may choose the form of education our children receive. Thus we do not feel obligated to the Department of Education for any divergence from the normal curriculum. Progress of the Old Order pupils in the key subjects measures up favorably when compared with public schools.

Urban expansion and related traffic problems are becoming a headache for planners, environmentalists, and agriculturalists. There seems to be no alternative except to continue to encroach upon prime agricultural fields and woodlands. As a group, we have no great need for more highways that stretch on endlessly. We can well do without larger cities, especially right in our midst. Single-lane gravel roads and small towns serve our purpose just as well, at a much lower cost.

Waste management is becoming a serious problem in and around large cities. Waste disposal sites are almost impossible to find, and alternative means of disposal are expensive. Old Orders contribute little to disposable wastes. We waste little and reuse a lot. Our children are taught to clean their plates. Any leftovers that cannot be consumed at a later meal are fed to livestock, and livestock waste is plowed down as fertilizer. We wear our clothing until it is worn out, and never replace it just because it is out of style. We buy few packaged foods, which also contribute to additional waste.

We are guilty of pollution to some extent, through animal waste runoff, fumes and smoke from tractors, and excessive use of chemicals. While we occasionally ride in cars or have trucks deliver things for us, we do not own motor vehicles and thus are much less responsible for pollution by fumes from traffic.

We are no great burden to our country through crime, vandalism, drug abuse, smoking, drinking, and violence. We do not perpetrate wars, but rather believe in loving others as ourselves, even our enemies. It is our conviction that by living in this manner, we are only doing what is expected of Christians. The only favor we ask in exchange is the continued privilege of being allowed to live according to our convictions.

"Am I misunderstanding you, or are you blowing your own horn?"

If this sounds like I am blowing my own horn, I did not intend it that way. I'm trying to say that if we have nothing to offer, there is no point in describing our traditions. As a group, it is our desire to live peaceably with all people, as far as possible. By taking inventory, I feel at least that it is still worthwhile for us to keep trying to do our part.

"I have to admit that I sometimes wonder how you can manage to survive without social benefits from the government. I suppose the reason is that you indulge in less sports and entertainment."

That is likely true. But we are convinced that we are just as happy without such entertainment. We never miss it, because we have never been used to it.

"I believe you. Happiness does not consist in the abundance of material things (Luke 12:15), but in peace of mind, and a clear conscience."

Of course, this does not mean that we have no problems. If we wish to keep from becoming involved with matters that under-mine our customs, we must be continually on the alert.

### Thank God for This Much

Several years ago, while I was parked beside the main road selling vegetables, a pickup truck pulled up behind me. The young man and his wife from Manitoba had driven east until they were in an area where they expected to find Amish or Old Order Mennonites. My covered buggy prompted them to stop and ask questions. I directed them to our home, where we entertained them, giving them a bed for the night, and a few meals. We enjoyed their visit, and they seemed to feel the same about their stay with us.

During the course of our conversation, we asked them about their weather.

"We have quite wet weather at present," the man replied. "We had fourteen inches of rain in two weeks' time."

How remarkable! Isn't that about the amount you sometimes have in a year?

He smiled. "Last year we had eleven inches, and the year before only three."

In two weeks they received as much rain as had fallen in the previous two whole years! Surely such scanty rainfall would have meant drought, if not a complete crop failure. Such an irregular rainfall pattern would have found most of us complaining in southern Ontario.

Since I had never been to Manitoba, I found it difficult to grasp this situation. How did they live through those two years? Were they able to irrigate? Did they live on crop insurance? I did not have the nerve to ask. In my experience, three inches of rain for a whole year would have meant barely any crop to speak of. I was reminded of our former neighbor who years ago had lived in western Canada. After a severe drought, one of his neighbors, a widow, had picked up a handful of shriveled grain and remarked, "Thank God for this much!"

My neighbor found it amusing to be thankful for a near crop failure. I didn't. To me, it showed an attitude lacking among us.

We have good reason to be thankful for even the most pitiful of harvests. How many areas in the world are blessed with such consistent weather as we are accustomed to? Where in the world would there be more reason to be thankful than here?

Are we as thankful for these benefits as we should be, or while the less-privileged say, "Thank God for this much," do we still complain? We complain when our mail does not go through on a certain day, and when the postal rates go up. In less-privileged countries, the mail service may be much less dependable and the costs higher, Yet they would possibly say, "Thank God for this much."

We complain if the stores do not have the exact brand of food we want. We go from store to store to find the best bargains. In third-world countries, people feel lucky if there is food on the store shelves. Even then, they may not have money to buy it.

In our country, the food wasted by many a family would feed another family quite well in some countries. If the poor people in some countries had access to our garbage cans, they would likely say, "Thank God for this much." We have the privilege of attending church every Sunday and listening to the preacher of our choice.

We have numerous Bibles in our homes, collecting dust. If the people of some countries had access to our neglected Bibles and the opportunity to attend any Christian church, would they simply say, "Thank God for this much"? No! They would count it as a blessing beyond their imagination!

If such people could see our country, where the average family has two cars, color TV, a cottage by the lake, and all manner of conveniences and luxuries, they would not imagine that such people would have any complaints.

It would be beyond their wildest fancy that one could spend as much time with amusements and recreation as at work, and still complain about the price of food! It would seem still more mystifying that in spite of their complaints, such people would refuse to buy meats available at less than a dollar per pound, and pay four times as much for fancy meats!

We are a spoiled nation. If anyone has reason to be thankful, it is surely us. Yet we take all our benefits for granted and forget to be thankful. Perhaps if we spent a year among some of the underprivileged people of the world, and tried to live as they do, we would learn to say from our hearts, "Thank God for this much!"

"Honestly, I think we have reason to be ashamed of our wastefulness."

Our neighbor's wife asked us some time ago what we do with pigs' feet, jowls, and trimmings when we butcher. We told her that we make liver sausage with them.

"My men don't like liver sausage," she said, "but I'll make something of it, and they'll eat it. After spending Christmas with our daughter on the mission field, and seeing how the natives eat, no meat will be wasted at our house!"

## Ontario's Legal Gambling Gambol

Reading daily newspapers is not my forte, if for no other reason than that I subscribe to none. I rarely see the work of regular columnists, and that lack may be reflected in my own writing.

A recent column by Pierre Berton, however, caught my eye. He echoed my views precisely. Or I should say, I echoed his.

Ever since Wintario made its appearance, I was forced to wonder at our Ontario government's attitude regarding gambling. Up to that time, I had understood that gambling was illegal in our province.

As the father of a sizable family, I knew that I could not expect to be respected if I did things that I forbade them to do. Such a stand would seem hypocritical to me and to my children, too! It was one thing for the government to make gambling legal. But now the government itself runs a gambling operation and promotes it. This hardly fosters respect.

Berton commented on the puzzling morality of the present government's casinos. One could almost assume that morality was missing. He asserted that poor people, who can least afford it, are the ones who will gamble, in the vain hope of growing rich.

Some years ago, I made a similar remark in a letter to the editor of the local paper. A personal letter from an executive of the lottery in question proved my point. He denied that poor people are the ones who gamble. Why would he have condescended to reply to my letter, if my assumption had not been correct?

Berton asked whether this is what we want. Is it prudent to foster a society that expects something for nothing? I pose another question: Is it primarily a vote-getter? As Mennonites, whose Christian principles hopefully are deeply imbedded in our very natures, we must carry the query one step further. Is gambling scriptural? There are numerous Scripture texts showing that we are expected to work for our bread (for example, Prov. 6:6; 2 Thess. 3:10-12). Nowhere do we find encouragement to win anything without putting forth an effort.

Our changing society induces many deviations from old, accepted values. Labor unions detract from a sense of craftsmanship. Instead, the only goals for unionized labor seem to be the paycheck and as many benefits as possible. The chief aim is getting the "mostest for the leastest."

To expect something for nothing, whether by gambling or by common inertia, is parallel to the story in our school readers of the lazy frog. He was waiting for Providence to send a fly.

Sooner or later, we all have to learn that there "ain't no free lunch." The sooner a person wins by gambling, the more certain his downfall. Such a person is destined to become a parasite, living off the honest working man.

In this respect, the Unemployment Insurance Commission unwittingly encourages such parasites. New social benefits would be much more effective if they were not violated by those who desire to have something for nothing.

We can feel thankful that we still have freedom of the press in our country, Writers such as Berton, David Suzuki, and our own Gordon Hunsberger, can be an inspiration to many. However, the discerning reader must still decide what is edifying, since the same freedom of the press tolerates undesirable views. It is up to the writer to express views that are edifying, prudent, and morally sound. We must remember that without freedom of the press, such columns could not exist.

"I well remember the story of the lazy frog. At that time, it was an interesting story. Now, thinking back, it is much more. By now I can see that we have many 'lazy frogs' among us. The sad fact is that our government feeds them at our expense. I know they don't mean to do that, but it is altogether too easy for freeloaders to cash in on such benefits."

I'm not trying to set myself up as some sort of expert, but I get no satisfaction out of winning something into which I put no effort. Possibly it is a form of pride in trying to prove that I can look after number one.

"That's nothing to be ashamed of. I can understand that especially from an older person's viewpoint. I can well remember when many honest workers refused to accept unemployment insurance, because they were ashamed to do so."

"I liked your comparison of the government to a father. In this instance, it works no better than if a father did things that his son was not expected or allowed to do. But then, maybe our government doesn't expect to earn our respect."

## Mennonites and Music

Sometimes it seems I have a mean streak in me. Whenever I come across anything written about Mennonites, I pull it apart at the seams to see how accurate or inaccurate it is. If I find something with which I agree, I pounce on it eagerly.

Sometimes such articles come from the most unlikely sources. A local police officer recently brought me a manuscript with the heading: "Mennonites and Music—Microsoft Internet Explorer." I must admit that my knowledge of the Internet is only a little less than the officer's knowledge of Mennonites—I hope.

I offer my responses to a series of quotations from this manuscript:

> Mennonite kids grow up making music an important part of their lives. It leads to a maturity of sound, and the ability to carry parts, and enjoy it. It's such a natural part of their environment that they are simply capable of doing things other people have to learn.

I agree. I have often been asked when I learned to sing a certain song. Often this precedes my memory. Hundreds of songs I learned over seventy years ago from my dad as he sang while milking.

> Although Mennonites regard singing as integral to church life, an affinity was not immediately apparent at the beginning of the Anabaptist movement in the sixteenth century.

I doubt that. First, Paul and Silas prayed and sang praises unto God (Acts 16:25). The Anabaptists were disciples of Paul, so to speak. Why should they not sing as well? Second, the Anabaptists composed hymns in prison, so they must have had an early affinity for music. Third, in writings taken from the time of the Anabaptists, it was stated that they sang at their meetings. In fact, the *Ausbund* was already in use among the Anabaptists in 1564.

Brought to North America, in the early eighteenth century, this hymnal [the *Ausbund*] is still used by the Amish in the U.S., and the Amish and Old Order Mennonites in Canada.

Try again. The Amish, yes; but the Old Order Mennonites, no! The early Mennonite settlers in Ontario brought the *Unpartheyisches Gesangbuch* (Impartial hymnbook, 1804), the Lancaster Conference hymnal, with them from Pennsylvania. In 1836, a pocket-sized hymnbook, the *Gemeinschaftliche Liedersammlung* (Common hymn collection), was compiled and printed in Canada. This has become the exclusive hymnbook among the Ontario Old Order Mennonites.

The Old Order Mennonites, a conservative group in southern Ontario, only permit unaccompanied unison singing.

Yes, at church services. At other, informal singings, there is un-accompanied four-part singing from English hymnbooks.

There is concern today that the Mennonite emphasis on quality four-part singing may be dying out.

Not among the Old Order Mennonites, whether in Ontario, Pennsylvania, Virginia, or elsewhere. Perhaps it should not be called "quality" singing; but at least it continues to be a combination of worship service and pleasure, enjoyed by young and old.

Music has long been important to Mennonite faith and life.

Amen. So shall it be.
"So you have an 'affinity for music'?"
I imagine that is what one could call it. I wouldn't like to say that I have the best voice, but I have always enjoyed singing. I

was a song leader in church, as well as at singings. So were two of my brothers, my father and my grandfather. I have the latter's hymnbook in my possession, which he used when a song leader in 1892.

"Did Benjamin Eby compile the *Gemeinschaftliche* hymnbook that was first printed in 1836?"

This is difficult to say. It is commonly supposed that he did, since he had an interest in the printery. Many of the hymns originated in Lutheran or Reformed hymnals. Whenever the composer's identity is not given with a hymn, it was likely composed by Mennonites.

"Are these hymnals used only in Ontario, by the Old Order?"

They are also used by the Old Order Mennonites in Elkhart County, Indiana.

"Are there still singing schools in operation among the Old Order Mennonites?"

Yes, although it is not necessarily practiced on a regular basis. There is always enough interest in singing schools to warrant their existence. Yet sometimes there is a lack of teachers. Our young people have singings every Sunday evening. There is always good singing at weddings, family gatherings, and frequently at nursing homes and with shut-ins.

## Happiness Is—

Are you happy? If not, why not?

Many of us are not too sure just what happiness is. The advertising media would like to tell us that happiness comes as a result of buying certain brands of clothing, food, or cars. Yet if our happiness depends on our favorable reaction toward TV commercials, it must indeed be quite superficial.

Doting mothers try to make their children happy at an early date. They tickle the baby's chin to make him or her laugh, which is considered to be a sure sign of happiness. As the baby grows older, he may sometimes fret and cry for attention. The mother picks him up to stop his crying, apparently making him happy by doing so. Later, the child wants candy, toys, or whatever catches his or her eye, throwing a tantrum if he does not get it. The mother gives in, to make the child happy.

About this time the mother realizes (if she has not done so before) that her indulgence is not bringing enduring happiness. It almost seems to her that the child's desires are addicting: the more he gets, the more he wants. If she fully realizes this, she has learned a valuable lesson. But it may already be too late for the child's welfare.

Quite obviously there are some who feel that the Old Order Mennonites are too narrow-minded for the good of their children. They believe that we are hampering their chances for development. According to them, if we even offer them guidance in making decisions for their future, we are not allowing them to make a personal choice, but are resorting to coercion to gain our ends.

"Train up a child in the way he should go; and when he is old, he will not depart from it" (Prov. 22:6). These are the words of the wisest man known to have existed. Although they appear in the Old Testament, they still offer sound advice, and there is little danger of being led astray by heeding them.

Happiness is definitely a state of mind. Through the experiences of my own childhood, and what I gained while raising a dozen children, I am firmly convinced that there is little if any relationship between happiness and the abundance of possessions or the lack of them. However, I am just as firmly convinced that there is a definite relationship between happiness and peace of mind. Happiness does not bring peace of mind; but peace of mind brings contentment, and contentment brings happiness.

As can be seen from the example of the doting mother, it is obviously necessary to be reasonably firm with children before they are able to make their own decisions. Naturally, we must be patient with them; but we must also be mature enough ourselves to say no when necessary.

As they grow older and have learned to know right from wrong, it should no longer be necessary to use such firm methods. However, if we truly love our children, we will still advise them to follow the paths that in our opinion will lead to their souls' salvation. We do not need to coerce or intimidate them. Nevertheless, it is our duty to try to lead and instruct them in the ways toward which our experience and our understanding of the Scriptures direct us.

If we do less than this, we are betraying them and may be held responsible for our actions on the great day of judgment.

"Do you think Old Order children are as happy as those who can have whatever they want?"

I think they are happier. Recollections of my own childhood reveal that there were indeed things I desired and couldn't have. Knowing that it was useless asking for such things, I soon gave up. My experience tells me that the child who expects to get everything he asks for is never happy for any length of time. He spends his time begging for the next thing, while he soon forgets what he just received.

"We don't usually refer to grown-ups as being happy, but rather as contented. Do you think Old Order grown-ups are as contented as those among the general public?"

In general, yes. Those who are satisfied to live according to scriptural teachings, who go the second mile in avoiding offenses, and love their neighbors as themselves—they are certainly the most contented.

"It seems your answer is redundant. You say those who are satisfied . . . are the most contented. Isn't that the same thing?"

You're right. Instead of saying "those who are satisfied," I should have said "those who are willing" to live scripturally, to avoid offenses, and to love their neighbors. Human nature does not bring this willingness, but humility, meekness, and lowliness does.

Such people will not necessarily react as do children whom we count as being happy, but they will show a meek and quiet spirit, which causes contentment. As Paul says, "Godliness with contentment is great gain" (1 Tim. 6:6).

"What about the rest?"

The rest are never satisfied. They react in the same way as spoiled children do. Here I am referring to extreme cases. The majority of church members are somewhere in between the two extremes. They know that too much leeway is not good for the church, so they satisfy themselves and are also contented.

## On the Road to Unbelief

A recent column in a local weekly newspaper had a bit of disturbing news for me. The United Nations no longer considers Canada as a Christian country. Even though about two-thirds of Canadians attend church, the figure is decreasing. The greatest decrease is among the long-established mainline churches. In some areas at least, Pentecostal, Baptist, and Jehovah's Witness churches are increasing. So are the New Age and similar organizations.

Perhaps the most disturbing trend is towards borderline Christianity. Many people attending church are no more than nominal Christians. There are even churches whose Christianity is little more than nominal.

Observers give several reasons for lukewarm Christianity:

• The church and its message have not changed enough with the times. Personally, I feel that they have changed too much already.

• People no longer look to the church as their social organization. In my opinion, there are too many other and more self-gratifying societies.

• Christian doctrine is incompatible with today's way of living. Instead, we say that today's way of living is incompatible with Christian doctrine.

• Too many people have seen the obvious inconsistencies among professing Christians. Yes, that's exactly the point.

There is a reason to be gravely concerned about this trend. It sounds quite similar to the Spirit's warning to the church at Laodicea:

I know your works, that you are neither cold nor hot; I would that you were cold or hot. So then, because you are lukewarm, and neither cold nor hot, I will spue you out of my mouth. . . . You say, I am rich, and increased in goods, and have need of nothing. (Rev. 3:15-17)

One can well imagine the thoughts of such nominal Christians today. They attend church and pay their dues. They are no drunkards, thieves, or murderers. They are respected citizens in the community. What more need we expect of them? It is not too difficult to understand why the Spirit said, "I would that you were cold or hot." The complacent ones, those who smugly believe that they are tolerable Christians, are harder to reach than gross sinners, whose guilt stares them in the face at every turn.

We have reason to be gravely concerned for such nominal Christians, and for Christianity in general. Lukewarm church members are not very receptive to living out the Christian faith in daily life. Especially the young people are wide open to anti-Christian doctrine and cults.

There is another and more immediate cause for concern. In the Mennonite church, how do we stack up on this issue? Are we free from lukewarmness, complacency, and smugness? We go to church every Sunday and are within the bounds of respectability. Our young people attend church and become baptized. The church is steadily growing. Is that all we need?

If our Christianity goes no deeper than this, we are in the same boat as the Laodiceans. We would do well to pay attention to what the Spirit further says to the church at Laodicea:

> I counsel you to buy of me gold tried in the fire, that you may be rich; and white raiment, that you may be clothed, and that the shame of your nakedness does not appear; and anoint your eyes with eyesalve, that you may see. (Rev. 3:18)

"I have a question I'd like to ask. I think I know the answer, but I want to hear it from the horse's mouth. Do you believe in the Bible in its entirety?"

Yes, definitely.

"Then you believe that the reasons given for lukewarm Christianity are really the result of partial unbelief."

I have no other answer for it. Why should the church and its message change with the times? Why should we expect Christ's doctrine to adjust itself to modern standards of living? At the risk of stepping on someone's toes, I ask, Why should we seek a social organization that is totally separate from the church?

"The answer to that, as I understand it, is so that the church need not bear the social load as well as the spiritual."

"Sometimes I wonder whether we are trying to carry too great a load of social programs. If our spirituality were greater, perhaps we wouldn't need such great separate social circles."

Yes, I think we could all benefit by a little more spirituality. That definitely includes our Old Order churches. We pride ourselves in having the church as the focal point of our young peoples' social circle; yet we would feel very uncomfortable about having their social activities in the church! That would never work.

## Institutionalism

Sort of an awkward title, huh? A little too highfalutin for ordinary people like us? Perhaps so; but 150 years ago, it caused a church division among the Mennonites.

My dictionary gives the meaning of the word as the emphasis on organization (as in religion) at the expense of other factors.

In 1847, John H. Oberholzer was an intelligent young Mennonite minister in the Franconia Conference of Eastern Pennsylvania. Among other things, he insisted that the minutes of the conference should be recorded. The rest of the ministers thought there were more important topics on which to focus. As a result, Oberholzer found himself at odds with the church, together with a number of members.

Several years later, he joined Daniel Hoch of Jordan, Ontario, who was likewise in disfavor with the church. This group was later joined by a sizable number of Mennonites who were emigrating from the Ukraine, to form the nucleus of the General Conference Mennonite Church. Some time ago, I had the privilege of translating the yearbook of their first ten years. It was so highly organized that a number of pages had headings with no entries underneath!

Organization in religion at the expense of other factors is positively not the way to go in the Old Order church. This reminds me of a young minister who asked an older one how to draw more people into the church. He had already tried box socials, bingo, strawberry festivals, and even a dance, without good results. "Why not try religion?" the older man suggested.

Institutionalism can take many forms. One common form is to elect committees for every function of the church. The *Mennonite Cyclopedic Dictionary* lists fifteen such organizations among the Mennonites. In the 1840s the Temperance Society was strong in some churches. The Mennonites conferred and decided that the church already had a commitment to temperance, so there was no need for a separate society to distract from the functions of the church.

The various lodges, secret societies, clubs, leagues, and the Legion—all function separately from the church and have a tendency to emphasize other institutions at the expense of the church. Of course, the church itself is an institution (and much more), but that is just the point. As Christians, we cannot allow any other organization to supersede God's church, the body of Christ. Jesus said, "Those who do not take their cross and follow after me, are not worthy of me" (Matt. 10:38).

The Old Order Mennonite church has a unique organization. The church is the center of the social circle. The young people's Sunday evening singings are planned on the church grounds. The visiting among the older, married people also centers on the church; the church district where (rotating) services are held, is the area where visitors are expected, usually unannounced. Rather than distracting from the church, this system ensures church attendance. Any other institution, that is not church based, would tend to distract from church attendance.

In the 1889 division in Ontario, the two senior bishops, Abraham Martin and Amos Cressman, both tried to lead their respective flocks according to Christian principles. They agreed that the church needed a revival. The problem was that those who spearheaded the revival leaned more toward Methodism than toward a revival of the Anabaptist teachings. Peter Sherk in his letters repeatedly wondered why they still called themselves Mennonites, when they were indeed more like Methodists. This methodistic leaning was more highly organized than the Mennonites were accustomed to having, smacking strongly of institutionalism.

In the 1893 division in Lancaster, there were several uncharitable incidents which hindered a peaceful settlement, if indeed one was sought. The aggressive act of the Lichty's building committee, superseding church authority by installing a pulpit without taking counsel, was without excuse. Even less charitable was the secretive removal of the same, by opposing parties.

"One would have thought John H. Oberholtzer's views would have been a trivial matter."

Probably; but he was far too aggressive in his views; his institutionalism ran hopelessly amok.

Since our churches enjoy a rural setting, they are intrinsically a part of the farming community, or more properly, the farming community is a part of the church—practically our only institution. That is as we want it to be.

# Elderhostel,
# Part 2

◆ ◆ ◆

# Observing the Sabbath

In the beginning, God created heaven and earth. During the first six days, God set the earth in order, to divide night and day, and bring all living creatures into being, including human beings. On the seventh day, God rested from all his work, sanctifying and hallowing the day.

In the Ten Commandments, the Lord decreed: "Six days shall you labor, and do all your work; but the seventh day is the Sabbath of the Lord thy God. In it you shall not do any work" (Exod. 20:9-10).

This is why we come together every seven days to worship God. Besides, it is a recognized fact that we need a day of rest after six days of labor. However, there is one thing that confuses most of us. Although we do work for six days, followed by a day of rest, our seventh day is not the Sabbath, but Sunday. In Germany and Switzerland, the calendar week begins on Monday and ends on Sunday, which then is the seventh day. Still, it is not really the Sabbath.

Personally, I am quite well satisfied with the system adopted in our country, since the ratio, six to one, is the same. However, some denominations adhere to the Jewish Sabbath and accuse us of changing the divine order from the Sabbath to Sunday. Some claim that the Catholic Church issued a decree to change the day of rest from Saturday to Sunday. By accepting that change, we are accepting the authority of the Catholic Church. I disagree.

The ceremonial law given through Moses directed how the Jewish Sabbath should be kept. For example, a man who picked up sticks on the Sabbath was to be stoned to death (Num. 15:32-36).

Christ ushered in the new dispensation of grace when he was raised triumphant from the tomb. Even in the Old Testament, there was a foreshadowing of the Lord's Day to supersede the Jewish Sabbath. In Leviticus 23:7, we read, "In the *first day* you shall have an holy convocation: you shall do no servile work therein." Verses 10-11 continue:

When you come into the land which I give unto you, and shall reap the harvest thereof, then you shall bring a sheaf of the *firstfruits* of your harvest unto the priest, and he shall wave the sheaf before the Lord, to be accepted for you: on the *morrow after the Sabbath* the priest shall wave it.

In 1 Corinthians 15:3-4, Paul says, "Christ died for our sins. . . . He was buried, and he rose again on the third day [the first day of the week] according to the Scriptures." Verse 20 continues, "Now is Christ risen from the dead, and become the *firstfruits* of those who slept." This holy convocation was on the first day, and consisted of the *firstfruits* of the harvest. Now, in the new dispensation, Christ arose from the dead on the first day of the week, to become the *firstfruits* (in resurrection) of those who slept (died).

Careful reading shows that the apostles gathered for worship on the first day of the week, surely in response to the appearances of the risen Lord on that day (Mark 16:2 and Gospel parallels). Acts 20:7 says, "Upon the first day of the week, when the disciples came together to break bread, Paul preached unto them." First Corinthians 16:2 also exhorts, "Upon the first day of the week, let every one of you lay by him in store, as God hath prospered him."

Justin Martyr wrote in his *First Apology*,

On the day called Sunday, all who live in cities or in the country gather together to one place, and the memoirs of the apostles or the writings of the prophets are read, as long as time permits. . . . Then we all rise together and pray. . . . Bread and wine and water are brought, and the president in like manner also offers prayers and thanksgiving, according to his ability, and the people assent, saying Amen; and there is a distribution to each. . . . Sunday is the day on which we all hold our common assembly, because it is the first day on which God, having wrought a change in the darkness and matter, made the world; and Jesus Christ our Savior on the same day rose from the dead. (chap. 67)

Justin (ca. 100-165) wrote this testimony about fifty years after the apostle John's death. John "was in the Spirit on the Lord's day" when he received the visions and messages in the book of Revelation (1:10). This shows that Sunday was the day for religious service during the time of the early church fathers. The apostolic fathers referred to the "first day of the week," "Sunday," or "the Lord's day" as the day for assembling together for divine service.

If the pope changed the Sabbath by decree, it had nothing to do with us. There is no doubt but that we observe the Lord's day because our forebears did so.

"Is there any scriptural justification for observing Sunday as the day of rest?"

Personally, I would say there is no absolute proof of it. In Revelation 1:10, John said, "I was in the Spirit on the Lord's day." This does not say when the Lord's day was, but almost surely it means what we call Sunday. In Leviticus 23:10-11, the Lord spoke to Moses, "You shall bring a sheaf of the *firstfruits* of your harvest; . . . on the morrow *after* the Sabbath the priest shall wave it." Paul builds on this in 1 Corinthians 15:20: "Now is Christ risen from the dead [when? on the day *after* the Sabbath] and become the *firstfruits* of those who slept." Jesus in Matthew 12:8 says, "The Son of Man is Lord even of the Sabbath day."

Christ arose on the Lord's day (Sunday). After the resurrection, the disciples gathered together on the first day of the week. This is no final proof in favor of observing Sunday; neither is there reason for observing the Sabbath.

The command to keep the Sabbath holy is indeed one of the Ten Commandments. But when faced with human needs on the Sabbath, Jesus Christ himself said, "The Sabbath was made for man, and not man for the Sabbath. Therefore the Son of Man is Lord also of the Sabbath" (Mark 2:28). With Christ and his followers, the Pharisees' rigid observance of the Sabbath fell by the wayside.

## Avoiding the Unequal Yoke

"Be not unequally yoked together with unbelievers" (2 Cor. 6:14).

Some years ago, a Mennonite businessman approached another Mennonite about joining his business association. When the latter quoted the above verses, the businessman exploded: "What? Are you calling me an unbeliever? I'm a Mennonite, too!"

Both men were right. What some people fail to understand is that if we join an association that includes unbelievers, we are associating with them, regardless of how many fellow believers are included. That is one of the reasons why we as Old Order Mennonites are not in favor of open communion.

A similar incident occurred about five years ago. A sincere Christian man and his family attended our Mennonite church for the first time. Since it happened to be our communion Sunday, the man expected to be able to take communion. When this was refused, he was deeply offended. To my knowledge, he has never attended a Mennonite church since.

Several of us have tried to explain why we cannot conscientiously give communion to strangers, without knowing more about them. On the other hand, on what grounds was he ready to have communion with us, not knowing whether we were worthy of his fellowship? He was unable or unwilling to understand this viewpoint.

What comprises the unequal yoke? We generally think of this in terms of a binding contract such as a marriage, a brotherhood, or an association where an agreement is signed. Paul gives us a clue to the intended interpretation in the passage that follows the quotation above (2 Cor. 6:14-18). He uses words such as "fellowship," "communion," "concord," and "part." Thus, any intimate relationship would be included.

Who should be classed as unbelievers? Not many of us would wish to have an intimate friendship with one who professes unbelief. However, anyone who professes partial unbelief must be considered as an unbeliever, because God's Word is indivisible.

Rejecting part of God's Word is in effect rejecting God. We

cannot serve two masters. Those who reject Christ's words, "Swear not at all," "Resist not evil," and "Love your enemies," are seriously tampering with unbelief (Matt. 5:34, 39, 44). So are those who reject creation and the virgin birth.

Old Order Mennonites believe that marriage should only be contemplated between those of like faith and belief (1 Cor. 7:39). We believe that membership in labor unions is contrary to the will of God, not only because of the unequal yoke, but also because of the unions' selfish aims and sometimes violent actions.

Membership in any association that is open to unbelievers constitutes the unequal yoke. To join a secret society is to become involved in more than the unequal yoke, since it detracts from the church.

Becoming involved in social activities that are open to everyone is probably on the borderline of the unequal yoke. Too much association with those of doubtful integrity has a tendency to break down one's own moral standards. Besides, many social functions are not compatible with our way of life.

We do indeed have a responsibility to minister to those who have not tasted the grace of God, whenever and wherever this is possible. However, this need not be in an intimate, social environment. Helping them in time of need will have more of an effect than socializing will have.

We are not of the world, but Christ has chosen us out of the world (John 15:19; 17:14-16). If we could more fully demonstrate and prove this to be true, our testimony would be more effective than it is at present.

"I have been told that the Old Order Mennonites are antisocial. Would you support this viewpoint?"

I agree that there are certain practices among us that could be interpreted as being antisocial. Were you told on what grounds this assumption was based?

"Yes, it was because you do not support the Kinsmen and Lions' Clubs. They claim that they are doing a good work, worthy of your support."

This is probably true; yet has anybody explained to you why the church could not accomplish the same service?

"No, I don't think so. Perhaps they would say they don't wish to load down the church with all the responsibilities."

This matter has been debated for a long time. In 1842, the Methodists introduced a Temperance Organization. The Mennonite conference decided there should be no need to join a temperance society, since intemperance had already been renounced at the time of baptism. In 1844, the conference endorsed the previous statement: that the influence of the Lord's church and the Holy Spirit should be sufficiently strong, that we do not need to join special societies, and make special vows and pledges in association with persons outside of the church.

This line of thought is no denial of the fine type of people commonly found in service clubs, nor do we wish to belittle the good work they accomplish. Instead, we suggest giving them our moral support insofar as it does not infringe upon the dictates of our consciences.

## Biblical Principles

When the Mennonite Church of today began in 1525, the main issue that separated the Anabaptists from the state churches was their firm belief in baptism on faith. This is still one of the chief tenets of our faith, as in the first biblical principle below:

### Baptism on Faith

Mark 1:15: "Repent and believe the gospel."

Acts 2:38: "Repent, and be baptized, every one of you."

Acts 8:37: "If you believe with all your heart, you may [be baptized]."

Romans 3:22: "The righteousness of God through faith in Christ Jesus is for all who believe."

### Nonresistance

Romans 12:17-19, 21: "Recompense to no one evil for evil. . . . If it be possible, live peaceably with all people. . . . Avenge not yourselves, but rather give room for [God's] wrath. . . . Be not overcome of evil, but overcome evil with good."

### Rejection of Oaths

Matthew 5:33, 37: "Swear not at all. . . . Let your communication be, Yea, yea; and Nay, nay. For whatsoever is more than these comes of evil."

### Pride

Romans 12:2: "Do not be conformed to this world, but be transformed by the renewing of your mind."

First Peter 3:3-4: "Whose adorning let it not be . . . the outward adorning of plaiting the hair, and of wearing of gold, or of putting on of apparel, but let it be the ornament of a meek and quiet spirit; which is in the sight of God of great price."

First Timothy 2:9: "That women adorn themselves in modest apparel, with shamefacedness and sobriety."

First John 2:15-16 "Love not the world. . . . For all that is in the world, the lust of the flesh, and the lust of the eyes, and the pride of life, is not of the Father, but is of the world."

### Role of Woman

First Timothy 2:12: "I suffer not a woman to teach, nor to usurp authority over the man; but to be in silence."

First Peter 3:1: "You wives, be in subjection to your own husbands; that if any obey not the word, they may be won by the chaste conversation of the wives."

Colossians 3:18: "Wives, submit yourselves unto your own husbands."

### Role of Man

Colossians 3:19: "Husband, love your wives, and be not bitter against them."

Ephesians 5:23, 25: "The husband is the head of the wife, even as Christ is the head of the church. . . . Husbands, love your wives, even as Christ also loved the church."

First Corinthians 11:4, 7: "Every man praying or prophesying, having his head covered, dishonors his head. A man indeed ought not to cover his head, as he is the image and glory of God."

### Women's Veiling

First Corinthians 11:5, 13: "Every woman that prays or prophesies with her head uncovered dishonors her head. . . . Is it comely that a woman pray unto God uncovered?"

### Compulsion

Matthew 18:28, 30, 34-35: "He laid hands on him, and took him by the throat, saying, Pay me that you owe. . . . And he would not, but went and cast him into prison. . . . And his lord was furious, and delivered him to the tormentors. So likewise shall my heavenly Father do also unto you, if you from your hearts forgive not every one his brother their trespasses."

### Feet Washing

John 13:14-17: "If I then, your Lord and Master, have washed your feet, you also ought to wash one another's feet. For I have given you an example, that you should do as I have done to you. Verily, verily, I say unto you, The servant is not greater than his lord, neither he that is sent greater than he that sent him. If you know these things, happy [RSV: blessed] are you if you do them."

## Church Discipline

Matthew 18:15-17: "Moreover if your brother [or sister] sins . . . , go and tell him his fault, between you and him alone. If he listens to you, you have gained your brother. But if he does not listen, take one or two others along with you, that every word may be confirmed by the evidence of two or three witnesses. If he refuses to listen to them, tell it to the church; and if he refuses to listen even to the church, let him be to you as a Gentile and tax collector" (RSV).

Luke 17:3: "If your brother trespass against you, rebuke him; and if he repents, forgive him."

Galatians 6:1: "If someone be overtaken with a fault, restore such an one in the spirit of meekness."

"Are these biblical principles still in force, and are they all being practiced by the Old Order Mennonites?"

"Yes, but taking human weakness into consideration. Sometimes we do slip and don't carry every one of them out as fully as we should."

"Do you have any particular ones in mind?"

"Yes, we must constantly keep struggling against pride. The lust of the eyes, the lust of the flesh, and the pride of life—these are a constant struggle."

## *Blessed Assurance*

If a stranger had come to Waterloo County when I was a boy, and inquired about the Old Order Mennonites, he would have received varied answers, depending on whom he asked. The most discreditable answers would likely have come from a liberal Mennonite. One of the answers would have been that they are "clothes Christians," that they depend on outward appearance and good works to get them to heaven.

About that time, a group arose, mostly young people, who claimed to have eternal security. Since this group and the Old Mennonites were poles apart, it was difficult for them to even discuss their differences rationally. Old Order members bent over backwards not to identify with the extremists. As a result, one young man told me that his (Old Order) mother might have a trace of the Holy Spirit, but his father had none at all. To this my father responded, "When he sits in church with the tears coursing down his cheeks, it shows the presence of the Spirit."

Paul, in writing to the Romans on the subject of salvation, presents a very positive attitude, especially in the closing verses of chapter 8: "For I am persuaded that neither death, nor life, nor angels, nor principalities, nor powers, nor things present, nor things to come, nor height, nor depth, nor any other creature, shall be able to separate us from the love of God, which is in Christ Jesus our Lord."

Quite positive, eh? Or has Paul omitted something?

Now turn to the closing verses of chapter 7: "O wretched man that I am! Who shall deliver me from the body of this death? I thank God through Jesus Christ our Lord. So then with the mind I myself serve the law of God; but with the flesh the law of sin." Thus a lifelong struggle follows. As long as we are faithful to God, nothing can take away our heritage; but if we fall into sin and refuse to repent, we can just as easily lose this inheritance.

So this is a lifelong struggle. How does this theory compare with Paul's teachings elsewhere? In Ephesians 2:8-9, he writes: "For by grace are you saved through faith, and not of yourselves; it is the gift of God: not of works, lest any one should boast."

Romans 6:23: "For the wages of sin is death, but the gift of God is eternal life through Jesus Christ our Lord."

Martin Luther taught salvation by faith alone. This is what most Christian churches teach today. Yet the early Christians taught more than that. In James 2:14, 17, we read, "What does it profit, my brothers [and sisters], though a man say he has faith, and have not works? . . . Even so, faith if it does not have works, is dead, being alone." In Revelation 14:13, John says, "Blessed are the dead who die in the Lord, from henceforth; yea, says the Spirit, that they may rest from their labors, and their works do follow them."

Both the doctrine of eternal security and the one on predestination offer a crown without a cross. As long as the theory is not carried to the extreme, the promise of God's care is there for the faithful ones. Predestination is scriptural insofar as it teaches the omniscience of God:

> He knows the present and the past,
>   He knows what is to be;
> and I can safely trust in Him
>   who plans my life for me.
>         (C. E. Breck, "He Plans My Life," *Life Songs*
>         [MPH, 1916], 224)

Some contend that, since God knows which will be the saved ones and who will be lost, it makes no difference how we live. They underestimate God's omnipotence. It is because God knows at the beginning what our choice will be, that he knows who will be the saved and the unsaved. If we throw up our hands and give up, he knows about that decision too.

Paul told the Corinthians, "I have planted, Apollos watered, but God gave the increase. So then neither is he that planted anything, neither he that waters; but God who gives the increase [or: the gift]. Now he who plants and he who waters are one; and every man shall receive his own reward according to his labor" (1 Cor. 3:6-8). That is what the Old Order Mennonites believe.

"You mentioned Paul's positive attitude in the closing verses of Romans 8. Then you asked, 'Has he omitted something?' Are you suggesting that something was omitted?"

I meant that we need to consult the whole Scriptures, rather than a verse or two. I believe that Romans 8:38-39 is indeed true: that nothing, nor anybody, can separate us from the love of God, if we steadfastly walk in the light, as he himself is in the light (1 John 1:7). However, I also believe that if we grow unconcerned, we can separate ourselves from the love of God.

"What do you mean by a crown without a cross?"

In part, I refer to Matthew 11:28-30. We must take Christ's yoke and bear it patiently; if we do so, the yoke is easy, and the burden is light. If we refuse to learn from him, and refuse to become meek and lowly of heart, we shall not find rest for our souls. The cross is easy to bear if we are meek and lowly.

## Elias Eby's Views

Elias Eby, second son of Benjamin Eby, pioneer bishop in Waterloo County, Ontario, was a well-informed man and a fluent writer. He kept a diary from 1872 to his death in 1878. This diary, housed in the archives in the Kitchener Public Library, reflects his views of current affairs. A few typical excerpts, translated from German, follow.

◆ ◆ ◆

August 5, 1872. Christian S. Huber of Bosanquet [near Sarnia, Ontario] was here today. He has much to boast of his piety and great conversion. This may be true, but we have only his word for it. [Huber was a brother-in-law to Samuel Schlichter, a minister with the General Conference Mennonites.]

November 24, 1872. We were at Ebys in meeting. Wismer and Solomon Eby preached. [Daniel Wismer had joined a more liberal Mennonite church for a while, then returned to the Old Mennonites and was ordained at Eby's meetinghouse. Solomon Eby was ordained for Port Elgin, but later helped to start what became the Missionary Church.]

I think Solomon Eby should first obey the church rules and regulations before he takes the liberty to preach in our meetinghouses. It is well-known and evident to him that it is not allowed for a preacher to baptize or to serve communion when a bishop is available, or offers to be at hand. On April 5, at the conference here in Berlin [Kitchener], Eby was told plainly by our bishops and other old faithful ministers, and told again, that it is not proper for him to encroach on the bishop's work.

Paying no attention to this, he went home to Port Elgin and

did according to his own judgment, baptized, and administered communion. Here, truly, a great disobedience is apparent.

Now this young man stands up in his own justification, in our meetinghouses, and tells us much about his conversion, and that out of love he would give his life for his Lord.

If he were to resign his own will and his obstinacy, I might possibly believe the above; but the way he conducts himself now, I can truly grant him little trust.

On this day none of our old ministers appeared here.

February 1874: Since January 23, D. Brenneman of Indiana is in this district. [In 1874 Daniel Brenneman, a minister at Goshen, and Solomon Eby of Ontario organized a group that became part of the Mennonite Brethren in Christ, now the Missionary Church.] He and D. Wismer hold meetings day and night, in schools, here and there in meetinghouses and in private dwellings, with would-be Mennonites, United Brethren, Methodists; in short, with anyone who accepts them. They carry on their work, German or English, without turning to our rules and regulations; but they wish to retain the Mennonite name, because they know that it stands fast and immovable.

These men had united and avowed themselves to this firmly grounded rule by their baptismal vows, and later through a decent walk of life gained the respect of the church. According to the church rules and regulations, they were called and instated as ministers of the Word, as teachers, preachers, and shepherds of the flock, which they also diligently practiced for some time by God's blessings. Too bad that such men now have strayed so far that they commune with those who despise our nonresistant faith, together with the church rules.

How can it be possible that these men wish to be our ministers, and also commune with those with whom they cannot be in agreement? Is this not being unequally yoked together? What can be the reason for all this confusion? Is it not willfulness and exaltation? Instead of the smallest, each wishes to be the greatest and foremost; instead of servants, they wish to be rulers and regents! That is not the meek spirit of Christ!

Brenneman handed out posters by which he advertised that he

would be at a certain hall in Berlin (Kitchener) on the evening of the twenty-fourth to proclaim Peace! Peace! Too bad that this self-styled peace messenger did not begin at home.

[The latter remark was referring to the troubles being experienced in Indiana at that time, when Wisler was excommunicated for being too conservative, and Brenneman the following year for being too liberal!]

◆ ◆ ◆

"Elias Eby must have had it in for the liberal preachers, Solomon Eby and Brenneman!"

Possibly; yet when Charles Eby, a Methodist missionary, gave a report on Switzerland, Elias attended, and he apparently enjoyed it!

### Social Assistance

Mike Harris pulled the rug out from under grants, subsidies, and social assistance. Since then, public outcries and complaints have been deafening. Nearly everyone seems to take it as a personal offense. Most people think that the man in the street suffers the most, while the filthy rich get by scot-free. This may be true; but we know that one cannot force the man with the whip hand. As for the rest of us, we know well enough that some have to tighten their belts. But there is no point in saying with Pooh, "Someone—but it ain't me!"

Some time during a tight spot in the recent recession, a non-Mennonite neighbor remarked, "This time, even the Mennonites feel the financial squeeze." This is natural. Many of them bear almost the same crippling overhead in interest on expensive equipment. They can no longer counterbalance this pressure through cost-effective measures of economy and frugality.

In one aspect of the economy, the Old Order Mennonites do come out on top. From the beginning, we have refused to share in personal benefits of social assistance. We have never accepted family allowance payments, partly on the grounds that our government administrators would have a better claim on our children in wartime, if they helped to raise and support them. Our reason for refusing to participate was partly because we did not approve of the principle. Old Age Pension, unemployment insurance, health and welfare insurance, and all similar forms of social benefits are among the personal benefits that we have refused.

Instead, we prefer to support a form of social protection among ourselves. Every father endeavors to raise and support his own children. If problems are encountered, other church members are willing to lend a hand. Aged and infirm members support themselves as long as possible. When funds run out, other family members take them in and look after them. If anyone runs into financial difficulties, the church will step into the breach if necessary.

Now, when social assistance is beginning to falter, our organizational structure is not dependent on governmental resources.

If pensions are cut, it does not affect us. Indeed, we have no big nest egg on which to draw. Our income is low, but so are our expenses. Why pay a high price to expand the waistline?

When grants, subsidies, crop insurance, and similar benefits were introduced, the church in general was reluctant to participate. Some members took advantage of dairy subsidy and other forms of assistance. Gradually a tangled web formed that seemed to draw us into too much dependency on the government. Finally, the church appointed a steering committee to identify and classify all forms of government assistance.

As a result, our church disapproved of all forms of grants, social assistance, insurance-type programs, and subsidies. Because of similar implications, we also placed milk subsidies on the disapproved list; earlier they had been granted rather reluctantly.

Rebates were tolerated. They were considered to be part of the farm business, since they represented a portion collected for a specific purpose, unrelated to the farming enterprise.

Recently I asked one of our dairymen whether he is satisfied with his milk check, without the subsidy.

He smiled. "I hardly notice the difference. The subsidy is being phased out for everyone. It's easier to accept this situation, now that we have decided to refuse it anyhow."

A voluntary sacrifice is easier to tolerate than one forged out with hammer and tongs.

"With public outcries against cutbacks in social assistance, what is the Old Order Mennonites view?"

In general, one hears little complaint about the economy and less displeasure with Mike Harris. Instead, the Old Order Mennonites are more inclined to feel that the complaints are generally groundless. Why should others complain of cutbacks, when we can do without altogether?

"Can you explain why this attitude is prevalent among the Old Order people?"

Yes, there are several reasons:

First, our doctrine forbids such an attitude. Paul wrote to Timothy, "Godliness with contentment is great gain" (1 Tim. 6:6).

Second, since we do not spend so much on entertainment and other luxuries, we are not as quickly affected by a recession.

Third, because we do not ask for government assistance or expect it, what's the point in complaining?

"Does the Old Order Church have its own organization that replaces social assistance?"

No. The church discourages every attempt at getting something for nothing. However, if the need arises, the church members see to it that no one starves or actually becomes needy. There is no need to keep up with the Joneses. The well-to-do and the poor are generally considered equal in the social circle.

"Is there no inequality in the job market, what with the Mennonites' relative lack of formal education?"

None whatsoever. The man with little education may be just as successful a farmer as an educated one.

### Old Order Insurance

Mennonite views on insurance changed greatly during the first hundred years after the first settlers came to Ontario. Our pioneer forebears trusted in God. They believed in the scriptural pattern of charity and good will, "especially unto them who are of the household of faith" (Gal. 6:10).

The conference statements of the last century bear this out.

The following resolutions were passed at the Berlin (Kitchener) conference of 1864:

◆ ◆ ◆

Resolved: that we manifest more activity in the way of mercy and charity toward the poor and needy brethren and sisters, as well as to all mankind.

Resolved: that since most professing Christians rely on institutions established by man as precautionary measures to protect their homes and buildings, to cover damage by fire, by which the members of such an institution, if not voluntarily, can be forced to pay their share; therefore, we see the need that we as members of one body, of which Christ is the head, return to the system of the apostles, help and assist each other among ourselves when we suffer damage by fire. At that time brethren shall be chosen to assess the damage and levy revenue accordingly, but to subtract a third of the total amount [church covers two-thirds, family suffering loss covers one-third]. We have confidence in the brotherhood, that each one contributes his donation voluntarily according to his ability, as his share.

◆ ◆ ◆

In later years, this policy was reaffirmed and strengthened. It is the basis of Old Order Mennonite policy today.

It is understandable that changes to this policy were warranted among many people. Although I have never owned or driven a car, I understand that insurance is mandatory for owners and operators. Possibly there are other factors which render the above policy obsolete in some circles. However, in the Old Order church, there has been no reason to abandon the policy, although minor changes have been made.

Our system is not like most other Mennonite aid plans. There is no organization or membership other than the church itself. The total amount needed to cover the loss is announced publicly, and members are expected to govern themselves accordingly. All funds are collected through voluntary offerings.

Every church member is eligible to receive help when needed. Main areas of coverage under this plan are for fire, wind, or water damage, hospitalization, and liability, besides help for the needy.

From an economical viewpoint, this method is unrivaled. No wealthy insurance companies get richer at the church's expense. Collections are taken up after a disaster, and then only in the amount needed. There are no administration costs.

Even those outside the Mennonite circle see the merit in the system. When a certain non-Mennonite sold his farm to a Mennonite and agreed to hold a mortgage, he inquired about insurance coverage.

"Don't you worry!" the lawyer assured him. "They have the best insurance policy there is!"

Above all, the policy reflects our trust in God rather than in human institutions. Why should we look for something better?

"Since this resolution regarding an alternative to fire insurance was established over 130 years ago, many changes have taken place within the Mennonite church. Would you be prepared to say that this policy is still carried out to the letter among your people?"

Yes, as nearly as we are able to do so. There may be slight variations of practice. Fifty years ago it was customary for the deacon to be at his local church to take up collections on a certain date. Now, for the sake of saving time, contributions are usually brought or mailed to the deacon.

"Since contributions are voluntary and human nature varies, it stands to reason that some are more conscientious than others, consequently giving more than their fair share, while others give less. Then, too, not all the deacons use the same ways for collecting. I recall one collection nearly fifty years ago, taken at the church; the deacon refused to take the whole offering of one young brother. Then he turned to an older, established man, saying, "And *you* could give more!"

"Suppose a man of limited means had a barn fire. His barn may have been rather old and decrepit. Yet it was all he had by which to make a living. How would such a situation be handled?"

That is why a committee is elected, in cooperation with the deacon, to be fair in all circumstances. Allowance is certainly made for circumstances. At the same time, if the one who lost his barn had limited means because of neglect, the committee will not make allowance to the point where someone would be encouraged in such neglect. Conversely, a rich man would not be reimbursed to the point where he would be encouraged to expand unnecessarily. In all these cases, discretion is the better part of valor!

### Living Comfortably Without Pensions

Is it true that by trying to avoid the pension system, we find it easier to cope as seniors than if we were to accept a pension? Surely that wouldn't make sense, and yet I wonder.

I have a statement issued by the Council of Canadians in 1990. Maude Barlow, volunteer chair of the council, says, "Did you know that three out of four seniors have incomes of $20,000 a year or less?"

Did I know? Is this supposed to be a joke? And she expects *me* to help these poor seniors, whose pensions just might be cut back!

I suppose there would be no possibility of getting Maude Barlow to understand that never in my life have I had an annual income even close to $20,000. It would likely be useless to show her that my wife and I are living quite comfortably, by our Old Order standards, on much less than half that amount per year.

These figures are so far out of proportion that it is useless to try to bring them into focus. Obviously, we have reason to be well satisfied and happy with our financial situation. At the same time, we need not feel guilty for not helping those who complain about their lot.

We do not feel deprived or underprivileged doing without television, radio, cassettes, video or tape players. We find good reading material more edifying and much cheaper.

Paul wrote to the Philippians, "I have learned in whatsoever state I am, therewith to be content" (4:11).

We have never spent any money to attend movie theaters, professional sports, horse races, shows, or exhibitions. We rarely eat at restaurants. Generally, we either have company for Sunday dinner, and occasionally supper, or we visit in the homes of friends. The meals compare favorably with $15 restaurant fare. These dinners are reciprocal, so no one gains or loses, and high-cost eating is eliminated.

Entertainment cost is eliminated as well. One might say that there is a four-tier visiting system among Old Orders in Ontario. The lowest tier is among closest neighbors. The second is the interrelation between the other districts in the Mount Forest area and our own. The first two tiers of visiting are carried out by horse-and-buggy travel.

The third tier is between the Mount Forest area and the larger Elmira area. Either a bus is chartered and numerous families take part, or vans are hired for smaller loads. Such methods of travel involve only one day.

The fourth tier takes the form of a tour, and the destination is usually across the border to a Mennonite community in Pennsylvania, New York, Indiana, Michigan, Ohio, Wisconsin, Virginia, Missouri, Iowa, Kentucky, or a combination of several states.

In earlier days, such trips across the border usually involved train or bus travel. More recently, the most common mode of travel is by van. This is especially common when attending funerals, weddings, or ordinations, when only a few days are involved.

Our young people, too, take such trips across the border, to any or all the above states. Usually, two teenage girls and teenage boys travel together, since this is the most practical arrangement for sleeping quarters; two girls in one bedroom, two boys in another. The drivers who take them from place to place, likewise are satisfied with this arrangement.

Both young and old enjoy such trips, and if decent behavior is shown all around, it can be quite edifying.

When not needed at home, our young people, ages 16 to 21, usually hire out by the year to church members in need of help. Girls work for busy mothers who need help with gardening, canning, sewing, childcare, and in some cases milking, on dairy farms. Boys help in field and stable.

In all cases, the hired help are considered as members of the host family, weekends as well as weekdays. This diversification helps them to gain experience.

"Your alternative to pensions poses a good question. How much do we really spend on entertainment in a year? I have never tried to figure it out; but it would not surprise me if we spent as much for entertainment as on food."

"Huh! There's no doubt in my mind. If we'd add together everything we spend 'for that which is not bread' [Isa. 55:2], it would be a lot more than we pay for food!"

"Catch 22 is, how to change our habits. Where would we start?"

"Throw out the TV!"

I'm afraid I can't help you much in working that out; but my guess is that you would be happier in the end if you could do it.

"What really amazes me, is that you pass by all the expensive entertainment, and replace it by something at least as good, without paying a cent!"

### The Liar's Subterfuge

During the past month I have spent most of my time in translating an old German book into English. In 1857 David Beiler, an Amish bishop, wrote *Das wahre Christenthum* (True Christianity); it was published in 1888. I am grateful for the privilege of translating it. (The result is now at Heritage Historical Library, Aylmer, Ontario.)

Beiler's book affords an in-depth study, not experienced by merely reading a book. One of the chapters concerns the swearing of oaths. I would like to present some of his views, along with supporting material from other sources.

What is an oath? It is a solemn affirmation or declaration made with an appeal to God, the Supreme Being, for the truth of what is affirmed. The person making the oath is understood to invoke God's vengeance on the liar if what is affirmed or declared is false or not performed as promised. Thus it is a risky thing to swear!

Certain forms of oaths were common in Old Testament times.

When Abraham sent his servant to take a wife for Isaac, he said, "Put thy hand under my thigh, and I will make thee swear by the Lord." When Isaac and Abimelech parted, they swore one to another. Again, Jacob swore by the fear of his father, Isaac, when Laban left him (Gen. 24:9; 26:31; 31:53).

One of the Ten Commandments even says, "You shall not take the name of the Lord your God in vain" (Exod. 20:7). This means not making wrongful use of God's name, as in false swearing and in other ways (Lev. 19:12). It thus leaves the door open for swearing and then performing one's oath, as we see in the Old Testament (sample: 1 Sam. 20:12-13; pagan swearing: 1 Kings 19:2).

However, this changed conclusively through Christ's teaching. He held truth so sacred that a person's simple word was as good as any oath if he truly followed Christ. In Matthew 5:33-37, Jesus says,

> You have heard that it has been said by those of old time, You shall not forswear yourself, but shall perform unto the Lord your oaths. But I say unto you, Swear not at all: neither by heaven, for it is God's throne; nor by the earth, for it is his footstool; neither by Jerusalem, for it is the city of the great King. Neither shall you swear by your head, because you can not make one hair white or black. But let your communication be Yea, yea; and Nay, nay; for whatsoever is more than these comes of evil.

This is a direct command from Jesus Christ. We are not to swear and thereby try to use God to establish our word.

In the letter of James, whom we believe to have been inspired by God, we find the following: "But above all things, my brothers [and sisters], swear not, neither by heaven, neither by the earth, neither by any other oath: but let your yea be yea; and your nay, nay; lest you fall into condemnation" (5:12).

The latter is short and to the point, but it brings out three points worthy of special consideration. James says, "Above all things," suggesting that this command is even more important than greed, fraud, wantonness, and bearing grudges, mentioned earlier in the same chapter. He says, "neither by any other oath."

This leaves no room for other forms of oaths than the ones mentioned by Christ. He adds, "lest you fall into condemnation." If swearing any form of oath leads to condemnation, there is no way of being excused by reasoning against the command.

John (Jan) Hus was one of the early reformers in Europe. When pressed to swear an oath, he made this statement: "I am afraid on every hand; if I swear, I am condemned to eternal death [by the Scriptures]; if I swear not, I cannot escape your hands. Yet I would rather fall innocently into your hands, than sin against God." He was burned alive as a heretic in July 1415.

History shows plainly that our Anabaptist forebears rejected the swearing of oaths. They suffered for their stand against oaths because governmental authorities thought this would undermine the state (*The Mennonite Encyclopedia*, vol. 4, on "Oath"). During persecution, when the oath of allegiance was required of all subjects in southern Europe, our forebears chose to leave the country with a clear conscience, rather than swear an oath and disobey the divine command.

As poor pilgrims, they wandered through foreign lands, trusting in the help, grace, and mercy of God to see them through (as in Ps. 107:4; Heb. 11:37-38). By divine providence they were able to establish homes here in North America, where we have long been living in peace and indeed in comparative prosperity. If our forebears knew that some of us today ignore the scriptural directives of nonresistance, baptism on faith, and nonswearing of oaths, I believe they would feel that they had labored in vain.

"Why would any Christian even think of swearing an oath? What is an oath but a form of subterfuge, to cover our lies with a pretext of respectability?"

I totally agree with that. If we tell the truth, no oath will improve on it. If we are lying, an oath makes it a twofold transgression.

"Is the common habit of swearing to confirm a statement included in Christ's statement to 'swear not at all'?"

I think it is, and in a way, it is even worse. Frequently it takes the name of the Lord in vain, in an attempt to make lies seem to

be the truth. Swearing is a profane practice with no value whatsoever. Why should it be practiced?

### Graven Images

Last Sunday, the minister who brought the introductory message discussed the first two of the Ten Commandments. When he
expounded on the second commandment, he stimulated my
thinking.

When I was a child, every store in town gave out calendars for
the coming year. Above the calendar pad, many of them had pictures, which I treasured. We were allowed to choose the calendar we wanted for our bedrooms. We were also allowed to
choose the pictures of the last year's calendar for keeping.

The kitchen-living room was not so favored. It was the domain of my mother, who was quite conscious of all display and
adornment. She picked a calendar with large clear figures and
cut off the picture, which she let me save for my collection. This
calendar was then the one that she displayed in the kitchen. To
her, a picture on the wall was a manifestation of pride. Besides,
it *was* a likeness.

Obviously, the pioneer Mennonite homes had no pictures on
the walls. Since my grandfather died when my mother was quite
young, she was raised in her grandfather's home. He had been a
pioneer, clearing off his own farm in 1844. Wall calendars likely
did not appear as such until the latter part of the nineteenth century. When cameras were invented about that time, they were
used only by photographers. Those who could afford it and
wished to do so, had their pictures taken in a photograph studio.
One might assume that the Mennonites would not have done
this; yet I have copies of such a picture taken of Elias and Anna
Eby, probably in the 1870s. Elias was a son of the pioneer bishop, Benjamin Eby.

When the Mennonite church divided in 1889, the liberal element no longer took much notice of traditional modesty. It
comes as a surprise, then, that "likenesses" or photographs were
*still* an issue among the more liberal branch of the church. Amos
Cressman was bishop of the church in Wilmot Township and made

some comments in a letter of 1893. He had been making house visits with Tobias Bowman, a preacher, and wrote the following.

"A frequent topic of conversation was how the devil comes with his wiles to bring vanity into the church through likenesses, which the good God commanded not to make nor to worship them. I feel that when we keep them and show them to the people, then we worship them."

About once a year through my school years, a photographer came to school to take a school picture. For this event, we were all expected to stand outside in a group. With the big, black box sitting on a tripod, the photographer draped a black cloth over his head, while the pupils stood in several rows before him. It was an awe-inspiring experience to me. But I was never allowed to take home a photograph.

Our attitudes have indeed changed regarding photography and pictures in general. We do not mind looking at pictures. If a photograph featuring Mennonites appears in a magazine, we are quite ready to look it over and see whom we can identify.

To be consistent, we must admit that the pictures themselves are not so much what we object to, as the way in which they are treated and displayed. Showing photographs to friends, or displaying them in prominent places, is a demonstration of pride. The same is true of posing for personal photographs. Decorating walls with pictures, even with flashy wallpaper, does not show a humble spirit.

When photography was first brought to our attention, most photographs were of people. Today, many people who travel through the world, especially in mountainous areas or other beauty spots, take cameras along to capture scenes. They take them home as mementos of their trips. In this case, it would not be comparable to graven images.

Whether or not taking such photographs and showing them to people can be considered as sin, it is something we can do without. The overall concept of indulging in sightseeing to a great extent is not compatible with the Old Order way of life.

There is little danger that we are hindered in serving the Lord because we have no camera. In fact, we have trouble thinking of good reasons why we should have one.

"Isn't it surprising that since your mother was so set against pictures, she allowed her children to save the pictures?"

My mother was not in the least imposing. She chose to have an undecorated kitchen for herself; but she would not impose the same on others.

"Would you say that Elias Eby was more modern than his father?"

I wouldn't really say so. Both were fairly progressively minded, yet cautious about introducing matters into the church which could cause trouble. Elias was quite concerned about the introduction of new doctrine into the church.

### No Old Order Sunday Schools

If Sunday schools were instituted for the spiritual improvement of the church, why do some people object to them? For Old Order Mennonites, the answer lies in the following: (1) The methods used in introducing Sunday schools. (2) The Old Order Mennonites' reluctance to change. (3) The fear of instilling a superior feeling in intelligent children. (4) The interpretation of Matthew 15:13: "Every plant which my heavenly Father has not planted will be rooted up."

Numerous letters have been preserved from the time of the Sunday school issue in the late 1800s.

John Weaver of Indiana wrote in 1878: "The Sunday school serves more to the spoiling of the children than to their welfare, especially the way they are held entirely after the fashions of the world."

Abraham Blosser of Virginia felt that the more progressive elements favoring Sunday schools bring the church closer to the worldly churches. He wrote in 1885: "There is no quicker way under heaven to exterminate a nonresistant church than by its going into a union Sunday school with fashionable, warlike denominations."

Bishop John S. Coffman proposed that Mennonite Sunday schools use no other books but the Bible and be conducted by our own ministers. Three months later, popular Sunday school books were purchased. Blosser found an ex-Methodist preacher teaching a Sunday school, with the aid of another outsider.

Samuel Musselman was a strong supporter of Sunday schools. He wrote to Bishop Jonas Martin in 1891:

> Now, dear brother, it appears to me that I see breakers ahead of you, if you make any false moves. I think all the other members are keeping themselves clear, and I would be very sorry to see you again get into trouble. Brother Burkholder is, I think, taking good care of himself. But I am afraid his actions will get some others in a wrong position, if they obey his counsel. You no doubt know he has his heart set on taking counsel, and keeping the school out of the meetinghouse.

From the facts available, it seems the Weaverland congregation was against Sunday school in general, for Musselman feared a vote. It also seems that Musselman hoped to intimidate the bishop through veiled threats. He did not dare challenge Burkholder, who took good care of himself, he admitted.

Bishop Christian Schaum of Indiana was alarmed by the Mennonites' tolerance of worldly churches and their tendency to copy the worldly practices. He saw many who sought praise from the world.

In 1894 he wrote,

> There are many professing Christians, but few cross-bearing ones. They wish to follow pride and conformity to the world. They now have their Sunday schools, whereby they are ever learning and never able to come to the knowledge of the truth.

J. Clayton Kolb of Pennsylvania wrote in 1904,

> Last fall my father resigned his place as a teacher in the Sunday school because he felt it was something that had no foundation in God's Word. As I was one of the ministers, I felt it my duty to also publicly denounce the Sunday school as idolatry. When I read God's Word, I can find no ground for any organization but the church.

From the information at hand, one can gather several sentiments. The introduction of Sunday schools was accompanied by
demonstrations of pride and worldliness there. Sunday schools
were held in cooperation with worldly churches, and the Old
Order Mennonite church declined to take part. The motives of
those who introduced Sunday schools were questioned. They appeared to be leading by human reasoning, self-esteem, and arrogance, rather than the lowly spirit of Christ.

The sentiments expressed by these writers are still felt in the
Old Order church today. Fear of falling into the same demonstrations of pride and undue self-esteem (Rom. 12:3), together
with the traditional Old Order reluctance to change—these are
the main reasons why the Sunday school, as generally conducted, has never been introduced into Old Order churches.

Today there are some Old Order Amish churches that operate
Sunday schools by humble, Christlike standards. Chiefly German language schools, they have no women as leaders. Only
members of the ministry explain the Scriptures. There is no competitive spirit among the pupils. Perhaps some day this course
will be followed by others.

"It is quite easy to understand why not everyone approves of
Sunday schools, considering how they were started among the
Mennonites. Nothing is gained by trying to force people to
change their minds, especially if leaders do not take enough efforts to conduct the schools acceptably. Naturally, people were
reluctant to change when they saw that their fears were well
grounded."

Yes, and when the supporters of the schools themselves show
arrogance, they defeat their own purpose in fostering the
schools. If those first three points had been taken care of by the
perpetrators, the outcome might have been entirely different.

## Foreign Missions Difficult
## for Old Orders

"Go and teach all nations." According to Matthew and Mark,
these were the words of Jesus after his resurrection, just before

he left his disciples (Matt. 28:18-20; Mark 16:15).

That was certainly a command. To many, it is considered so important that it has been called the great commission. But the Old Order Mennonites do not literally fulfill this command.

Mark goes on to say, "They went forth, and preached everywhere" (16:20). It would be difficult to prove that the disciples actually preached everywhere in the populated world. The *Martyrs Mirror* and other histories indicate that the gospel message was indeed taken to all parts of Europe, much of Asia, and at least the northern part of Africa.

Dietrich Philip, in his *Enchiridion* (Handbook), plainly states his views on this matter:

> The apostles were commanded by the Lord to preach the gospel to every creature, which by the grace of God, they did (Col. 1:6). If this were to be followed out, then the teachers now would have to preach not only to the Christians as mentioned, but also to the Jews, Turks, and all the heathen. But Paul declares to the teachers and bishops of the church that they shall take heed unto themselves, and to all the flock, over which the Holy Ghost had made them overseers. (Acts 20:28)

Since Philip was a co-worker with Menno Simons, laboring for the same cause, we assume that their views were similar. The same statement also appears in Colossians 1:23: "The gospel, which you have heard, and which was preached to every creature which is under heaven." Also, in Romans 10:18, we find these words: "Have they not heard? Yes, verily, their sound went into all the earth, and their words unto the ends of the world."

Since Paul asserts in several places that the gospel has been preached in all the world, the so-called great commission has apparently been fulfilled. This is likely one of the reasons why the Old Order churches have never supported or encouraged foreign missions. Another reason was probably because nonresistance and standards of dress, as highly regarded by most Mennonites, were frequently neglected among the missionaries. There is also evidence that when foreign missions are overemphasized, the home church is frequently neglected.

There is another logical conclusion to be reached regarding our reluctance to engage in foreign missions at this time. First, though Paul was the missionary to the Gentiles (nations) and traveled extensively, we find nowhere in his writings that he encouraged others to do the same. Instead, he encouraged them to take heed unto themselves and to all the flock, as stated above.

Second, in Romans 10:18, Paul quotes the prophetic words from Psalm 19:4, indicating that the great commission was being fulfilled, as authorized in Matthew 28:18-20. This corresponds with Matthew 24:4-44, the prophetic description of the destruction of Jerusalem, as well as of the end times: a twofold cataclysm, with the first being a figure of the second. There Jesus says, "This gospel of the kingdom shall be preached in all the world for a witness unto all nations; and then shall the end come" (24:14).

From available history, it is obvious that the Christians were dispersed through persecution (Acts 8:1). Following the destruction of Jerusalem, they spread into the known world. They did not go with the intention of fulfilling the great commission, but fulfilled it as a result (Acts 8:4). Likewise, one can expect a similar dispersion before the end of the world, possibly to avoid the mark of the beast (Rev. 13). It would be reasonable to assume that the final great commission will be fulfilled then.

A similar instance of "Going to teach, or make disciples of all nations" occurred during and after the Reformation and the resulting persecution. The Mennonites and Amish did not migrate to America to spread the gospel. They came to gain freedom of religion. Yet when the tourists flock to Amish and Mennonite areas to see the phenomenon, they are subjected to a faith and doctrine that "shall not return to me empty, but it shall accomplish that which I propose" (Isa. 55:11).

In his 1961 booklet *As You Go*, John Howard Yoder has also explained and supported this pattern of every member of the church living and sharing the gospel wherever they are. He was a Mennonite who grew up in a congregation with Amish roots (Oak Grove, Smithville, Ohio). The title comes from a literal translation of the Greek in the first part of Matthew 28:19, in the great commission. Yoder calls this "migration evangelism" and says that missions are at our doorstep. This approach is similar to our Old Order view.

"If the Old Order Mennonites and Amish find it difficult or impractical to support foreign missions, are they doing all they can as witnesses to their neighbors?"

You are definitely right in mentioning that point. I am sure we could do better than we do, without infringing on our faith and doctrine. In fact, being a consistent witness to our faith at all times could definitely bring just as positive results as foreign missions would. Thanks for reminding me of our shortcomings.

## Mennonites and Voting

From a human viewpoint, it seems necessary for all Christians to vote. Perhaps we are courting trouble if we leave voting to unbelievers. If unbelievers do all the voting, what else could we expect but an unbelieving government? Why not vote in Christian officials, or even Mennonites? Why not wipe out evil by force?

This is not what the early Christians taught, nor is it what our forebears taught over a hundred years ago. There were indeed men of Mennonite background who dabbled in politics, but there is no evidence to show that they were faithful members or adherents of the Mennonite church.

In 1864, at the conference at Christian Eby's place, a resolution was passed on the matter: "According to our understanding of God's Word, campaigning and voting for candidates to serve in public office does not conform to our nonresistant Christian confession of faith."

In 1884, another conference passed a resolution: "According to the Gospel of Matthew 6:24, 'No one can serve two masters,' and 2 John 9, 'whosoever transgresses': when brothers accept the office of councilor, or when a brother nominates another brother for councilor, they cannot be considered as brethren until they have again reconciled themselves, through admission and confession in front of the church, and have been taken up by the bishop with hand and kiss."

Regarding the wiping out of evil by force, God did occasionally support so-called "just" wars in Old Testament times. The first of these occurred when the Elamites and others defeated Sodom and Gomorrah, and took Lot captive. Abram, with 318 men, defeated the Elamites and rescued Lot. As a result, Melchizedek, king of Salem, blessed Abram.

That was a just war, supported by God. In the new dispensation, we have no evidence of any just wars. Christ said, "Resist not evil" (Matt. 5:39). That is the final word for us.

Despite this, some Mennonites have in the past tried to resist evil, contrary to Christ's command. In 1960, some Mennonites who had never before voted, changed to support voting. They did not think that they should depend on God only when a Catholic, John F. Kennedy, was a U.S. presidential candidate. Some of them even resorted to "stumping" for Richard Nixon, the other candidate. Twelve years later, the man whom they supported was responsible for the Watergate scandal. So much for human reasoning!

There are numerous reasons why we, as descendants of the Anabaptists, should not vote. If we are what the apostle Peter calls us, "strangers and pilgrims," we literally have no vote (1 Pet. 2:11). If we vote, we are in effect asserting that we are not strangers and pilgrims.

Almost five hundred years ago, when our forebears baptized each other and formed the first Anabaptist church, they officially separated church and state. To turn around and vote in a state election is to render their confession void.

All true Christians profess to believe in an omnipotent God. Why would we confess this and then refuse to prove our faith? If we as Mennonites believe that God needs our votes, strength, and insights into man's character to achieve the results God wants, we must be Münsterites instead of Mennonites! (see *The Mennonite Encyclopedia*, vol. 3).

Paul told the Romans, "Let every soul be subject unto the higher powers, for there is no power but of God. The powers that be are ordained of God" (Rom. 13:1).

Yes, John F. Kennedy was ordained of God, regardless of how

many Mennonites voted against him! We also need to realize of whom Paul spoke those words. The Roman emperor at that time was none other than the cruel Nero. He was responsible for the death of his own mother, and later, for Paul's own death. By this we realize what Paul was saying: all rulers, good or bad, are ordained by God.

Let us remember, though, that even if they are ordained of God, they are not necessarily godly powers. In fact, it is doubtful that any worldly powers can be called godly. God can use any powers.

It is our duty to be subject to the powers that be; to honor, fear, and respect them, and to pay taxes and dues as required, as long as such requirements do not conflict with God's laws (Mark 12:17; Acts 5:29; Rom. 13:6-10).

Tertullian, one of the strongest defenders of the early Christian faith, said,

> I owe no duty to forum, campaign, or senate. I occupy no platform, I seek no office. I shun the voter's booth, the juryman's bench. I break no laws and push no lawsuits. I have withdrawn from worldly politics. Now my only politics is spiritual.

I think this position is supported by the New Testament. "For here have we no continuing city, but we seek one to come" (Heb. 13:14).

"Is there reason to believe that a Catholic president is worse than any other?"

Not to my knowledge. But then perhaps I am too indifferent about who is elected. In recent years, there seems to be little that politicians can and do accomplish.

## Shunning or Love?

> I wrote to you in my letter not to associate with . . . any one who bears the name of brother if he is guilty of immorality or greed, or is an idolater, reviler, drunkard, or robber—not even to eat with such a one. . . . "Drive out the wicked person from among you" (1 Cor. 5:9-13, RSV).

That is a command from the apostle Paul. The Dordrecht Confession of Faith (1632), which the Old Order Mennonite church has adopted as its own, supports this command (art. 17). Yet from the inauguration of the Anabaptist church, the Swiss Brethren did not observe such literal shunning. As with so many scriptural mandates, there is a difference in how such Scriptures should be understood.

Jakob Ammann, a young bishop in Alsace in the 1690s, felt that excommunicated members should be totally avoided and shunned. In its strictest sense, this meant that the excommunicated person must be shunned by family members, so that he must eat and sleep alone.

Hans Reist, the older bishop living in Switzerland, had a different viewpoint. (Don't tell anyone, but he may have been my ancestor. The name of my great-great-great-great-great-great-grandfather was Hans Reist, who lived at the same time, in the same general area.) He understood such avoidance to be limited to spiritual matters, barring him from communion and from meals at social functions such as weddings and funerals. To this day, most Old Order Mennonites observe shunning as Reist did, while the Amish and several small groups of ultraconservative Mennonites observe strict avoidance.

In the backs of our minds there is still a nagging doubt: Are we practicing shunning in the scriptural way or not? If the above command is to be taken literally, Ammann's method is the correct one, and we are wrong. Yet is that compatible with the Christian doctrine of love and charity?

However, there can be a difference. There are cases among us where members lost their membership because of material matters. They are not necessarily immoral, idolaters, revilers, drunkards, or robbers, and even may be members of another Christian church. Or they may have committed a gross sin, but have repented. None of these cases would fit the description of which Paul writes in 1 Corinthians 5:11-12.

Too often, strict avoidance contradicts Christian love ethics. However, perhaps we are wrong and should practice stricter shunning, trusting in divine providence to teach us love in discipline. Perhaps our faith is just too weak.

One point is obvious. For every reference to avoidance, there are dozens of exhortations to love one another and practice forbearance. If it becomes necessary to choose between exercising charity or practicing avoidance, there would be no doubt about which to choose. Charity, as love in action, is the bond of perfection. How could anything else supersede it?

Paul also eloquently says, "Charity suffers long, and is kind; charity envies not; charity does not vaunt itself; is not puffed up. . . . It bears all things, believes all things, hopes all things, endures all things" (1 Cor. 13:4-7). The Revised Standard Version says,

> Love is patient and kind; love is not jealous or boastful; it is not arrogant or rude. Love does not insist on its own way; it is not irritable or resentful; it does not rejoice at wrong, but rejoices in the right. Love bears all things, believes all things, hopes all things, endures all things. (1 Cor. 13:4-7)

Those are truly the important points of the Christian life: the ones that demonstrate true discipleship. Unless we can reconcile strict avoidance with love, we lose much more than we gain by practicing strict avoidance. Both exhortations were written by the same man, to the same people.

If Paul had intended that a strict avoidance be practiced, as 1 Corinthians is understood by some, he must have considered it possible to reconcile the two. He must have seen it possible to exercise charity, as he taught in 1 Corinthians 13, while practicing strict avoidance.

However, if he did not intend it to be carried out in the fullest sense, we are forced to choose. Our choice is in favor of exercising charity.

"If the Old Order Mennonites adopted the Dordrecht Confession, and the Swiss Brethren did not observe strict shunning, how is that reconciled, since you are descended from the Swiss Brethren?"

The Swiss Mennonites had not adopted the Dordrecht Confession before they moved to America. Here they were a small group and decided to accept the Dordrecht Confession, even though they did not fully agree on the issue of shunning.

"I would understand you to say that strict avoidance may be the answer when a person is living in immorality or any of the other vices mentioned, but not if a man is overtaken by any trespass, and is willing to repent when reminded of his sins."

That is what I would suggest is the answer. Just as Paul told the Galatians (6:1), we should gently restore anyone overtaken in a fault. We need to distinguish between deliberate immorality or vice, and stumbling or being overtaken in a trespass. If we can do that and govern ourselves accordingly, we might be able to carry out what Paul was teaching.

## Faith or Gullibility?

Our pioneer forebears in Canada did not have highly educated doctors to attend to their physical needs. Most of the doctors at that time combined a smattering of medical education with existing folk medicine. Others combined sorcery, invocation, and faith healing, known in German as *Brauchen*.

Many of the pioneers learned home medical arts from the Indians, who combined their knowledge of herbs with sorcery. The result of such education was a mixture of faith and gullibility. This would seem quite ignorant to us today. But before we pass judgment, we must remember that they made the most of what knowledge was available to them.

As more medical knowledge was gained, less dubious healing methods were practiced. However, a certain amount of gullibility remained. This mixture of faith and gullibility carried over into the spiritual life, so that it sometimes was difficult to tell one from the other. So-called old wives' tales are examples of this syndrome.

Possibly some of you have heard the story of the "Bohemian farmer who sits sleeping in the forest," an account of an incident that supposedly took place over two hundred years ago. It was translated some years ago by Noah Good and published by

Lester Sauder, Clay Book Store, Ephrata, Pennsylvania.

This German farmer supposedly desecrated the Lord's Day by forcing his servant to draw wood on Sunday. When the servant headed for home with his load of wood, the farmer sat on a stump to smoke his pipe. When the servant returned, the farmer was supposedly rooted to the stump.

A more recent case of a similar nature came to light in the Jacob Mensch letter collection. Elizabeth (Ziegler, Kolb) Wenger wrote to Mensch on October 6, 1878:

> Now a remarkable occurrence took place near Stratford here in Canada, when a man intended to dispute with God. It had rained so much, and he still had grain in the field. He became so angry that he started cursing in the house. Then he went out into the field with a knife in his hand, and went to a stump to fight with God. There he still stands, the people say, with the knife in his hand, pointed toward heaven, and petrified like a solid rock.
>
> The breast and the head are alive, but the rest is dead. He consumes nothing but water and wine. We have often heard this, and when he is touched, he screams, they say. No one of our neighborhood has been there yet, so we do not know whether it is true, but we have often heard that it is supposed to be true. . . .
>
> Preacher Cressman mentioned it over the pulpit, but he said he is not certain whether it is true, but with God all things are possible. He turned Lot's wife into a pillar of salt, and just as easily he could turn such a bold talker to stone. Be not deceived: God is not mocked.

Since Stratford was only fifteen miles from Amos Cressman's home, one wonders why he didn't check out the incident before using it in his sermon. Mrs. Wenger did not mention it in her letter of several months later. To me, something seems to be lacking, and the story is not plausible. Perhaps they hoped it was true. If it was not true, why was it less important to correct the mistake? On the other hand, if it had been proved to be true in the meantime, why would they not have verified it later?

It might have been temporarily possible; but in the long run, it lacks credibility. Possibly the man was stricken through his mounting blood pressure, causing partial paralysis, or something similar.

"Since the Scriptures give us no explicit rules about observing the Lord's Day, one would not expect that such a thing would take place. However, it is obvious that we do need a day of rest, every so often."

That is true enough. Yet we do feel uncomfortable with our neighbor's disregard for Sunday, and with stores being open on Sunday. I think this proves that we are not too sure how we should observe the Lord's Day, except that we use it to worship the Lord.

"In times past, one heard much about the supposed effect of the moon's position for doing certain things. Is that something that is observed among your people today?"

There are any number of signs and omens that are mentioned today, but few are seriously believed or observed. Here are some examples: When shingling a roof, the horns of the moon should be turned down, otherwise the shingles will curl up. Fence posts are to be planted under the same sign, so they do not freeze up.

"That is much the same among us. We talk about a rainbow in the morning, bringing bad weather; but few people are concerned about it. A common saying is that we plant in the earth, and not in the moon!"

## The Magdenburg Letter

The natural man is a strange creature. He can be extremely skeptical if it suits his purpose to be so. If something bizarre appears that suits his natural inclination better, he can be just as extremely gullible. Long-term benefits seem too vague for him. Immediate pleasures, though short lived, look much more inviting. He prefers the spectacular at hand than what is realistic but distant.

An example of such gullibility may be found in the Magdenburg Letter. Supposedly written by God himself and dropped down from heaven, it was discovered at Magdenburg, in central Germany, two hundred years ago. It contains some scriptural instruction, especially regarding the observance of Sunday (not the Sabbath). Having the letter in one's possession was supposed to protect one from lightning, fire, and flood. Anyone who had the letter and did not reveal it to others was accursed.

There is little reason to take the letter seriously. To my knowledge there is no record in the Scriptures of such a letter acting as a charm to ward off disaster. Such a practice does not seem to be compatible with Gospel teaching on the need for faith in God. Yet some biblical accounts of ancient practices seem strange to us today (Matt. 9:20; 14:36; Acts 5:15; 19:12). Possibly the Magdenburg Letter was written by a well-meaning but misguided person who hoped to instill Christian teachings by using scare tactics.

Such gullibility was rampant in earlier days. Before the medical profession had reached such a high degree of knowledge, it was quite understandable that this should occur. In the absence of reliable doctors, our pioneer forebears had to rely on home remedies to combat ailments. In every district there were usually one or more people who professed to understand such aids to health. Many of those remedies combined the medicinal properties of herbs with magical or occult methods referred to in German as *Brauchen*, seemingly a blend of faith healing and black magic.

After many years of lurking in the fringe areas of the Mennonites' faith and credibility, this custom seems to have practically disappeared. Few people today admit to a belief in the practice. Alas! An obviously greater menace is ready to take its place among the gullible.

Subtly, stealthily, as an angel of light, the new menace is creeping into our midst. It is being gradually introduced through seemingly harmless means. Literature is available in some health food stores, chiropractic offices, and organic gardening centers. It is shrouded by a religious aura, yet more closely related to Eastern mysticism than to Christianity. The Thing is so ethereal, so elusive and intangible, that it is difficult to name. Those involved with it rush to its defense at any contradiction.

In most cases, it seems to be directly or indirectly related to the New Age Movement, which is quite different from Christianity. It is characterized by supernatural rituals, behavior, and properties. Supposedly, electric currents bridge incredible gaps, inanimate objects take on unusual characteristics, and strange powers override normal human actions.

Like a drug ring, whole matter seems to be motivated by some intangible, central power. To me, it seems foreign to the power of the Spirit. There is only one alternative, because there are only two main powers. If it is black magic, the author is the devil. I hope I am wrong in my suspicions. However, until someone proves me wrong, I have no wish to become involved. To me, the Magdenburg Letter looks mild by comparison.

"Do the Old Order Mennonites no longer practice or believe in sorcery or *Brauchen*?"

I would be inclined to say it is no longer openly confessed or practiced among us. Those who still practice this art are so far in the minority that they would be reluctant to mention it in public.

"What is your opinion about faith healing?"

I have mixed feelings about the subject. There is a vast field open before us, including faith healing, anointing with oil, praying for the sick (James 5:14-16), drinking herb teas, and using various home remedies I believe each has its merits. On the other hand, there are crusaders who claim that since Christ healed all the sick and infirm who desired to be healed (Matt. 4:23-24), Christian ministers should and could do the same today.

If the apostles and disciples were expected to heal everyone, why did Paul leave Trophimus sick at Miletum (2 Tim. 4:20)? Why did he tell Timothy to drink no longer water, but use a little wine for his stomach's sake, and his frequent infirmities (1 Tim. 5:23)? Why was Epaphroditus sick nigh unto death? Paul says that God had mercy on him; but there is no indication that Paul or anyone else healed him (Phil. 2:25-27).

If sick persons desire to be anointed, or ask others to pray for them, their wishes should by all means be granted. Yet it seems to me like presumption if we do so without placing the matter into the hands of God, and saying "Not my will, but thine be done" (Luke 22:42).

## Are We Environmentally Friendly?

There is a saying that the mills of the gods grind slowly. This aptly describes the Old Order Mennonites. Any change comes very slowly with us.

We react slowly to the environmental issues: so slowly, in fact, that I have sometimes wondered whether there was any interest whatever in the environment. Of course, we contribute little to the waste problem. Food waste is minimal. No leftovers are thrown out. Even food that may be partly spoiled is fed to farm animals.

Clothing waste is infinitesimal. Except for outgrown children's clothing, all clothes will be worn out. Children's clothes are passed down from one to the next, so that nothing is discarded until the youngest child has outgrown all of them. Even then, they may be shared with another family or used for rags. When clothes are no longer suitable for dress occasions, they are worn for work.

This point was reinforced for me recently when a busload of twenty-five people from our area in Ontario traveled to Hawkesville in the Waterloo Region. The Mennonite-sponsored Christian Aid Ministries has a used clothing depot there, in a recycled old schoolhouse. Here we sorted, bagged, and baled several thousand good used garments for delivery to the needy of Romania, the former Soviet Union, and Nicaragua. These clothes are surplus that accumulates at thrift shops, rummage sales, and so on. Although the workers were all Mennonites, I feel sure that less than 5 percent of the clothes came from Mennonite homes.

Old Order Mennonites are historically skilled in recycling remnants and used material. Woven, braided, and hooked rugs are created from such material, and they find their way into fashionable homes. Comforters are made from coarse woolen material, such as heavy coats, which are then shipped to needy countries.

In the past, Mennonite farmers have been guilty of indiscriminate chemical use. Today, most farmers have cut back on chemicals. Most of them are licensed operators and periodically at-

tend seminars on chemical use. Besides, an increasing number
are experimenting with organic farming. Whether it will prove
satisfactory remains to be seen.

In our market gardening operation, we have been following an organic program, only resorting to chemicals as a last resort, such as to control potato beetles. Hopefully we will be able to find some method of control soon that is more compatible with ecology.

"Have you ever tried planting beans with potatoes to ward off potato beetles?"

Yes, and it didn't make one whit of difference. We also tried rhubarb leaf juice, with the same results. We even tried sucking the beetles off by vacuum; but it took off the leaves as well!

"Why not pick off the beetles by hand?"

May I ask you how many potatoes you grow?

"Oh, we have a row about forty feet long."

That's what I thought. Those who try to be the most helpful, and think they have an answer to the potato beetle problem, have no idea whatever about handling a commercial operation. We grow only one acre of potatoes, and last year we picked 20,000 bugs, after which we stopped counting. Then we gave up and sprayed them. Can you imagine how long it would take to pick the bugs off a hundred acres? Have you any idea what the price of potatoes would be, if the bugs were all picked by hand? Nobody could afford the potatoes!

There is another matter to be taken into consideration. Most Mennonites are cautious about carrying ecological concerns to extremes. If an environmental issue is taken to the point where it is practically a religion, that is incompatible with Christianity and strongly discouraged among us.

We find too many instances of a package deal being offered, including the environment, ecology, organic farming or gardening, animal rights, health fads, New Age medicine, and Eastern mysticism. Extreme caution must be exercised to prevent involvement in such organizations.

In general, Old Order Mennonites find any reasonable form of environmental program acceptable. They desire to adapt to the whole community when it does not encroach upon their own conscience. Concern for the environment is a healthy attitude as long as it remains within the sphere of reason.

"What makes you so critical of the New Age movement?"

We have a son who subscribes to the New Age cult. He had to sell part of his business to pay for his brainwashing course. He told me he was looking for a god with whom he could identify. A god whom we can mold after our own desires is not one with which I care to commune.

## Is Vegetarianism Scriptural?

During the past twenty years, there has been a strong trend towards decentralization among the urban population of Canada. This has been especially noticeable in our area, seventy-five miles northwest of Toronto. Farms were cheap here twenty-five years ago. City people could buy a farm here for far less than the price of a decent house in the city. They could have lots of elbow room, where they could get away from it all, and also experiment with growing their own food.

This trend coincided with the interest in antiques, country crafts, bird watching, ecology, organic gardening, healthful living, vegetarianism, and animal rights. With some, this interest inspired them to build or restore their own log house, heat it with a wood stove, use coal oil lamps, bake their own whole wheat bread, and furnish the house with solid wood furniture.

All this is quite commendable, especially to us, who still live simpler lives in general. The trend in our country had gone unnecessarily far in discarding the old and accepting the new, flimsy furniture. To us it would have made more sense to keep an even keel and not go to extremes in the first place. When the pendulum starts to swing, no telling where it will stop.

The greatest danger, from my viewpoint, is the package deal, including most of the above seemingly worthwhile aims, which is offered under the blanket of the New Age Movement. (Naturally, it is not always referred to as such until the noose is ready to be tightened.) This infiltration of New Age doctrine into such a variety of virtuous causes is part of the networking system through which the doctrine of human's inherent goodness and self-sufficiency is propagated.

At this point, I have no quarrel with bird watching, antiques, and crafts. Organic growing is desirable insofar as it is practical. The same may be said of healthful living. If it is pursued to the point where meals are no longer palatable, especially where young children are concerned, the baby may well be thrown out with the bathwater.

Animal rights, too, has its place. Although most farmers know that cattle need to be comfortable to be profitable, some farmers need to be reminded of this occasionally. Nor have I any objection to those who wish to pursue a vegetarian's life. The accounts of creation clearly assign plants and the fruit of trees for human food (Gen. 1:29; 2:16). After the flood, humanity is allowed also to eat animals, birds, and fish (Gen. 9:2-3). The prophet Daniel proved that a vegetable diet can be quite healthful, and he thus managed to keep from eating food not permitted by Jewish dietary rules (Dan. 1).

Any diet, whether vegetarian, partly so, or heavy with meat, must be well-balanced to be satisfactory. However, it is unscriptural to make a religion of a diet and condemn the eating of meats and other animal products. Paul wrote to Timothy of some who depart from the faith, commanding to abstain from meats, which God has created to be received with thanksgiving. "For every creature of God is good, and nothing to be refused, if it be received with thanksgiving" (1 Tim. 4:3-4).

Jesus "declared all foods clean" (Mark 7:14-19, RSV), and Peter had to learn that lesson (Acts 10:9-16). Therefore, according to Jesus, Peter's vision, and Paul, even pork, forbidden in the Old Testament (Lev. 11), is good and suitable to be eaten by Christians. Yet there are brotherly considerations. Christians must not judge other believers who follow their consciences to be vegetarian (Rom. 14). They also must not be a stumbling block to others by eating meat routinely offered to an idol (1 Cor. 8).

In 1 Timothy 4:8, Paul further states, "Refuse profane and old wives' fables, and exercise yourself rather unto godliness. For bodily exercise profits little; but godliness is profitable unto all things." This warning is likely aimed at "the seducing spirits, and the doctrines of devils," mentioned earlier (4:1).

"Okay, so Daniel and his companions refused to eat the king's meat, eating vegetables instead. When Cain and Abel brought their first offering to God, Abel's offering was acceptable, and Cain's was not (Gen. 4:3-5). What was their offering?"

H'm, that's a good question. I'll look it up. You wouldn't guess! The Lord rejected Cain and his offering, of the fruit of the ground; Abel and his meat sacrifice were accepted. What made the difference was likely not *what* they offered, but with what kind of life they offered it. The Lord told Cain, "If you do well, will you not be accepted? And if you do not do well, sin is lurking at the door" (Gen. 4:7). Yet the fact remains that the meat offering was the one accepted.

"Could you explain what the profane and old wives' fables were?"

In my opinion, old wives' tales are based on superstition and are similar to the occult, or Eastern Mysticism; a supposedly supernatural power, yet not emanating from God.

"Can you explain the New Age doctrine?"

The New Age movement is too complex to be defined in a few words. If we believed in the New Age theories, we would not need God's grace. Instead, we believe in ourselves, that we can attain to celestial heights by our own power.

"Sounds eerie to me. I think I'll steer clear."

## Animal Rights

 Our North American environment has created a strange paradox. Around the turn of the century, many farm boys grew tired of life on the farm. They were bored by the loneliness, the lack of entertainment, and the drudgery of plowing with horses. So they went to the city, then eventually made enough money to afford a place in the country, with room to keep a horse.

From among these people, as well as among some of their city cousins, a distinct species of animal lovers developed. Some of them had little more knowledge of animals, wild or tame, than they learned from books. Others went to the farm, the zoo, and the park, to learn all they could about animals. Even so, they saw only their friendly, playful traits.

They refused to believe that these same animals can be dangerous and vicious. As an obvious result, they would go to Algonquin Park with their children. Oblivious of fear and even of warnings from guards, such children would venture too close to wild creatures, with disastrous results.

Such people also do not realize how stubborn and even dangerous farm animals can be, and that they need to be trained to become safe and friendly. Thus they think farmers are cruel when they seek to control and subdue such animals.

From these people, the Animal Rights movement was born. Their views of animals did not coincide with those of farmers. They were right in assuming that animals should be treated humanely and compassionately. Yet Jesus declared all foods clean, and Paul called every creature of God good, which even Peter learned (Mark 7; 1 Tim. 4:4; Acts 10). Hence, we have scant reason to avoid meat. Naturally, the slaughtering should be done as humanely as possible.

However, the Animal Rights people had limited contact with all manner of animals. They thus did not realize that farm animals need to be disciplined and trained, just as humans do, so that they learn to submit to authority. Yet just as with humans, this is not necessarily cruel. Even the Scriptures inform us, "For the moment all discipline seems painful rather than pleasant; later it yields the peaceful fruit of righteousness to those who have been trained by it" (Heb. 12:11, RSV).

A horse lover, like my son-in-law, can testify to this. Though he is firm with his colts while breaking them, there is a close bond of love and friendship between him and his horses.

Some people take exception to our practice of tying horses in the open during church services. It is only under the most extreme weather conditions that horses grow uncomfortable from the cold. Usually a horse feels quite warm and cozy under his blankets during the winter.

Naturally, not all people show the same amount of consideration for their animals, covering them insufficiently. On the other
hand, in cold weather one sees horses in the fields of hobby
farms; that is never found on Mennonite farms.

There has been some complaint about crowded quarters for
livestock and poultry. There is not too much cause for alarm.
Only comfortable livestock will be profitable for farmers. Most
Mennonite farmers do their utmost to keep their livestock comfortable, because they know that it is to their own interest. Contented cows give more milk. There is less danger of tail biting
and feather picking among contented swine and poultry.

In short, all good Mennonite farmers know that it is to their
advantage to give their livestock tender loving, care. These facts
have been drilled into them since boyhood.

"Isn't it ironic? Boys leaving the farm because they were tired
of horses, then going to the city to make enough money to return
to the farm and have a horse? That has been aptly called the
American way of life."

I actually believe that the whole concept of leaving the farm in
favor of the city is somewhat warped. City wages do look tempt-
ing to a farm boy, because it is so difficult to tell what a farm
worker's income actually is.

"As far as the Animal Rights movement goes, part of the problem is that they equate animals with humans, not realizing or be-
lieving that man has a never-dying soul, with which the lower
animals are not endowed."

In other words, the problem is much more deeply rooted than
any concern for dumb animals.

"From what I have seen, the Old Order Mennonites' horses
don't seem to be suffering. As far as the rest of the livestock is
concerned, it is obvious that if your farming practices were far
out of line, your farms would not flourish as they apparently
do."

"Yes, if the rest of us were as closely associated with Mother
Nature as the Mennonites seem to be, we would not need to be
greatly alarmed about the environment and ecology."

## The Bobolinks Are Still Singing

A recent editorial headline asked, "When Did You Last Hear a Bobolink?"

Headlines such as this are common today. Environmental articles are popular and often quite pertinent. The deterioration of the ozone layer, air pollution, and water contamination are popular subjects, and for good reasons.

Factories discharge thick clouds of polluting smoke and poisonous fumes into the atmosphere. The large manufacturing corporations running them need to be reminded of their transgressions. The cost of preventing such pollution is so high that they would continue to violate human rights except for the application of pressure. Farmers may apply chemicals to their fields beyond reasonable levels. They sometimes allow barnyard runoff to pollute public waterways. We all need to be reminded of our responsibilities towards our fellow human beings.

All this does not mean that we need to be unreasonable in the adaptation of our principles. There is no need for scare tactics. Rachel Carson, in her 1962 book *Silent Spring*, awakened a healthy awareness towards the unrestrained use of chemicals. At the same time, she stirred up those who carried environmental issues to fanatical extremes.

Close to the large manufacturing centers, especially those involving chemicals, wildlife has indeed suffered to some extent. Concern for human health is no idle fantasy. In remoter and more-wooded areas, the impact is minimal. Fish are still plentiful in the clear streams. Wildlife is so profuse that it borders on being a nuisance. Birds are abundant.

One morning after a light spring rain, I walked toward our church to start the fires. As I passed a wooded area, a chorus of myriads of birds greeted me. Orioles, rose-breasted grosbeaks, red-winged blackbirds, wrens, and warblers—all vied with each other in presenting their music. Across the road in a meadow, the bobolink with its unmistakable warble made its first appearance of the season.

There is a parallel between our environmental and church issues. A considerable amount of deterioration and "pollution" has appeared in today's churches. In one church, the issue concerns "gay" preachers; in another, the problem involves AIDS. Within the Mennonite churches we hear of such issues as women in the ministry, tobacco, nonresistance, and nonconformity.

We could use scare tactics to promote public awareness. We could foster fatalistic or quietistic views, by washing our hands of the problem and blaming everyone but ourselves. We could throw up our hands in despair. On the other hand, we could do our part to improve the church and promote peace.

The Rachel Carsons are helpful in fostering an awareness of our problems, but let us not despair. In remote areas, farther from polluting influences, the birds are still singing. People still gather together in loving, Christian fellowship. Dedicated ministers preach the loving gospel to large, attentive audiences. Yes, the bobolinks are still singing.

"When you say the birds are still singing in remoter areas, away from polluting influences, to what are you referring?"

In general, we find that smaller congregations, away from the root of contention, find it easier to preserve the peace, in spite of controversies elsewhere. In my opinion, peace, love, and unity are far more to be valued and treasured than differences, be they from ever so noble motivations.

"Would you suggest that while the bobolinks are singing, people are so concerned about 'the environment' that they can't hear the song?"

That is possible. In the end, "scare tactics" may be doing more harm than the "pollution." For the past ten years or more, we have been warned about the weak spots in the ozone layer, and that the summers are beginning to grow hotter. Yet thus far, there has been no particular trend in that direction. I believe that we may benefit the most if we continue to listen to the bobolinks' song.

## Should Christians Defend Their Country?

To many people, laws are made for breaking. This includes God's laws, the Ten Commandments. Some people will argue that since we live in the new dispensation, the whole Mosaic law is no longer in effect. This is true to some extent. But Christ said, "Think not that I am come to destroy the law, or the prophets; I am not come to destroy, but to fulfill" (Matt. 5:17).

In Matthew 5, Jesus verifies this. He not only forbids killing, but also anger, insulting others, revenge, and resistance. Matthew 5:44 makes it impossible to justify war, as do other Scriptures (Matt. 26:52; John 18:36; 2 Cor. 10:3-4; Eph. 6:12-13; Rom. 12:17-21; 1 Cor. 4:12).

The early Christians stood firmly on nonresistant principles. From the second and third centuries, we hear leading voices from the early church speaking earnestly against war:

• Justin Martyr (110-165) was a philosopher who converted to Christianity and became an evangelist. He was executed during the reign of Marcus Aurelius. Justin wrote, "We who formerly murdered one another now refrain from making war upon our enemies."

• Tertullian (140-230) was an elder in the church at Carthage and wrote formal justifications (apologies) for the Christian church. He asked, "Can it be lawful to make an occupation of the sword, when the Lord proclaimed that he who uses the sword shall perish by the sword?"

• Origen (185-254) was an elder in the church at Alexandria, the first Christian writer of Bible commentaries, and a pupil of Clement of Alexandria. He wrote, "Nowhere does [Jesus Christ] teach that it is right for his own disciples to offer violence to anyone, however wicked."

• Cyprian (200-258) was overseer of the church in Carthage, and many of his letters survive. He said, "The whole world is wet with mutual blood. Murder, which is admitted to be a crime when committed by an individual, is called a virtue when it is committed wholesale."

• Arnobius (ca. 260-330) was the teacher of Lactantius and

also wrote formal justifications of Christianity. He explained the Christians' position in these words:

> We have learned from [Christ's] teaching and his laws that evil should not be repaid with evil; that it is better to suffer wrong than to inflict it; and that our own blood should be shed rather than stain our hands and our conscience with that of another. As a result an ungrateful world has now for a long period been enjoying a benefit from Christ; for by his means the rule of savage ferocity has been softened, and the world has begun to withhold hostile hands from the blood of a fellow creature.

So what about helping to defend our country? Origen's answer to this question corresponds with the statement of Arnobius (above). When urged by the Romans to help in the preservation of justice by fighting under the Roman banner, Origen replied,

> We do help, by putting on the whole armor of God, in obedience to the apostles' injunction: "I exhort, therefore, that first of all, supplications, prayers, intercessions, and giving of thanks be made for all men; for kings, and for all that are in authority" [1 Tim. 2:1-2]. The more one excels in holiness, the more effective is his help to kings. Indeed, we refuse to fight under [the emperor], although he may require it. But we do fight on his behalf, forming a special army of righteousness, by offering our prayers to God.

There is every indication that this method worked for the early Christians. As Arnobius stated, the Roman empire enjoyed an extraordinary period of peace for two hundred years, which the early Christians believed was a result of divine intervention.

Where is our faith today? We give lip service to the same faith, although our actions belie our words. If Christians everywhere practiced the same faith as did the Christians of those early centuries, a golden age of peace would be possible. Certainly there would be less harm in trying it out than in helping to fight an unholy war.

"You say a certain verse makes it impossible to justify war.

How can it be impossible?"

Jesus Christ said, "But I say unto you, Love your enemies, bless them that curse you, do good to them that hate you, and pray for those who despitefully use you, and persecute you" (Matt. 5:44). If we loved our enemies, how could we justify war? Isn't there a contradiction there somewhere?

"Well, I suppose we should pray for those with whom we are at war."

While you're at it, perhaps you should include all those who are at war, on both sides. By then, the war might no longer be necessary.

"How is it that such teachings of those early Christians were not passed down to us through the established Christian church?"

Because it was not compatible with their viewpoint. From the time of Constantine (Roman emperor, 306-337), so-called Christianity was spread far and wide. Christian teachers such as Augustine (bishop of Hippo, 396-430) began to teach the doctrine of a "just war," in which Christians supported Rome with the sword, for the good of society. Incidentally, after this change of doctrine, the Roman empire collapsed in short order (by 476).

"It would almost seem as though those early Christians had instilled peace into the hearts of the Romans at that time."

Perhaps that is stretching the point. There was nothing peaceful about Nero, and later emperors had their armies. Tolerance would be closer to the truth.

## Is War Necessary?

Sixty-five years ago, our history textbooks gave us the impression that wars waged by Christian countries were necessary, honorable, and ethically moral. The War of Independence, the Civil War, and the War of 1812 were treated with respect by Americans, and tribute was paid to their respective heroes. Isaac Brock, Wolfe, and Montcalm, held places of honor in our history books.

Today, the tables have been somewhat turned. Even thirty-five years ago, a Canadian history text for grade 10 brought a different viewpoint before students of history. Instead of granting exploitive publicity to warfare in general, it exposed some of the evil influences that fostered warfare.

In the chapter on "The Road to War" (World War I), there are a number of positive statements bolstering our firm belief in the inconsistency of war.

1. When Archduke Ferdinand was shot by a Serbian sniper, he was not the victim of a lone assassin, as claimed by the Allies: France, Russia, and Great Britain. The murder was planned in advance by Serbian authorities, and was known by the British, who ignored this information to shelter the Serbs and condemn the pro-German Austrians.

2. As a result of the Bolshevik revolution, the filed documents in the archives of many European countries were made public. These proved that our revered leaders were far from being honest.

3. Preparations for a European war had already begun twenty-five years before the Great War (WW I) broke out.

4. Wars do not usually begin between a powerful country and a small one. For some reason, too remote to discuss here, wars usually break out when there is a balance of power. Europe was divided into two rival camps: the Triple Alliance of Germany, Austria, Hungary, and Italy on one side: and on the other, the Triple Entente of France, Russia, and Great Britain. All of these major powers had selfish interests in the war, hoping for financial gain by winning.

5. Although these alliances were lined up on opposite sides of the bargaining table, a considerable amount of bargaining passed back and forth under the table, such as "If you help us in the Suez, we will help you gain Morocco." This two-timing helped to aggravate the issues.

6. In 1909 Winston Churchill wrote, "A serious antagonism between two nations is not caused by natural hatred. It is the result of the vicious activity of a comparatively small number of individuals, and the credulity of the masses."

7. In wartime we hear much about the propaganda spread by the enemies. This in itself is propaganda. No mention is ever made of the propaganda spread by our own nation. To make young soldiers passionately inflamed against the enemy, some

218  A Separate People

facts are distorted, and others invented. In wartime, no nations have any qualms about spreading untruths if it helps their cause. Hatred must be encouraged and justice discouraged.

8. Our civilians, too, were fed on propaganda before, during, and after the war. Even today it is difficult to separate truth from fiction.

If we truly believe that war is forbidden in the New Testament, we must believe that it is not necessary. We must all resist the types of propaganda that glorify war and encourage hatred for our fellow human beings. Knowing that warfare is morally wrong, we must put forth every effort to be peace-loving ourselves.

A school history text deserves to be commended for exposing such inconsistencies and propaganda. We laud the frankness and sincerity of those who reveal such unacceptable behavior, not only among our enemies, but also among those in authority in our own country.

"What is the name of the history book to which you referred?"

*Decisive Decades*, by A. B. Hodgetts (Thomas Nelson & Sons, 1960).

"If I still had some doubts about whether it is right to go to war, your evidence would certainly be sufficient to convince me that no wars are ever justifiable."

"It still seems difficult to know what to do. We still are expected to obey the powers that be."

Yes, insofar as it doesn't violate the divine law. However, Peter said that when there is a clash of authorities, "We ought to obey God rather than men" (Acts. 5:29). Christ said, "Render to Caesar the things that are Caesar's, and to God the things that are God's" (Mark 12:17).

"I wonder what would have happened if war had broken out while that history textbook had been in use."

I suppose they would have done one of two things. Likely they would have told the pupils that this war is an entirely different thing, our country is totally innocent, and it did not spread any propaganda. If they were afraid the pupils would not believe that, the textbooks would have been exchanged for other, less-honest ones. I can't imagine that they would have taken a chance on leaving such books in the school, while being involved in war.

"Gives you sort of an eerie feeling, as if someone might be peeping in the window!"

I know. However, in all seriousness, if the time came, and your convictions proved to you that war is not right, what could you do? You would have no choice but to stand firm, as Moses told the Israelites, "Fear not, stand still, and see the salvation of the Lord" (Exod. 14:13).

That is the final test.

# Why Speak German?

Some time ago, I chanced to talk with a group of tourists from Hamburg, Germany. I was asked how long it has been since we left Germany. When I told them that it is over 250 years, a young man among them remarked that I was still quite well for my age!

I am willing to admit that I am still well for my age; but that has little to do with how long we are in Canada.

When the Mennonites first came to America, they settled in the wooded wilderness. There were no other people in the area, and thus no schools or churches, until they established their own. To a large extent, they were self-supporting. What they could not produce, they did without. Therefore, it was obvious that they continued to use their native language. There was no need to change.

The same conditions prevailed when our forebears moved to Canada a hundred years later. Nearly all of the original settlers were German, since the Mennonites had purchased the land en masse. The towns and villages were generally populated by European Germans who immigrated several years later. Thus, business was for the most part conducted in the German language during the first fifty years.

In the latter part of the nineteenth century, when Sunday schools and other innovations were introduced, English preaching was also included. Those of the Old Order, who did not favor Sunday schools, likewise rejected the English language for church, family, and their own community life. Invariably, when and where English was introduced, other modern practices followed. Usually this included a change from simplicity in dress and manners to more worldly forms.

Although the Old Order Mennonites and Amish kept using the German language in America for these 250 years, we do not consider it as a sacred cow. Yet the above facts prove the dangers of discarding the German language.

In part this reflected the general reluctance to change on the part of the Old Order Mennonites. Partly it represented a rejection of conformity to the world. The language barrier guarded us against being absorbed into the social life outside of the Mennonite circle.

Old Order Mennonite children learn Pennsylvania German as their mother tongue. Before they start school, most of them have learned English as well. All classroom work is conducted in English in Mennonite parochial schools, except for a few hours of German lessons per week. English speaking is recommended on the playground as well. Thus the pupils are truly bilingual by the time they finish school.

Most Mennonite men converse quite freely in the English language. Some of the older women, who have fewer dealings with the outside world, are more inclined to falter during an English conversation. Although church services are generally conducted in German, many of the ministers will switch to English when they are aware of English-speaking visitors in the church.

After 250 years, the Pennsylvania German language has become a part of our heritage. It is as much a part of our legacy as the black hat and the horse and buggy. Although we are not so naive as to believe that these customs are necessary for our salvation, we also realize that discarding customs because we are ashamed of them could be a hindrance to our salvation.

Why should we discard our mother tongue?

"How much difference is there between the Pennsylvania German dialect and Plautdietsch?"

A great deal. Our dialect comes from the Palatinate in southwestern Germany, where our ancestors lived for several generations.

Plautdietsch or Plattdeutsch is a dialect of Low German, spoken in some form in all of North Germany and related to Dutch and English. Mennonites from Holland used it in the Danzig area and along the Vistula River, and later carried it to the Ukraine, and eventually to North and South America. There are local variations, as one would expect.

In church services, however, both sets of Mennonites tend to use more High German in place of the Pennsylvania German or the Plautdietsch of daily living. This is influenced by the use of German Bibles, old hymns, and traditional vocabulary for speaking about our faith.

"Has the Pennsylvania German dialect changed much through the years?"

There is a gradual change from generation to generation. Some German words are replaced by English ones. To a certain extent, this is unavoidable. Since we don't learn the German name for all the new inventions and developments, we are inclined to Germanize English words.

"Does the younger generation continue to teach their children the dialect as their first language?"

Yes, as far as I know, even our great-grandchildren are taught the dialect from childhood. There are indeed other plain people around us who are losing out; but German is still going strong among us. To some people, it may seem foolish, and yet it helps to preserve our heritage. As long as we have so many differences between us, there is so much less danger of being assimilated into mainstream society with our own language. That to us is a definite advantage.

## The Changing Mennonites

Possibly fifteen years ago, Frank H. Epp introduced me to his 1977 book, *Mennonite Peoplehood*. I agree with many of his fundamental statements, even though I may not agree with his solutions. Here is the gist of his basic statements, with which I wholeheartedly agree.

He states that the modern Mennonites have sacrificed the

image of community on the altar of modernism. Few things remain that draw local people together. The Roaring Twenties did not promote a traditional community. To the American world, it was the passing of tradition. To us, it was the parting of the ways.

Modernism has in many ways destroyed traditional society, and according to Epp, it was replaced by shoddy substitutes. With the advent of the motor car, the social circle was no longer confined to the neighborhood. Sermons on radio and television supposedly now fill the need for the church, which formerly was the center of community activity.

Our close relationship with our neighbors is gone. This affinity was for keeps. The family, the school, the church, and the neighbors all traveled the same road. The social circle is lost in space. The community has been suspended.

Brotherly love is at the center of the social circle. With the social circle gone, brotherly love is weakened. It is sacrificed on the altar of progress.

When those of foreign races sacrifice their identity, they frequently sacrifice traditional values, breaking their common bonds. This is a case of throwing the baby out with the bathwater, which often happens when progress is ruthlessly introduced.

Another force that weakens the community is when modernism is too highly honored. Everything new is called progress.

"How aptly stated! In the spiritual sense, modernity is not necessarily progress. There is a grave danger that the opposite is the case. In fact, what reasoning is used when progress is unquestionably called good?"

With the introduction of technology, and financial security, neighbors did not need each other any more. In a real sense, they ceased to be neighbors. Independence does not contribute to community, friendliness, and hospitality. This is the antithesis of the good Samaritan (Luke 10:25-37).

As Old Order Mennonites, we take quite seriously the points mentioned above. On these points I agree fully. Even with these views, we find it a continual struggle to preserve our community in the face of modernism. The loss of rural intimacy and ethnic identity, the passion for modernism, and increased prosperity are all threats to our community. We find little or no spiritual benefits to counterbalance this threat. For us, there seems to be no choice if we expect spiritual blessings. We listen to Jesus saying, "What I say unto you, I say unto all, Watch" (Mark 13:37).

"Isn't it surprising how often modern writers admit that the new views are not necessarily better, but that they blend better with modern technology and theology?"

Yes. The passing of traditional society is not really compatible with our views based on the Scriptures. The writer to the Hebrews was referring to "traditional community" when he wrote,

Let us hold fast the profession of our faith without wavering,
. . . and let us consider one another to provoke unto love and to good works; not forsaking the assembling of ourselves together, as the manner of some is; but exhorting one another. (10:23-25)

"How often we have seen that 'their replacements were poor substitutes'! I have to think of the flimsy furniture that replaced the solid pine."

Yes; nor can radio and television ever replace the old country church, where the congregation sang and worshiped together.

"The family, the neighborhood, the school, and the church: doesn't that portray a picture of the Old Order community?"

It certainly is one of the basic concepts that binds us together. Continuity is what the Old Order community thrives on. Epp also mentions the loss of ethnic identity. To many, our adherence to the German dialect seems foolish. In a sense, it hampers our witness to neighbors. Of course, when strangers attend our services, at least part of the service is in English, if the minister is aware of such strangers. Yet ethnic identity is a strong bond to hold community together.

"To me, it has always seemed sad that modernity and progress have become so linked together, when obviously all they have is an appearance of commonality. I think we should never speak of progress, unless the subject actually shows improvement."

# The Mennonites and the New Deal

As a senior citizen I can well remember the Great Depression. I recall the ridiculously low prices of grocery items, such as cornflakes at three boxes for 25 cents or even less. I also remember that not many groceries of any kind were purchased, regardless of how low the price. With potatoes as low as 15 cents a hundred-pound bag, wheat at 50 cents per bushel, and hogs down to three dollars per hundredweight, it was only natural for farmers to eat what they had.

I realize that we Ontario farmers, with a mixture of crops, suffered little from the Depression. We came through without a scar. Those who bore the brunt were the Western wheat farmers and the city wage earners. With only one cash crop on which to depend, and several years of drought that destroyed even the gardens, the Westerners were on the brink of starvation. Unemployed laborers had saved nothing during the good times, had not so much as a garden, and were equally destitute.

As the Depression continued, many people grew desperate and became critical of the government. In the cities, they expressed themselves through Communist movements, unions, and strikes. In some rural communities, the United Farmers, granges, farmers' unions, and youth movements sought answers for the low returns received for their labors.

In the United States, President Roosevelt proposed his New Deal. He promised old age pensions, unemployment insurance, wage and price supports, shorter work weeks, and a whole bag full of social benefits. Canadians watched attentively and wondered whether the plan would work.

Young people were enthusiastic and wondered when Premier Bennett would wake up to establish similar programs. Although he did introduce such legislature toward the end of his term in office, he was not ready for such radical measures in 1933. His advice to the young farmers was "Save your money, be honest, pay your debts, work hard, and keep quiet."

One might consider it strange that the Old Order Mennonites would not even passively support governments such as the United Farmers, the CCF (Cooperative Commonwealth Federation, a Canadian political party of the early 1930s uniting farmers and labor), or any other New Deal government that champions the working classes. Why do they seem to favor the old democratic governments with their capitalistic tendencies?

First, the newer, left-wing parties operate on an aggressive principle, not compatible with nonresistance. Second, our Lord himself took for granted governments that were unfavorable to the poor people. He advised his followers to pay tribute to Caesar, rather than to reform the government. Third, the New Deal, with all its social benefits, would cause us to rely on temporal powers for our support; then we would no longer be pilgrims and strangers on this earth.

The young men of the New Canada Movement scorned Premier Bennett's advice. Today, few of those young men or their descendents are actively engaged in farming. The Old Order Mennonite community continued to operate on the principles suggested by Bennett. They saved their money, tried to be honest, paid their debts as well as they could, and in general worked hard and kept quiet. The community pulled through the Depression without much suffering and is as strong as ever. If they had clamored for a New Deal, the results might have been less favorable.

"With the Western farmers and the city people suffering, how did the Ontario mixed farmers respond?"

Thinking back, I recall at least three ways in which they helped. First and most important was the food sent out west. Nonperishable foods, such as potatoes, turnips, cabbage, beets, and carrots were loaded at the station in Elmira—a carload per week, if I remember correctly, throughout the fall.

Farm products were made available for townspeople on a pay-as-you-can basis. Many townspeople walked out to farms to hoe corn and potatoes in exchange for food.

"Wages would likely have been quite low, I assume."

Yes, if any jobs were available. In our local town, Elmira, less than one-third of former wage earners were employed. The four largest factories were closed. Hundreds of men stowed away in boxcars, traveling from town to town, seeking employment.

## Old Order Pharisees

Some people have compared those of the Old Order churches to the Pharisees. Perhaps the similarity is not as far-fetched as it may seem. In fact, I have had similar thoughts myself.

In Luke 18, the Lord told a parable about a Pharisee and a publican. The Pharisee prayed, "God, I thank you that I am not as other men are."

Although I have never prayed in this manner, there are times when I am indeed glad that "I am not as other men are." "Other men" may be just as good or better than I am. I have no argument with that. I refer more to economics.

Take my wardrobe, for example. As long as my clothes are in decent shape, I wear them. Sometimes I would still wear them when my wife thinks they are no longer in decent shape. They always remain in style, at least, as close to style as they ever are.

My wife, too, wears dresses similar to those she wore fifty years ago. When she does get a new dress, which she naturally makes for herself, it will be similar in color and style to her old one. I never need to buy a new buggy or horse just because the old one happens to be the wrong color or style.

Our furniture is another example. Fifty years ago, many people discarded their heavy, solid wood furniture in favor of new and lighter-weight furniture made in factories. The "hardware" on the new kind was plastic; the surface was veneer over cheaper material. The Old Order Mennonites kept their heavy furniture or bought their neighbor's.

Today, that lightweight furniture is falling apart. The trend is a return to solid wood. Unless the Old Order people stand firm, all their solid wood furniture will fall into the hands of people who had discarded it fifty years ago.

Half a century ago, young men and women left the farm for jobs in the cities. The young men were tired of driving horses. The young women wished to get away from the drudgery of the farm kitchen. Today those same people or their descendants return to buy their own places in the country, where they can keep a horse or two and get away from the rat race in the city. That is the American way of life. The Old Order people do not need to come back. They never left in the first place.

Fifty years ago it was considered a luxury to eat in a restaurant. We heard of hot dogs and hamburgers, imagining them to be food fit for kings. Now even poor people look down their noses at hamburgers.

Today a home-cooked country meal is a luxury for city people. If it consists of stone-ground whole wheat bread, with herbs, and honey instead of sugar, so much the better. Here on the farm, we never strayed far from wholesome foods.

When the Old Order Mennonites build their next new church, they will need to pay more than ever. Even with rising prices, it will likely cost less than a hundred thousand dollars for a building to accommodate up to five hundred people. There will be no towering steeple, no stained glass gracing the windows, no carpeting, wiring, or plumbing. Every square foot of the interior will be put to practical use.

Many people long to live as the Old Order Amish and Mennonites do, but they think it must be a hard life. For those of us who were born and raised under these conditions, there is nothing hard about it. Considering what it takes to live in high society, the Old Order life by comparison seems easy and undemanding.

"Don't the Old Order women's dresses change in style at all?"

Very little. It is true that patterns change slightly within a hundred-year span; yet it is so little that it is barely perceptible to a stranger.

"Would the Old Order Mennonites eat hot dogs and hamburgers today?"

Possibly, if they were eating at a restaurant or fast-food outlet. At home, they rarely do. Old Order meals do gradually change. Many of our women are fond of cookbooks and keep trying out new recipes. Fifty years ago, no meal was complete without pie. Today pie is more of a rarity.

"Do Old Order Mennonites use whole wheat flour?"

Some do and some don't. There are health food faddists who follow all the latest twists for healthful living. There are others

who feel that a meal is not healthful unless it can be fully enjoyed.

"Are you suggesting that whole wheat baking can't be fully
enjoyed?"

That depends on whether it rises properly. I have eaten whole
wheat bread so hard that I needed to soak it before I could chew
it. That is not my type. I prefer a meal that is easily eaten and di-
gested.

## Old Order Shopping

During the past, I have had numerous interviewers who
wished to know how we Mennonites live. One question was
how our shopping methods differ from those of others. At first
thought, it seemed to me there was little difference. We buy our
groceries, hardware, drugs, and lumber where everyone else does.

On closer reflection, I changed my mind. When we go to the
grocery store, we buy the staples needed for cooking, baking,
canning, and so on. We buy few prepared foods. Besides, our
daughter has a bulk-food store, where we make our greater purchases. My wife does all our cooking and baking, so our chief
purchases are flour, sugar, vinegar, and shortenings. We buy seal-
ers for canning. Because at our age we consume so little meat, we
buy picnic hams, chicken legs, and sometimes hamburger, at re-
duced prices.

Most Old Order women do their own sewing. So instead of
buying from the numerous ladies' and men's wear stores, we buy
fabrics for making our clothing. We never go to barbers, hair-
dressers, beauty parlors, or manicurists. In our fifty-six years of
marriage, my wife has always cut my hair. Naturally, she also
puts up her own hair.

My wife is a good cook, so we never eat out except at friends'
homes, where the food is free, because our visits reciprocate.
Sometimes when traveling we may eat at a restaurant or fast-
food outlet, but rarely in our hometown. Why should we? It
seems like foolishness to pay up to $10.00 for a meal that would
probably cost us one dollar at home.

Since our tractor fuel is delivered to our doors, we never go to service stations. New and used-car dealers are not required, since we do not drive cars. To a certain extent, this is offset by what we pay to blacksmiths, harness makers, and repairers. Yet such shops are in rural areas and have no bearing on our shopping in town.

Our church organization takes care of financial emergencies, so we do not frequent insurance offices. We do patronize banks, and some of our people use the Mennonite Credit Union. This could raise a thorny issue about being unequally yoked together with unbelievers. However, the Mennonite Credit Union is quite conscientious about who can become a member. I believe membership is reserved for those of the nonresistant faith.

We in the Mount Forest area buy most of our fuels from local dealers. But because of longstanding relationships and better deals, we purchase most of the livestock feed from Waterloo Region feed companies (about thirty miles away). Competition in that area is so strong that feed prices are more competitive than local ones. Another reason for lower prices may be that Waterloo area farmers are more stable, but in this area non-Mennonite farms may frequently change hands, making credit a greater risk.

The greatest difference between our spending and that of non-Mennonites is in the entertainment field. We attend no theaters, shows, horse races, exhibitions, hockey, baseball, or any other professional games, amusement parks, or arenas. We do not participate in sports such as bowling, card parties, billiards, curling, golf, or skiing. We need no recreational equipment such as campers, trailers, mobile homes, cottages, or swimming pools.

As already mentioned above, our daughter has a bulk-food business at the farm. She also sells all kinds of fabrics, notions, religious books, and giftware. Her sons operate a bike shop alongside, where they service and sell new and used bicycles. Across the road from her, a neighbor sells footwear along with his harness repair business.

Appliance dealers are rarely patronized. Photographers, florists, travel bureaus, jewelers, carpeting sales, and radio or TV salesmen get little, if any, of our money.

It makes one wonder: are we any benefit at all to the trade and commerce in our local towns? If not, we can at least be sure that we are no burden to the local population.

"You ask whether you are a benefit to the businesses in your town. No one is under any obligation to buy what he doesn't need. I know there are economists who claim that we must spend money to create a strong economy; but if that undermines our financial stability, then what?"

We as Old Order Mennonites don't mean to be stingy, but it is up to us to discern what we can afford.

"I agree that we spend too much on entertainment. But do you imagine we do that because we owe it to the entertainers? Don't ever let anyone tell you that you owe anything to Wayne Gretzky!"

There is such a great difference in what we consider as our priorities. Should we accept social assistance, just so we can spend it on entertainment? Isaiah, a prophet inspired by God, said, "Wherefore do you spend money for that which is not bread?" (Isa. 55:2). Although this is not in the New Testament, it does make sense. Paul is of the same mind: "Having food and raiment let us be therewith content" (1 Tim. 6:8).

"I think you are right. I guess we just find it difficult to understand how anyone can live a contented life without indulging in entertainment. I do respect you for it, though."

I don't find it difficult to understand. Television is the most powerful mass media of the day. Those of us who never watch TV are not subjected to such pressure. In our opinion, we are probably more contented than most of those who are addicted to TV.

"I'll support that view! At my age, I sometimes feel like throwing my set out the window!"

"You're not the only one. Right now, I'd trade my set for a slice of good homemade bread!"

# True Savings

Several years ago, our local newspaper, in cooperation with local merchants, sponsored its First Annual Gift Certificate Program. There has been none since, so apparently it didn't work out as well as anticipated. For $44.95, selected "lucky" people were entitled to receive up to $500 worth of savings, gifts, and services. The operator draws telephone numbers out of a hat to find the lucky winners.

We happened to be among the "lucky" winners. When I answered the phone, the operator congratulated me and started to read off the list of gifts and savings to which we were entitled: free oil change, brake inspection, car wash, radiator test. . . .

"Wait a minute!" I cut in. "We don't even have a car!"

"You don't have a car?" She sounded incredulous. "Then what about flowers, hair styling, shampoo, and sun tanning?"

"I'm sorry, but none of that interests us."

"Oh!" She began to show frustration. "Well, you would be entitled to two movie rentals and three tickets for cross-country skiing."

"We don't indulge in movies or in skiing."

"Here's one that you can't resist, though. You're entitled to three family portraits, for a total value of $239.85. I'm sure you would appreciate that."

"We do not sit for portraits."

"Do you eat out sometimes? There are several meals available which, if you buy one, you get the second one free."

"We never go to a restaurant just for the sake of eating out. We only eat out when we are too far from home at lunchtime, and then we usually pack a lunch."

That's when the operator gave up. The only item on the long list that would have been of any value to us was two pounds of nails, which would not have been a bargain at $44.95.

I did not regret the fact that we could not benefit from these savings. Instead, I realized once again how blessed we are that we are not compelled by our society to spend money for such a wide range of items and services.

Obviously, few people in developing countries would have benefited by any of these savings, any more than we could. Until recently, all of these were considered luxuries, and poor people could well do without them.

We do not live in a rich country. Our national deficit is so high that it seems too close to bankruptcy for comfort. Yet the public is constantly clamoring for more social services and benefits.

If more people would live within their means, there would be less need for social benefits. If more people spent their leisure time at home, baking, gardening, and canning, instead of going to the cottage or the beach, they would have cheaper and more wholesome food. They would save on traveling expenses and would cause less air pollution.

Those deeply ingrained habits that came with prosperity are difficult to break. Yet we are firmly convinced that we live happier and more fulfilling lives than those who have everything and still ask for more.

"That story sounds familiar. Wasn't that featured in Peter Etril Snyder's annual catalog a few years ago?"

That's right; it was. Does that mean that you are an art fancier?

"Oh, now, I wouldn't say that. And yet, I do enjoy Snyder's work. He specializes in Mennonite art. Were you the man who was lucky enough to get two pounds of nails for $44.95?"

I didn't bother getting them. They're cheaper at the hardware store.

"I think you were lucky that nothing more was interesting to you. Such bargains can be expensive in the end, when we cash in on what we may not need."

"I like your choice of words. We don't want to be compelled or pressured by our society to spend money for luxuries. We should be ashamed that we have no more backbone than to allow the Joneses to control our finances."

Yes, if they simply *controlled* them, it wouldn't be so bad. I would say they try to expropriate our money.

"You know, it's really marvelous that you people do without so many things that we consider as normal expenses. Are we really so wasteful?"

Your ordinary car expenses should not be considered among your wasteful spending. Then again, the local merchants didn't offer free horse feed, buggy wash, or harness repair.

"I'm sure we could do with less restaurant food. As for hair styling and shampoo, I suppose I *could* do my own. At least, I've never paid for sun tanning. If I need a tan, I can get one on the deck or at the beach; but then I would spend money to get there. Oh, dear, I didn't realize how wasteful we are!"

"Well, I haven't heard you complaining about the pension being too low, either."

You're beginning to make me feel cheap, as if I were blaming you for being wasteful. That's not the idea. We *want* to live the way we do.

## Roles of Retired Farmers

Traditionally, the Mennonites have always taken care of their own. When a younger son was ready to take over the farming, the old people retired to the *Daudy* (grandparents') house, a small home attached to the farmhouse. Grandpa groomed the horses, oiled the squeaky garden gate, and patched the veranda floor. Grandma knitted socks and mitts for her grandchildren, and occasionally peeled potatoes for her daughter-in-law.

When the Canada Pension Plan was adopted, the Old Order Mennonites wanted no part of it. They felt that the younger, able-bodied people were responsible to care for their parents, according to the Scriptures: "If any provide not for his own, and especially for those of his own house, he has denied the faith, and is worse than an infidel" (1 Tim. 5:8). "Honor your father and mother, . . . that it may be well with you, and you may live long on the earth" (Eph. 6:2-3).

For this reason the Mennonites appealed to the government for exemption from the pension plan. After several years, this petition was granted.

In the course of time, the position of the retired Mennonite farmers changed. Cottage industries sprang up throughout the Old Order farming community. The elderly women found a lucrative trade in quilts, both in piecing and in quilting. To accommodate a large quilting frame, the *Daudy* houses needed to be enlarged.

Shops were built on many farms. Here retired farmers build cabinets and other furniture, repair machinery, and manufacture stabling. Some have harness, shoe, and carriage repair shops. Others weave carpets or make horse blankets. Still others make or assemble parts for larger shops.

Many of those who have no shops of their own are employed in the shops of others. They voluntarily work for less-than-average wages, but can work at their own pace. They take time off whenever they want to take a break.

The horses are no longer groomed as regularly. The garden gate continues to squeak. The veranda floor must wait until it is replaced by a new one. Socks and mitts are purchased ready-made.

The psychological effect of gainful employment among seniors is positive. Life continues to be meaningful. Greater longevity seems to result, when compared with those who sit on park benches.

In many cases such seniors remain self-supporting until they are eighty years old. When they are no longer able to work and do require help, the young people are close by to render assistance. Because of their continued employment, the old people are often in a position to pay for their needs.

We hope such a system of home care can be continued indefinitely. The mutual benefits are too great to be sacrificed.

"Why did the Old Order Mennonites object so strongly to the pension plan?"

Because they did not believe in the principle of the thing. If the pension plan were reserved for those who were unable to support themselves, the cost of pensions could easily be cut in half.

"It seems to me that the Old Order plan is self-destructive. Seniors who are self-employed take jobs away from younger men.

Doesn't that cause more unemployment?"

Not if the working mothers stay at home to take care of their children, prepare nourishing meals for her family, and do the family's laundry and housecleaning. She would be there to keep her young people off the streets. If she is a true mother, she is in a much better position to raise her children than any babysitter. So that leaves more jobs outside the home for the younger men.

"You are deviating from the point, aren't you?"

Not really. I'm presenting a natural course of events.

"I think I can follow your line of thought. If gainful employment means greater longevity, then conversely, sending them to retirement homes, with nothing to do, is shortening their lives. Isn't that part of the point you are making?"

Well, yes, it amounts to that. If we honor our parents, we will not deliberately shorten their lives. Being a senior myself, I see a whole cycle of events that make life meaningful for seniors. The extended family is a social circle in itself, and it fosters continuity and social security, without draining the public coffers.

The horses do not seem to suffer for lack of regular grooming. Mother will give the garden gate a shot of WD40 to stop its squeaking. As for Grandma, she will still sit in her rocker for knitting, after her quilting days are over.

## Leisure Time

One question frequently asked of the Old Order Mennonites is what they do in their spare time. They have no television, radio, or video. They attend no theaters, shows, or fairs. They frequent no places of amusement, entertainment, or professional sports. They participate in no public hockey, baseball, tennis, bowling, or card games. They do not go to the beach, nor do they take extended hunting or fishing trips. So what do they do?

The answer is varied. There are indeed a few who literally work from dawn to dusk, except for mealtime. They are workaholics. Work is their only interest, besides eating and sleeping. Others—men with heavy workloads who cannot afford help, and mothers with numerous small children—have little time for recreation, except for the few moments they spend with their children.

The vast majority do have some form of recreation in spare time. In some cases, this takes the form of work bees. Women of all ages gather in homes for quiltings, by invitation, of course. They regret it when they are unable to attend a quilting! Although practical work is accomplished, quilting is definitely also a social function. Men and boys find a similar form of work-play by attending farm auctions, livestock sales, and barn raisings.

In the evening, after the day's work is done, there is a leisure hour in most Old Order homes. Where there are young children, families sometimes play games. Mennonites enjoy singing, so some evenings are spent in this way, especially during the winter.

However, in most homes, evenings are spent in reading. This is where a pertinent question arises: What do they read?

Because there are fairly rigid criteria on suitable reading material, it is easier to say what they don't read. This varies greatly between homes—to say nothing of what young people read on the sly!

Pornography, or even books with pornographic references, are strictly prohibited in most homes. Murder mysteries and Western thrillers are strongly discouraged. Such reading material may encourage immorality, lust, and violence.

Romances have a tendency to lead to divorce, since they present an entirely false impression of love and marriage. Those who read such stories are inclined to become disillusioned when they encounter real-life marital conditions. Popular writers who produce Christian romances can be almost as misleading, since they also present unreal views of married life, masquerading as Christian ideals.

Among stories for juveniles, the Hardy Boys, Nancy Drew, and Danny Orlis series are discouraged in many homes because of the quasi-violence portrayed in most of them.

So what is left? Actually, there is no lack of good reading material. There are numerous books, both fiction and non-fiction, dealing with our Anabaptist heritage. Many of them, though true, are as thrilling as some mystery novels.

More and more books are being written from the Old Order Amish and Mennonite slant. Anyone who doubts the availability of sound reading material should check the Pathway Bookstore catalog put out by the Old Order Amish.

"I can understand how the older people can get by with what you mentioned; but what about the young people?"

That varies too. It is not so much a matter of killing time, as there is in finding time to do all the things they would like to do. Among the boys, there are haircut meetings.

"Now that's something new to me. You mean to say that they would get together to have their hair cut?"

Exactly. Every three weeks, on a certain day, half a dozen boys get together to cut each other's hair. Naturally, it tends to be a social gathering. The housemother probably serves lemonade or apple juice, with cookies or squares; although there is no fixed rule. It is possibly eleven-thirty or twelve o'clock before they get home.

Some of the boys, who wish to make extra money, go with a gang to catch broilers during the night. This highly remunerative work is done on the boys' spare time, or sleeping time, so they must decide how much they are able to do.

"What about the girls? Do they have nothing similar to do?"

During the winter, quiltings are a common thing among both girls and women. Most girls get at least six quilts from home, besides hooked rugs, comforters, and other bedding. This accounts for the many quiltings during the winter. If the girls have a knack for quilting, they can find a well-paying source of income in the evenings and spare time, by quilting for others.

Another form of pastime for girls, besides reading, is writing circle letters. This is also common among older women. To start a circle letter, a social letter is sent to a friend, who adds a letter and sends the two on to a third, and so on, until the desired number of correspondents is reached. The pack is then sent back to the first, who removes her old letter and adds a new one. Such circle letters continue indefinitely.

"We certainly see that time does not weigh heavily on the hands of Old Order Mennonites."

## The Dachwaggeli

There are certain words in the Pennsylvania German dialect which have no counterpart in another language. One such term is *Dachwaggeli*, the one-seated, covered buggy with square corners. For a hundred years or more, this vehicle has been the means of transportation among the majority of seniors among us. There has also been a certain stigma attached to the vehicle, as a

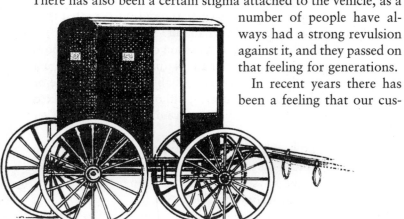

number of people have always had a strong revulsion against it, and they passed on that feeling for generations.

In recent years there has been a feeling that our cus-

toms deprive two classes of people who would need a covered vehicle the most: the elderly who no longer drive their own horses,
and those with a number of young children in their families. In
these two cases, a two-seated roofed vehicle is useful. However,
some people prefer to see the *Dachwaggeli* done away with altogether, and they are not about to see its use expanded, especially not among younger people.

Such people have indeed a legitimate claim to protest against
covered buggies for young people. In Pennsylvania one may see
Old Order young people driving buggies similar to our *Dachweggelin*, rigged out with plush upholstery, heaters, ceiling lights,
and in some cases even built-in radios and tape players. Colored
lights adorn the buggy. The horse is decked out with colored
loops, shiny brass, and nickel.

The casual observer cannot tell whether youths driving these
rigs are members of the church or not. If the same things happened here, we would certainly discourage our young folks from
driving such vehicles.

The situation seems to be undergoing a quiet, unobjectionable
transition here. A number of covered carriages are now in use to

transport invalids and wheelchairs. Gradually others appear with two-seated, covered carriages to accommodate sizeable families. So far, none have appeared that seem to be defying the ruling against modernity. Even younger people now drive plain, simple, *Dachweggelin* in the prescribed order.

The ones who favor a greater use of covered vehicles have the key for acceptability in their own hands. If they keep their vehicles simple and free from adornment, there is little difference in how many seats the vehicle has, or how many horses are hitched to it. There is no reason for pride and liberalism to gain ground as a result. The stigma will burn itself out.

Instead of being a stepping-stone toward driving a car, such vehicles will to a large extent eliminate the need for a car. If, on the other hand, decorations and displays of pride become evident in the new type and use of vehicles, it will prove what motive was behind the change of vehicles.

The trend among younger people to pattern themselves more closely after the manner of their elders should be encouraged rather than repressed. Closing the generation gap strengthens the church. If single people are not ashamed to copy the manners of older people, there is a greater chance that they will be ashamed of ridiculing them. Why should they need to be different?

"Just how is the word *Dachwaggeli* translated?"

Literally, it would be "a little roofed wagon." In Pennsylvania, the vehicles that look similar are called carriages. However, what we call a carriage is more similar to their spring wagon, except that our carriages have low sides, rather than a flat rack, and have two or three removable, cushioned seats.

"I can't figure out who rides in open buggies, and who has the *Dachwaggeli*. Is there a slide rule to say who does what?"

Traditionally, only people over fifty rode in *Dachweggelin*. Today, there is neither a fixed rule nor a certain custom to say who drives a *Dachwaggeli* and who doesn't. There was a certain stigma at one time; some people reached the age when others ride in covered buggies, and they did not wish to be seen in one. On the other hand, some young people are eager to have a covered buggy before they are the age to be driving one normally.

# *Grandpa Says*

◆ ◆ ◆

# Canada 130 Years Old

"Grandpa, how far can you think back?"

The old man put down his book and peered over his glasses at his granddaughter.

How far? Well, Sarah, I clearly remember the sixtieth anniversary of Confederation. How long would that be?

"Umm: that would be—71 years, right?"

Right. My brother subscribed to the *Family Herald* at that time. Our mailbox was a mile from home, so I usually brought the mail along on my way home from school. Of course, I always read the children's page before I left the paper at Menno's. There was a children's story under the heading "1867-1927." That was water for my mill.

"What was it like to walk to and from school then?"

Our side road was mostly dirt and sand, although soon afterward, Emanuel Soehner hauled gravel for the road, stony pit-run, with his one-ton Rugby truck. At that time there were mostly teams and wagons on the road, with a few cars: the Model T Ford, Chevrolet, Star, Essex, Willys-Knight, and Durant. Some, like the Model T, were square-cornered, with glass doors and windows. Most of them were touring cars, with folding tops, like top buggies.

"If there were no big trucks, how did you get cattle to the stockyards, and hogs to the butchers?"

There were no stockyards then, either. We drove our cattle five miles to the station, on foot, where they were weighed, and the drover paid us in cash. Then we chased them into pens, ready to be loaded directly on train cars, for shipping to slaughterhouses. Fat hogs went to the station on horse-drawn wagons with stock racks.

For helping to drive cattle to town, we were rewarded with a quarter each, and perhaps a five-cent ice-cream cone.

On one such occasion, Father took me to the fire hall, where the harness hung overhead, just inside the doors, ready to be dropped down on the horses' backs when the bell tolled. However, neither the harness nor the bell was now in use because the town had invested in a truck and a siren.

At that time, all the factories were steam-powered, and had whistles that were blown at twelve o'clock. From our home, we could hear the whistles of the Elmira and Elora factories, five and six miles distant.

"There must have been lots of whistles then. Didn't the trains have whistles too?"

Yes, but they were different, at least with a different timing: two medium, a short, and one long "Toot." Factories gave just one blast, but each had its own tone. Stearn engines for running threshing machines had a long, sharp note, and two high-pitched short ones.

In those days we hauled all our grain into the barn to be threshed. When the wheat was all drawn in, and a few loads of oats, the threshers would come, so that each farmer could thresh for about half a day. Then there was room for drawing in the rest of the grain, to be threshed in November or so, when the fall work was done.

"How did you get the grain sheaves up into the mow?"

With a rack lifter. This is a heavy, wooden windlass that hoisted the loaded rack from the wagon nearly to the barn roof. From there, the sheaves were thrown into the mow. We hitched the team to the rope for pulling up the rack.

"What about hay making? Did you have balers?"

No. Balers were first used in the field about fifty years ago. We cut the grass with a mower pulled by a team. Most people raked the hay with a siderake and loaded it with a hayloader. In the barn, they unloaded it with a hayfork.

We were a little more old-fashioned. My dad believed it was too hard for a team to pull a partly loaded wagon towing a hayloader over our sandhills. We raked it with the dumprake, then forked it on the wagon by hand. At the barn, we unloaded the hay with a hayfork on a rope through pulleys, with a team to pull the hay up into the mow.

"How did you grind your grain for feeding?"

We had a roller chopper for grinding cattle feed. We had a six-horsepower gasoline engine for running the chopper. For pig feed, we took the grain to the mill in town, where it was ground. We took home bran, shorts, oil cake, and meat meal to mix with the chop, using the scoop shovel.

"Did you use any chemical weed spray in your fields?"

No. We always hoed the corn, potatoes, and mangels at least once. We also went through the grain fields and hoed all the thistles. The only sprays we used were for potato bugs. Neither mustard nor sow thistles grew on our sandy land, but we had lots of twitch grass!

"My, that must have been a lot of hoeing! Didn't you get tired?"

Of course we did! But then we didn't have as much corn. Five acres was all we needed.

## Growing-Up Years

"Grandpa, what were your growing-up years like?"

Would you really like to know?

"Well, yes, unless you'd rather not tell me."

All right; but I warn you, not all of it is pleasant. When I look back over the years, I often think of one of our hymns, as it would be when translated into English:

> If one is up in years,
> his past oft reappears,
>     and brings only regrets;
> of all those moments fleeting,
> few stand out, worth repeating,
>     from which one satisfaction gets.
>
> (*Die Gemeinschaftliche Liedersammlung*
> [Berlin/Kitchener, Ont.: 1836], 198, verse 2)

I was the youngest of six boys, and a weakling at that. By the time I could have participated in their sports, they had outgrown them. As a result, I never learned to play any active games such as baseball, hockey, or anything else that required and built mus-

cle. I had many lonesome days and looked forward to school. Even there, I was unable to keep up with others of my age in active games and spent much of my recess time in reading.

"You mean you never helped to play ball?"

Very little. Occasionally someone would say, "Come on out and help to play ball." Sometimes I would give in; but soon they would say, "Why didn't you catch the ball? Why didn't you hit it? Why didn't you throw it to me?" Then I would go back in and read. To this day I can't hit, throw, or catch a ball.

"I guess I never noticed."

You'd soon find out if you threw a ball to me. At home it was the same story. Our egg baskets were always lined with newspapers or magazines, to save the eggs from breakage. When I was supposed to be gathering eggs, I would read those papers, inside and out. There were few books around, but all the farm magazines had children's pages, which I devoured until I graduated to the serial stories: sometimes a Western, sometimes a mystery. My mother did not approve at all. I respected my mother greatly and tried hard to please her. But when it came to reading, I let her down disgracefully.

"I understand. You were not the only one. Some of my brothers were the same."

Church services were not held as regularly then as they are now. During my school years, we had services in our home church only every four weeks. The whole family attended then. On the intervening Sundays, our parents would attend services at one of the other churches, or visit in the neighborhood. Frequently the children would then stay at home. Sad to say, when a group of boys was at home alone all day, we sometimes did things we were ashamed of later.

"So it might sometimes have been four weeks before you would have gone to church again?"

That sometimes happened. Some Sundays the neighboring boys all gathered at one home. During the summer we would go swimming. When the boys gathered at our place during the summer, we usually spent the afternoon at the fish pond, on a property next to ours, owned by several local businessmen.

The sign TRESPASSERS WILL BE PROSECUTED awed us but did not keep us from going on the property. It even inspired us to snoop around the buildings when no one was there. If we happened to be in swimming when a car drove in the lane, sounding the horn, we ran, clothes in hand, back to the orchard to get dressed, no doubt to the amusement of the "intruders."

We milked our six cows by hand. Many other machines were hand or foot operated: cream separators, butter churns, washing machines, turnip pulpers, sewing machines, and water pumps, except those operated by windmills. Fridges, coolers, and electrical appliances were unheard of among us. In the winter, the roads were traveled by cutters and sleighs, to the tune of ringing and jingling bells. If the roads were closed, fences were opened for driving through the fields.

"Would you open a neighbor's fence and drive through without asking him?"

Yes, we would, because we knew he would do the same on our farm. That was still part of the pioneer spirit of pulling together.

"Where did you go to school?"

The old public school stood a little to the south of the present

North Woolwich Old Order parochial school. It was large for one room, but there were sixty-four pupils when I started school! In the middle of the room, toward the back, there was a large furnace for coal or wood, which usually kept the room quite warm. When I started school, we still wrote on slates. Within a few years, that changed to workbooks or scribblers, as we called them then.

"What subjects did you learn?"

Much the same as today. The three R's came first, then spelling, geography, history, composition, grammar, and art covered most of the subjects.

The woodstove was the only source of heat in the home. We slept on straw ticks on top of rope beds. Our bedroom was cold, but the heavy comforter was warm. Everyone went to bed early, as the coal oil lamp gave barely enough light by which to read.

"What was your work in the winter?"

Cutting wood to keep us warm the next winter. With a two-man crosscut saw, axes, sledge, and wedges, we spent many a day in the woodlot. Later in the summer, we cut it short with the buzz saw and piled it in the woodshed to dry.

Yes, there have been some changes in seventy years; some for the better, but not all.

## Old Order Vacations

"Grandpa, have you ever gone on a vacation?"

Well, Sarah, that depends on what you call a vacation. When we go visiting in the United States, you could call it a vacation. You see, my mother-in-law came from the States, and so did my grandfather. So we have relatives and many friends across the border. When we visited my brother in Virginia, we traveled on Skyline Drive and visited the Luray Caverns, both of which are scenic vacation sites. Even visiting in a far country is a form of vacation.

Nine years ago we had a different vacation. We were gone for sixteen days, early in September. The weather was ideal. We did not stay at a cottage nor visit a beach. We saw neither mountains nor oceans. We visited no historical sites, museums, nor parks.

We spent no money for meals, lodging, or travel. Yet only once before had we been away from home for a longer period of time in our forty-six years of married life.

"How could you take such a long vacation without spending any money? Did you travel with someone who paid the expenses?"

No, we traveled alone. But wait—there was a slight traveling expense. Our first stop, before we even left the community, was right here with the blacksmith, your father. He reset two of our horse's shoes!

"Oh, so you traveled with the *Dachwaggeli!*"

Yes. From here we traveled on with our covered buggy to Shady Lawn, your aunt's dry goods store, where we had supper. Then we continued to the home of one of our most southerly church members, where we spent the night.

The next morning we headed toward the south. For the next two weeks, we received three square meals a day, a bed to sleep in every night, feed and accommodations for our horse—all in exchange for the dubious privilege of being our hosts.

"How many places did you visit?"

We visited in over fifty homes. Many were homes of those our age and older, and quite a few were shut-ins. We attended church services twice and also visited two schools and a few stores.

"Were the people expecting you? I mean, didn't they mind having you come any day of the week?"

To people who are not acquainted with our methods of visiting, this would indeed seem as though we were taking advantage of their hospitality. As it stands, I hardly think anyone took it amiss. Our home is always open for visitors. On several occasions, we have supplied beds for a dozen or more visitors in one night, who came unannounced. This open-door policy is an accepted standard among the Old Order Mennonites.

"I think that would be exciting, traveling with the *Dachwaggeli* for over two weeks!"

A similar situation arises when our people visit Mennonite communities across the border, or when they visit us. Sometimes one family is notified in advance about visitors arriving from a distance, but not necessarily always.

As soon as visitors arrive, arrangements are made for having them hauled from place to place the following day. Generally those who provide night lodging also have the privilege of being drivers the next day, with their horses and carriages.

Local travel agencies offer bus tours to Pennsylvania, to visit the Amish and Mennonite communities. For a price, visitors can see the well-kept homes and sample Mennonite cooking at local restaurants. They can spend the night in a bed right in the heart of Mennonite country.

When we visit Pennsylvania, we pay only our fare to get there and back again. All the rest is free: the authentic Mennonite meals, lodging in the homes, and entertainment or enjoyment. We see the whole panorama from the inside.

"I can hardly wait until I am old enough to go on a trip."

Don't worry; your time will come soon enough. We Old Order Mennonites consider it a privilege to host visitors from across the border or out of state. It is an interesting and edifying experience, and even exciting. Sometime we might even be entertaining angels (Heb. 13:2; Gen. 18–19) or welcoming the Lord, "the King," by giving hospitality to needy strangers (Matt. 25:31-40). If healthy attitudes prevail, such visiting exchanges help to strengthen the bonds of friendship and the "household of faith" (Gal. 6:10).

Besides, it presents an excellent opportunity for freeloading!

## Old Order Expansion

"Grandpa, you were one of the first Mennonite people to move to Mount Forest, weren't you?"

Yes, we were the second family to move up there. Your parents were the seventh.

"How did you ever get started? I mean, weren't you afraid it wouldn't work?"

Yes, I was afraid, and I think Grandma was more afraid than I was, but I believed it could work. It all started fifty years ago, while I worked in the St. Jacobs mill. One of the men I worked with had a dream of buying a cheap farm outside the Mennonite district, for about eight thousand dollars. He believed that one could make a living on such a farm, with a team of horses, a few hundred hens, half a dozen cows, and as many sows. I was partly convinced.

Over a hundred years ago, there was a small Mennonite community in Wallace Township, north of Listowel. Circumstances prevented the church from growing. There was a division in the Mennonite church. Those who were more old-fashioned moved back to Woolwich Township.

"Are there still Mennonite people living there?"

There are Mennonites living there again. The Mennonites who had first lived there built two meetinghouses, one at Brotherston and one at Kurtzville. In recent years, the Markham people started having church at Brotherston again, and the Conservatives use the Kurtzville church. There are quite a number of Mennonites scattered throughout the area.

I stuck my neck out by inserting an ad in the *Listowel Banner*, asking about available farms. Response was good. Quite a number of farms were offered at about a hundred dollars per acre. A number of friends were willing to join me in a tour of inspection.

Just one little monkey wrench can stop the biggest machinery. The Perth Agricultural Representative talked with the one from Waterloo. The former informed the latter that some war veterans were being settled in Wallace Township, just beyond the western edge of the present Old Order community. Since this was soon after World War II, the wound was still raw. The veterans did not want nonresistant Mennonites as their neighbors. The Perth agent suggested letting the matter cool off. We did.

The years rolled on. Farm prices kept rising. The church kept growing and expanding, and my feet grew itchy again. In 1962, on Civic Holiday, I made a tour of Wallace Township.

"How did you go?"

With my bicycle, an old standard.

"How far was it?"

About twenty miles. Oh, don't look so shocked! I was younger than I am now, and seven years younger than your father is. Wallace Township looked good to me, but farm prices had risen. I had hoped for something cheaper. Meanwhile, I told a Record of Performance milk inspector about my problem. He advised me to look in the Conn area. He had two farms northwest of Conn and was sure there were still good farms available for eight thousand dollars!

"Where were those two farms?"

Where Uncle Ivans and John Gingrichs live now. The next year, on Civic Holiday again, I pedaled up through Arthur toward Conn. The road was totally strange to me. All I knew was that one of our old neighbors lived near Conn. I watched mailboxes as I went until I found what I was looking for.

When I told the man what I was after, he offered me his two-hundred acre farm for eighteen thousand dollars. The house was new but too small for our family. I did see several cheap farms that day.

"You didn't buy a farm that day, though, did you?"

No. When I came home, I received a cold reception. Nobody wanted to live near Conn, with its cold, wet land. Why, it was just at the edge of "Floatin' Proton"! Proton Township was well-known for its wet land.

The next year, again on Civic Holiday—

"Why always on Civic Holiday? Is that the day to buy farms?"

No, but it had to be on a holiday because I was working in the feed mill. It would have been too cold on Christmas Day. Anyhow, I went and talked with my cousin, whom I respected for his good judgment. He didn't think starting a new settlement was a good idea. "It's been tried before, and it never works. If the others all failed, why do you think your plan would prosper?"

My wings drooped. I was about to give up—until I talked with another man whose views were quite different. "There is no reason why such a community should not prosper. It isn't necessary to go about it in a big way. Let's just go quietly ahead and buy a few farms."

"Did your wings still droop?"

No! I was ready to soar away on the wings of an eagle! In fact, one of our group bought a farm soon afterward, and shortly afterward I bought a two-hundred-acre farm for eleven thousand dollars.

"Is that where you lived then?"

Yes, we built our *Daudy* house at the back of that farm.

"What does your cousin say now?"

He told me once that he did not expect it to work out; but it did, and he was glad.

"My, you sure had some experiences!"

# The World

"Grandpa, what do we mean when we talk of the world? When I was little, I learned that the world was round. In school I was taught that it was the earth which was round. Later, in history class, I learned that when Columbus sailed toward the west, some of his sailors thought the world was flat and were afraid they would sail over the edge. Columbus knew better, and as a result, he discovered America. He had sailed from the Old World to the New World. This is really confusing."

Yes, it can be confusing, because so many words have more than one meaning, depending on how they are used. The dictionary tells me that the world is the earth with its inhabitants, which all belongs to God (Ps. 24:1). It also means the whole human race. When Columbus sailed to America from Europe, to the New World from the Old World, he found that the two were worlds apart. In this case, the word means two distinct classes or forms of existence.

"When I first heard of the Old World and the New World, I thought it referred to the world before and after the Flood."

That could make sense, too. However, at the time of the Flood, God used the word "earth" rather than "world." We read in Genesis 6:12-13 that "all flesh had corrupted their way upon the earth." God said, "Behold, I will destroy them with the earth" (RSV).

"I have heard a lot through our ministers, and in the Scriptures about 'the world,' 'worldly,' and 'worldliness.' Is it true that we use those words more than most other churches?"

True enough. Many Christian churches do not use those expressions, perhaps because they do not fit into the picture they see. We frequently mention being separate from the world, meaning from the sin of the world. Someone might ask what we mean by "the world." This is one of the easiest questions for us to answer, for it comes directly from the Holy Scriptures. Let me quote a few such passages:

The children of *this world* are in their generation wiser than the children of the light. (Luke 16:8)

You are of *this world*; I am not of *this world*. (John 8:23)

Now is the judgment of *this world*; now shall the prince of *this world* be cast out. (John 12:31)

Not as *the world* gives, give I unto you. (John 14:27)

Love not *the world*, neither the things that are in *the world*. If any man love *the world*, the love of the Father is not in him. For all that is in *the world*, the lust of the flesh, the lust of the eyes, and the pride of life, is not of the Father, but is of *the world*. And *the world* passes away, and the lust thereof; but he that does the will of God, abides forever. (1 John 2:15-17)

We know that we are of God, and *the whole world* lies in wickedness. (1 John 5:19)

Jesus answered, "My kingdom is not of *this world*: if my kingdom were of *this world*, then would my servants fight. (John 18:36)

Has not God made foolish the wisdom of *this world*? For after that in the wisdom of God *the world* by wisdom knew not God, it pleased God by the foolishness of preaching to save those who believe. (1 Cor. 1:20-21)

If any man among you seems to be wise in *this world*, let him become a fool, that he may be wise. For the wisdom of *this world* is foolishness with God. (1 Cor. 3:18-19)

God was in Christ, reconciling *the world* unto himself, not imputing their trespasses unto them; and has committed unto us the word of reconciliation. (2 Cor. 5:19)

Demas has forsaken me, having loved *this present world*. (2 Tim. 4:10)

That by these you might be partakers of the divine nature, having escaped the corruption that is in *the world* through lust. (2 Pet. 1:4)

For we wrestle not against flesh and blood, but against principalities, against powers, against the rulers of the darkness of *this world*. (Eph. 6:12)

Now is the judgment of *this world*; now shall the prince of *this world* be cast out. (John 12:31)

[Jesus,] who gave himself for our sins, that he might deliver us from *this present evil world*. (Gal. 1:4)

For the grace of God that brings salvation, has appeared to all men, teaching us that, denying ungodliness and *worldly* lusts, we should live soberly, righteously, and godly, in *this present world*. (Titus 2:11-12)

"I must look up all these Scripture verses."

Then you would be noble, like the Bereans to whom Paul preached (Acts 17:11).

"I can understand that people who like fancy clothes, go to war, go to college, vote in elections, or are members of parliament—such people would not use those words, because they themselves are so close to the world."

There is certainly nothing very gratifying about the descriptions of evil in this old world. Many people try to get all the sinful pleasure out of this world that they can. We call such a person a *Weltmensch*, a worldling.

"That gives me plenty of reason to stay away from worldliness."

Yes, the Scriptures tell us that we can't serve two masters. We can't serve God and mammon (Matt. 6:24). I'd rather be a pilgrim and stranger in this world, and let others seek their fleeting pleasures (1 Pet. 2:11; Heb. 11:25). We "look for new heavens and a new earth, in which righteousness dwells" (2 Pet. 3:13).

## Toward Sodom

"Grandpa, why do none of our people live in cities?"

Well, would you like to live in a city?

"No-o. I just wondered if there is a special reason."

Have you read *The Trail of the Conestoga?*

"I think so."

When Mabel Dunham wrote that 1942 book, she gave a vivid picture of the trials and triumphs of the first Mennonite settlers in Ontario. Her next book, *Toward Sodom,* described how the liberal and modest people separated in Waterloo County. Those closer to the cities grew more liberal than those toward the north, in the more secluded area.

When Abraham and Lot separated, Lot chose the fertile plains of Jordan and "pitched his tent toward Sodom" (Gen. 13:12). This was an evil city, founded by the descendants of Ham. Lot and his family became absorbed into the city, so much so that when the city was destroyed, only Lot and his two daughters were saved (Gen. 13-14, 18-19).

The Old Order Mennonites have traditionally been a rural people. The simple farm life, the closeness to nature, and the rural environment have always seemed more compatible to the Old Order pattern than the city environment, higher wages, and worldly social involvement.

In the past, it has been obvious that as cities expanded, Mennonites who lived closest to the cities became absorbed into the urban environment, like Lot, unless they moved farther away. This does not necessarily mean that all cities are evil, just because they were not suitable for Old Order living.

Today, by far the majority of Canadians live in cities. It is no longer necessarily true that the cities are founded by ungodly men, as the first cities were (Gen. 4:17; 10:2-12; 11:1-9). The groundwork for the city of Kitchener was laid by Mennonites. Bishop Benjamin Eby encouraged and supported its early development, and it was first named Ebytown, later Berlin, and now Kitchener. There is an indication, though, that Benjamin's views in this respect had changed toward the close of his life.

"Was Benjamin Eby one of our bishops?"

Benjamin Eby was the first Mennonite bishop in Waterloo County, before the church had divided. He lived right in the middle of the present city of Kitchener.

Living a simple, godly life seems to be somewhat easier in a rural area than in the city. We are closer to nature, to God's good creation. How would you know about giving thanks to God the Creator and Provider (Ps. 104), if you didn't see how the garden grows? We see the necessity of rain and sunshine, heat and cold.

We are walled in, not by high-rise apartments, but by wood-lots and hills. Instead of the roaring of motors, we hear the lowing of cows and the hum of bees. We smell freshly plowed fields and new-mown hay instead of fumes from trucks and smoke from factories. We live in the midst of growing things. People born and raised on a farm find it difficult to see how city folks can feel as truly thankful for food. They mostly see it simply coming from supermarket shelves.

"I just can't imagine how that would be. I can see that I would not want to be cooped up in a city."

I didn't think you would like it. There is no doubt but that a rural setting is more suitable for raising children. In the morning they wake up to the crowing of roosters and the singing of birds. They can roam in the fields. They enjoy the feeling of freshly plowed earth between their bare toes, and the reeling and swaying while riding on a load of hay, especially when it is loaded with the hayloader.

As they grow older, they can plant seeds in the garden, and then watch the plants sprout and grow. There are eggs for them to gather, and calves to feed. They enjoy animals and learn how to relate to them. All these are experiences in growing and maturing.

"Couldn't they even have a dog or cats in the city?"

That depends on where they live. If they lived in a big apartment building, there is a small chance that dogs and cats would be allowed. There would be no room for a garden or even a flowerbed.

"That's not all. If we lived in a big city, we couldn't have a horse and buggy. We couldn't even go to our church, unless we took a taxi. I think I asked a foolish question. Of course, none of our people would want to live in a big city."

Naturally, we don't know what the future holds for our people. The more modern the farms become, the dimmer is the future of the church as a truly Old Order institution. The more high-income, off-the-farm employment that is available and considered necessary, the closer the ties with modern society.

The course open to us is clear. As the cities encroach on our farmland, and when our community expansion is necessary, we must seek remoter areas, if possible. If we wish to preserve our heritage of simplicity, we must keep ourselves at a respectable distance from expanding cities. We need not compete with developers, as long as cheaper land is available in outlying areas. The privilege is ours.

"I hope I can still live on a farm when I grow up, even if I become a hired girl or a schoolteacher, or if I ever marry."

## Our Poor Deprived Children

"Grandpa, have you never felt like pitying me?"

Frankly, I've never really given it a thought. When we think of pitying people, the ones who come to mind first are the grumpy, grouchy ones, who are never happy. You don't answer that description at all. I can't recall ever seeing a frown on your face. However, if you really think you should be pitied, I can give it a try. Do you feel as if you need some pity?

"Not really. But in a report from Ottawa, ten years ago, it showed that over one million children lived in poverty in 1984. By 1988, the figure had dropped to under a million. Likely by now it will be higher again."

How did they figure out the poverty level?

"It says that a rural family with five children and an annual income of less than $24,209 was considered to be living in poverty."

Oh, our poor, deprived children and grandchildren! No wonder you think we should pity you! We and all our descendants must indeed be living in poverty! Besides, we did not accept

Family Allowance, Child Tax Credit, and personal subsidies. Thus we deprived our children and grandchildren of an additional sum in our schools, and we deprived them of qualified teachers and education beyond the eighth grade. We even deprive them of that greatest of educators, the TV set. They are robbed of the opportunity to watch movies, exhibitions, baseball and hockey games. They do not have the privilege of going to the beach, the cottage, or summer camp.

Instead of having all such advantages, they are expected to feed the chickens, sweep the floor, and fill the woodbox, after coming home from school. On Saturdays and holidays, they help with planting the garden. Later they pick berries and cherries, peas and beans, corn and cucumbers. They help to dig potatoes and carrots. They drive a tractor or team for loading hay or cultivating. Besides all that, I've seen you hurrying back from school to babysit your little niece. You really have little leisure time.

"Yes, but that's fun! I like playing with my nieces!"

I know you do. That's just the point that city people don't understand. There is no actual sign of deprivation. You likely eat more and better food than city children do. Most of our food is homegrown, homecooked, and fresh. The work you do builds up a healthy appetite. You sleep nine or ten hours every night.

The lack of TV watching does not seem to hamper your education. In fact, what you learn from other sources is more practical and may be at least as beneficial.

"I sure hope so! From what I've heard others talk about TV programs, I'm sure they do more harm than good."

I think you're right. Besides, you learned German before English, so that by now you are bilingual. You can talk two languages reasonably well. Some of those who watch TV can hardly read or write. Many cannot speak even one language without dropping in bad words or repeating fillers: "like wow," "cool," "you know." Though our teachers are not highly educated, they are dedicated.

After the eighth grade, our children are apprenticed to their parents for several years, to learn their trade by practical application. We think their farming and homemaking skills serve them

better than a college education. This program was approved by
the Ontario Department of Education in negotiation with the
Mennonites.

"We have lots of fun, too! There are lots of pets to play with:
baby chicks to cuddle, cute little kittens, and playful puppies.
There are baby calves who lick your hands. Squirrels chatter in
the trees. Woods and meadows are alive with the song of birds.
The bees buzz in the orchard. If people think we are deprived,
they don't know our life."

Some people give another reason to prove that our descendants are being deprived. Statistics show that it costs $54,000 to
raise one child up to age eighteen. Since we raised twelve children, and obviously did not pay out $54,000 for raising the
whole family, somewhere along the line the calculations must
have gone haywire. If we had educated them to the nth degree,
we could have spent so much money in raising them, if we had
it! But to what end? So that they could go to the city to join the
ranks of the unemployed?

"Doesn't that seem silly? But perhaps we are just too dull to
understand."

Yes, if we had a higher education, likely we could understand!

"I don't think I want to go to college just to find out how stupid I am. I would rather stay simple and enjoy myself."

That sounds like a good idea. Happiness is a state of mind and
can't be purchased with money. There is a greater chance of
being happy if we are content with what we have, than by want-
ing more.

# The Author

ISAAC R. HORST was born at the close of World War I, on the Sand Hills twenty miles north of Kitchener, Ontario. Physically unsuited for strenuous exercise, he spent his spare time in reading, at school and at home. This condition also kept him from developing an active interest in farming.

After his marriage to Selina Bauman and the arrival of children, the family teetered between unsuccessful farming and off-the-farm jobs. Neither seemed to provide enough income.

Horst then taught school for two years in the Mennonite parochial system established in 1966. He became a reasonably effective teacher by bolstering his eight grades of schooling with correspondence courses in high school English (grades 9 and 11) and creative writing.

Those extra courses ignited a literary spark in Horst. For twenty years, the ink has flowed steadily from his pen. During that time, he self-published twenty-three books; eight were religious and historical, and fifteen were cookbooks.

His published books include titles such as *Separate and Peculiar* (1979), *Conestogo Mennonite Cook Book* (1981), The *Man Who Could Do Anything* (1983), *Wildlife Vittles* (1983), *Why, Grossdaudy?* (1985), *Closeups of the Great Awakening* (1986), *Until Jacob Comes* (1990), *Breakin' the Fast* (1991), and *Liedersammlung Commentary* (1997). He also has lodged numerous unpublished books in Amos Hoover's Muddy Creek Farm Library, Denver, Pennsylvania.

Horst also wrote regular columns in local newspapers and several periodicals, especially for the *Mennonite Reporter*. He still enjoys translating texts from German to English, especially old hymns or manuscripts. He is about half finished transcribing and translating the Jacob Mensch collection of 1,600 letters.

In the mid 1960s, Horst explored the suitability of having an Old Order Mennonite settlement in the Mount Forest area, about thirty miles north of Elmira, Ontario. His family was among the first to settle there in the late 1960s. In the early 1990s, three members of his immediate family and three grandsons were among the first Old Order Mennonites settling in the Chesley area, forty miles northwest of Mount Forest.

Both new communities are flourishing. Mount Forest has four churches, and Chesley built one in 1998. None of this has made the author rich or famous, but he says the pioneering is more exciting than his farming experiences.

For ten years after Horst retired from farming, he ran a business of dismantling old buildings for salvage. Usually he wrecked a barn with the help of one or two other retired farmers.

Isaac Horst and his wife, Selina Bauman Horst, have eleven children, sixty-four grandchildren, and fifteen great-grandchildren. They are members of the Cedarview Old Order Mennonite Church, where Isaac has served as janitor and as a song leader.